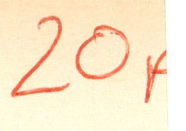

CONTENTS

Introduction 1

1. Clause 28 in Practice 4
   KATH PRINGLE, TARA KAUFMANN and PAUL LINCOLN

2. Louder Than Words 13
   ANNA TAN and MICHELLE BUTLER

3. Meetings, Management and Leadership 20
   JONATHAN LOUW

4. Disabled Lesbians and Gays Are Here to Stay! 29
   KIRSTEN HEARN

5. Nuremberg Revisited? 40
   TARA KAUFMANN

6. Don't Break Our Arts: The Arts Lobby
   And Section 28 48
   DAVID BENEDICT, SUE SANDERS, CAROLE WODDIS

7. Lifestyle or Practice? A New Target
   for Legislation 57
   DIANE HAMER, PAUL LINCOLN and TARA KAUFMANN

8. The Moon is Shining as Bright as Day:
   Parents, Children and Section 28 68
   NICOLA FIELD

9. The Making of a Radical Blackgay Man 93
   PETER NEVINS

10. Sells Papers, Ruins Lives: Homophobia
    and the Media 109
    JAMES BAADEN

11. Out Of The Box 126
CAROLINE SPRY

12. Approximations: Image, Desire
and Lesbian Identity 137
HEATHER SMITH

13. The Limits of Tolerance? 155
BOB CANT

14. Labour and the Natural Order:
Intentionally Promoting Heterosexuality 179
SARAH ROELOFS

15. Living with HIV 197
IAN FRASER

16. Caring, Campaigning and the
Dehomosexualisation of AIDS 205
CHRISTOPHER SCOTT

17. Pulpits, Courts and Scandal 210
SAVITRI HENSMAN

18. It Couldn't Happen Here:
A European Perspective 221
ROBERT G. and GERARD V.

19. Porn Again 232
COLIN RICHARDSON

20. New Year Revolutions 251
DEBBY KLEIN

Afterword 256

Notes on Contributors 266

Introduction

Two years after the introduction of Clause 28, where are we and who are we? After some of the most exhilarating events in ten years and the most extreme publicity, both good and bad, that any campaign could wish for, is there a lesbian and gay movement? Is there a community, and do we have an identity above and beyond the dramas with which we became identified in 1988?

Nearly two years on, David Wilshire, the Conservative MP who first proposed Clause 28 in committee, described his work as 'a warning to the liberal and the trendy that you can go too far for society to tolerate', and gloats, 'The strident boasting arrogance of the homosexual community seems to have quietened down a bit' (*Guardian*, 11th October 1989). There has been much self-censorship, much cutting off of funds and many threats. Yet local councils are retaining their equal opportunities policies and their lesbian and gay units. Hackney, Haringey, Camden and Islington councils all supported the 1989 North London Lesbian Strength and Gay Pride Festival. Gay cultural life continues, lesbian and gay projects receive funding, and not a single case has come to court. Has Clause 28 lived up to our worst expectations? And if so, how?

At the start of the 1990s, what we do see is an increasingly fragile conservative government but also an increasingly fragile lesbian and gay movement. The alliances of 1988 have largely collapsed. The political groups which were created in this period are less powerful and command less support than might have been expected. Now that the immediate threat appears to have passed it is worth considering what actually happened. There was an absence of leadership. We acquired some heroes, but who chose them? We learned how to lobby the House of Lords, but did we really have any faith in parliamentary process? We discovered the political language of Westminster, but this took us back to a world which ignored both gay liberation and feminism. It is necessary to consider why this happened. What were the compromises we made without thinking? What routes to our own survival did we ignore without a moment's thought?

Clause 28 was significant for many reasons. Lesbians became sufficiently recognised by Government to be discriminated against in their own right. AIDS provided the backdrop to a vindictive campaign that brought together those at high risk and those at low risk of infection. The debates about identity politics within lesbian circles and the debates about the creation of services for people with AIDS were time-consuming and did not lend themselves to the specific organisation of lesbian and gay political activity. In a severely fractured world it was a remarkable achievement that so much happened, that so many people marched and that so much was done publicly to make the discussion of lesbian and gay lives central to public debate.

This book charts some of the achievements of the period from 1988 to the present. It offers a critique and a review and it looks to the future. Whilst the clause excited passion and commitment, it also forced us to fight for our lives in a way that, with hindsight, might have been done differently.

Contributors examine the rise to fame of the actors who spoke out against the clause, and analyse some of the dangerous analogies which were made with the Holocaust. Those involved in direct actions speak about their experiences, and the roles of the Labour Party and the Established Church are examined in some detail. We look at the way in which the media has reported lesbian and gay lives and the way in which it has damaged them.

Introduction

The position of local authorities and the voluntary sector is questioned, and there is discussion on who 'represents' our community.

This collection also deals with how issues of race and disability are negotiated in our media and communities. There are thoughts on the ways in which AIDS campaigning has challenged and reformulated lesbian and gay organisation, and a consideration of our developing attitudes to childcare and to children.

This book chronicles some recent aspects of lesbian and gay history and offers comments on the next stage of that story. We could not hope to present an exhaustive representation of the diverse and complex communities which make up modern lesbian and gay culture: this collection is intended to provoke further debate about important issues in lesbian and gay life. We hope that readers will develop the ideas contained on these pages so that the authentic voices of protest and experience can fertilise the seeds of our liberation.

Tara Kaufmann and Paul Lincoln
October 1990

Chapter 1
Clause 28 In Practice

Kath Pringle, Tara Kaufmann and Paul Lincoln

Clause 28 of the Local Government Act 1988 inserted a new Section 2A into the Local Government Act 1986:

[1] *A local authority shall not*
   [a] intentionally promote homosexuality or publish material with the intention of promoting homosexuality;
   [b] promote the teaching in any maintained school of the acceptability of homosexuality as a pretended family relationship;
[2] *Nothing in subsection [1] shall be taken to prohibit the doing of anything for the purpose of treating or preventing the spread of disease.*
[3] *In any proceedings in connection with the application of this section a court shall draw such inferences as to the intention of the local authority as may reasonably be drawn from the evidence before it.*

On 16th December 1986 the following exchange took place at a meeting of South Staffordshire Council:

'Those bunch of queers that legalise filth in homosexuality have a lot to answer for and I hope they are proud of what they have done. The film said how to try to avoid AIDS but it did not specifically say stop being queer. It is disgusting and diabolical. As a cure I would put 90 per cent of queers in the ruddy gas chamber. I would shoot them all. Are we going to keep letting these queers trade their filth up and down the country? We must find a way of stopping these gays going round.'
      Cllr Bill Brownhill, Leader of the Council

'Every one of us here will agree with what has been said.'
      Cllr Jack Greenaway, Leader of the Labour Group

Clause 28 In Practice

This is indicative of the social and political climate which put Clause 28 on the statute books, and explains why surprise was not the most obvious characteristic of lesbian and gay response. Indeed we had already witnessed the Earl of Halsbury's attempt (at that time not supported by the Government) to promote a bill which was almost the exact prototype for what was to follow.

On the morning of 8th December 1987 a network of telephone calls spread the news to lesbian and gay activists London-wide that the Government had slipped a nasty surprise into the Local Government Bill, which was being debated in committee that afternoon. Dozens of us packed out the committee room to witness a democratically elected government actually taking the lead in campaigning for *more* discrimination against a sector of the population, cynically whipping up fear and hysteria in a deliberate attempt to create a scapegoat on which to focus moral panic. Worse, we witnessed the almost total collusion of the Opposition, with the notable exception of Bernie Grant, Labour MP for Tottenham, who warned:

> 'If the new clause is accepted, it will be a signal to every fascist and everyone opposed to homosexuality that the Government are on their side.'

Accepted it was, and within days had stimulated enormous opposition and a new single issue campaign, 'Stop The Clause', based on a rather fragile coalition between lesbians and gay men.

The following week saw a mass lobby of Parliament. In January there was a march in London, capped by an exhilarating protest in Manchester which formed the largest ever lesbian and gay demonstration in Britain. Even this was exceeded by the 50,000 present at the London demo in April. The scale of the opposition was enormous. Stop The Clause groups sprang up all over the country, and regional demos were held in towns that had never before seen any kind of lesbian and gay political activity. Special interest groups also proliferated: trade union groups, Stop The Clause Education Group, Jews Against The Clause, and so on. The Arts Lobby were spectacularly successful in gaining media attention for the campaign by mobilising the showbiz world in our support. Some, indeed, felt that the Arts Lobby may have become a victim of its own success in diverting attention and resources to the 'easy' areas of the campaign, and exploiting scare tactics to the stage of crying wolf.

Arguably of even greater impact, however, were those lesbians who engaged in some of the most imaginative and effective direct action in recent years: the most famous examples of this being the abseiling raid in the House of Lords, the invasion of the 'Six O'Clock News' on BBC television, the picket of Harrods, and the occupation of the Daily Mail Ideal Home Exhibition.

Although it may at times have seemed that way, Clause 28 was not the only event in the 1986-9 lesbian and gay calendar. Other struggles were continuing, usually without the resources and public recognition of the Stop The Clause campaign. There were, for example the struggles to establish gay lifestyles as valid within the Church of England; the Haringey Black Action/Positive Images campaign; continuing work around AIDS which produced the London Lighthouse (an AIDS Hospice and Day Support Centre) and a British ACTUP group (AIDS Coalition To Unleash Power). Yet is was Clause 28 which most successfully mobilised our communities and placed lesbian and gay rights on the political map so dramatically.

From the outset, the wording of the Clause was described as 'obscure and badly drafted' (Madeleine Colvin, National Council for Civil Liberties Legal Officer, *Guardian*, 11th October 1989), and considered almost unworkable as a piece of practical legislation. There was, in fact, considerable suspicion that the Clause had been deliberately constructed as a piece of legislation which would not need to be legally watertight, but would be effective merely through the threat of its possible use, and

Clause 28 In Practice

through self-censorship. Clause 28 may be vague and woolly, yet it hit bang on target in feeding the high level of social prejudice, and playing upon fear.

Attempts to assess the possible impact of Clause 28 were constantly frustrated by its failure to define its terms: 'homosexuality', 'pretended family', and, most particularly, 'promote'. Legal interpretation of the concept of promoting homosexuality varied from explicit and directive homosexual propaganda, to *any* representation of homosexuality which was not explicitly negative.

That the Clause did not need to be fully functioning as law in order to take effect became evident early on in its progress towards the statute books. Long before it came into force, long before it had been voted, the Clause was being used against lesbians and gay men. As protests against it helped to raise the issue's profile, so the level of homophobic abuse seemed to increase. As early as February 1988 the Woolwich police threatened to close down Greenwich Lesbian and Gay Centre on the grounds that it was illegally funded under Clause 28; councils in Strathclyde and Essex warned local college heads not to allow lesbian and gay clubs or meetings on their premises; GALOP (Gay London Policing Group) reported alarming increases in gaybashing on the streets; and the London offices of *Capital Gay* were badly damaged by an arson attack.

Once the Clause was passed, broad interpretation of the concept of 'promotion' proliferated and was used to justify widespread abuses:

— the BBC delayed transmission of a programme about the experience of gay teenagers, rescheduled it to a late-night slot, and finally insisted on censoring out its more positive representations of homosexuality.

— in Wolverhampton, a video made to protest against the Clause was banned from being shown on Council-owned premises, so as not to 'promote homosexual activities'.

— in an electioneering smear campaign in Gateshead, a

High Risk Lives

councillor was accused by his Liberal and Social Democrat opponents of 'promoting' homosexuality, simply because he had spoken publicly of his acceptance of his son's sexuality.

— Essex County Council used the Clause to ban meetings of the Colchester Institute Lesbian and Gay Group.

— in Hounslow, a Conservative councillor accused the local library service of 'promoting ... abnormal behaviour' when they produced a guide to books of interest to lesbians and gay men.

— Hereford & Worcester County Council refused to consider funding a lesbian group for fear of contravening the Clause.

— in East Sussex the County Education Officer decided to stop using a National Youth Bureau publication (despite its having been approved, and financed, by the Home Office) because it included an advertisement for the London Lesbian and Gay Centre.

— Kent County Council excluded Benjamin Britten's opera *Death in Venice* from a schools' festival because of its theme of homoerotic obsession.

— an exhibition on Clause 28 mounted by Aberystwyth University students in the town library was forcibly removed by the Chief Librarian.

— Hull City Council refused to allow the screening of a Jean Genet film at a local arts festival.

— Lambeth Council withdrew funding from Converse Pictures, the only — and award-winning — lesbian and gay production group.

— Strathclyde County Council refused to include lesbians and gay men in their new equal opportunities policy.

— the headteacher of an Avon secondary school banned a touring theatre production due to be shown in his school because of its representation of a gay character, which he feared would contravene the Clause.

— attempts to ban a student Lesbian and Gay Society

were made in Strathclyde, but the National Union of Students (NUS) successfully negotiated an agreement.

— Scotland has, on the whole, been affected rather differently from England and Wales, as local authority funding tends to be provided in the form of one-off payments for specific events, rather than as running costs for groups. The Scottish Homosexual Action Group did receive funding from Edinburgh District Council for their successful Lark In The Park festival, but this support was withdrawn in 1989 following legal advice that such payments risked prosecution under Clause 28.

Clearly, then, the Clause is being used, and only vigorous protest from lesbian and gay activists is containing the excesses of similar attempts. Yet all these manifestations of the powers of Clause 28 rely on fear, confusion and misinformation: it is unlikely their interpretation would stand up in a court of law. Legal opinions commissioned by the Association of London Authorities and the National Council for Civil Liberties concluded that 'promotion' could only be taken to mean deliberate and active encouragement to people to become homosexual or to experiment with homosexual relationships.

Further, a Department of Education and Science circular to schools stated that Clause 28 does not render illegal any objective discussion of homosexuality in class, counselling pupils concerned about their homosexuality, or dealing with homophobic bullying and victimisation. Nor does it preclude the implementation of equal opportunities policies which cover the needs of lesbian and gay employees, or groups applying for grants. Indeed, in a letter to the Organisation for Lesbian and Gay Action (3rd March 1988) the Prime Minister herself declared that, 'The Government is against discrimination in any form, and it is in no part our intention in supporting Clause 28 to remove the rights of homosexuals.'

Manchester City Council summed up the powers of the Clause in their reports of July 1988 and February 1989, concluding, 'there is a grave danger that the Section will compound hostility towards lesbians and gay men, simply by playing upon people's fears and prejudices, and through encouraging employees of local authorities, teachers and governors to censor all mention of lesbians and gay men, either out of fear and ignorance or because the law now appears to justify their existing prejudice.'

Manchester was not the only municipal authority to oppose the new law. As early as February 1988 leaders of local authorities form Edinburgh to Ealing were working together to produce a united response to the proposed legislation. As a group they urged MPs and Peers to throw the clause out, warning that it could help increase the spread of HIV by creating 'a level of uncertainty and even confusion about what local authorities can do in the area of preventative health care and in combatting discrimination.' Only in a climate of open and informed debate, they argued, could they meet their responsibilities for health education. On this specific issue, we did manage to get the Clause amended.

During the run-up to the Clause being accepted, some authorities supported local and national campaigns. Once the law was in force, however, their priorities changed and attention was focused on educating their employees on how their responsibilities were affected. Some councils, as in the examples above, met this challenge with what can only be described as panic measures, acting on distinctly over-cautious legal advice to batten down the hatches and make themselves invulnerable. Other councils have taken rather more liberal legal opinion, and have resisted pressure to abandon wholesale their lesbian and gay electorate. Those authorities with lesbian and gay units were at an advantage here, in having the resources and knowledge needed to understand the issue and work through existing channels of communication with local gay communities. But even the Conservative Hampshire County Council issued an altogether sensible circular to its employees, emphasising that the Council's work would continue as normal.

Clause 28 In Practice

It is notable that, despite many threats, no case has yet been brought to court. In the case of the Colchester Institute, the NUS campaign seemed likely to culminate in a test case, but in the event the council climbed down. While its admission of error was welcome, the legal implications were still unresolved. There is some suspicion, indeed, that anti-gay activists have been consciously avoiding a test vase in order to maximise the Section's confusing and intimidatory effect. Indisputably, self-censorship has become endemic in the post-Clause political climate. Bob Hall, Leader of the Conservative group on Haringey Council, boasts that the council officers reporting on North London Pride's funding application 'took great pains to explain that the money was not designed to promote homosexuality' (*Guardian*, 11th October, 1989). All too often illegality is not ascertained, but merely assumed — that is how the law works.

Clause 28 gave new legitimacy to an already deeply rooted homophobia, which — in practice — subjects many lesbians and gay men to terror campaigns and literally murderous attacks, and which burdens the wider population with repression of individual choice.

But our response produced many positive effects. Thanks to our resistance, the Clause 28 issue became a *public* issue. People came out in their droves to declare which side of the fence they were one. New groups such as the South Asian Lesbian and Gay Group, and Jews Against The Clause, did invaluable work in challenging heterosexism in their own communities and racism in lesbian and gay culture; there was an explosion of growth in black lesbian and gay culture, and the establishment of both a Black Lesbian and Gay Centre and a Black Communities AIDS Team. LANGUID (Lesbians And Gays United In Disability) hosted the first-ever conference for lesbians and gays with disabilities in Manchester. OLGA (the Organisation for Lesbian and Gay Action) continued, against all the odds, to survive as an active campaigning force. And the advertising agency which sold us Margaret Thatcher went on to have a go at promoting homosexuality on television's first (late-night) lesbian and gay magazine series. We were active, we were vocal, we established unprecedented visibility. We may have lost the battle, but we can no longer be ignored.

Acknowledgements

Thanks to the following for supplying information:

Brighton Area Action Against Section 28
Camden Borough Council Lesbian and Gay Unit
Cara-Friend, Belfast
Gay London Policing Group (GALOP)
Haringey Borough Council Lesbian and Gay Unit
Jews Against the Clause
Lesbian and Gay Employment Rights
Lighthouse Media Centre, Wolverhampton
Manchester City Council Equal Opportunities Unit
North West Campaign for Lesbian and Gay Equality
Organisation for Lesbian and Gay Action (OLGA)
Scottish Homosexual Action Group
Terrence Higgins Trust
The Pink Paper
York Lesbian and Gay Solidarity

Chapter 2
Louder Than Words

Michelle Butler and Anna Tan

I never thought that school needlework classes would ever come in handy, but there I was, sewing lentils into two twenty-one-foot banners to weigh them down. Four women from our group had decided to do something in protest against Clause 28.

Suicide Bridge in Archway, North London, was chosen for our action. We were going to spraypaint the bridge with symbols of the fight against Clause 28, with angry words, but when we checked out the bridge a week or two before the planned action the spikes sticking out from the top put us off climbing over it, and anyway none of us knew how to abseil down. The bridge was used by some people as a means to an end, literally — hence the name. Looking at those spikes I found it hard to imagine anyone scaling it and jumping to their death onto one of the busiest routes into London. The bridge seemed to me to be a symbol of how some of us felt about Clause 28, as if somehow all those rights for which young lesbians and gays had come out were going to be brutally snatched away. I felt angry standing on that bridge watching the traffic pass under me. I felt angry at having to fight a battle that had already been fought. Was it only a few years ago that I was being told how lucky I was to be able to come out, go to my own clubs, not have to get married, stay in the same community I had grown up in? Now all that was going to change, and all I could do was write letters to MPs and demonstrate. It felt futile.

I was scared of being caught. I had heard all about the local police station and didn't fancy it much. Nor did I fancy my family reading all about me in the local papers. This made me feel resentful at having to consider so many people's feelings, agonising over how much to tell them and how it would affect them. I wanted them to see their daughter as strong and capable of sticking up for herself, not as a 'trouble-maker'. Even though I left home over four years ago, even though I am independent of them, what they think still matters to me. I felt like I wanted it all. I wanted all of my rights and I wanted my family to respect me for who I am and not for what they wanted me to be. To me the fear was of being misunderstood, of being made to feel abnormal and deviant just because I was fighting for what I considered to be my rights. But I suppose I realised that there comes a time when trying to justify myself is not enough, when action is needed to find a bit of self respect.

I had been one of the handful of lesbians who spent the night outside Harrods in the pouring rain the night before the Sale that year. I had seen the reporters and camera crews carefully pass by our banners on the morning of the Sale, ignoring our protests, ignoring injustice in favour of stories about who was going to buy what and what a bargain it was. It's strange how people look at you when you carry a banner proclaiming that, as a lesbian, you demand your rights. It's a look mixed with embarrassment, fear and the sort of gory fascination people have when there's been an accident.

However, the fight against Clause 28 was not just about responding to injustice: it was also about finding strength through unity, and control through facing the situation. Being involved in direct action can also be exciting. I began to really feel a part of lesbian herstory. Facing the prospect of Clause 28 gave me a surprising sense of belonging and acceptance. It also made me feel like I was fighting real and concrete laws, and not unspoken agreements between bigoted people.

Louder Than Words

I did find it incredibly easy to feel overwhelmed by it all. Britain in the 1980s is a hard place for anyone who isn't rich, white, heterosexual and able-bodied. Facing the reality of Clause 28 means facing the possibility of losing the right to be an 'out' lesbian who is also valued within society. Somehow we must not accept that reality and thereby not play their game. In the short term it would be easier to go back into the closet and pretend it isn't happening, because it seems almost too absurd. But in the long run I now feel that taking action means claiming some control of the situation, and if that means breaking the law then sometimes I will do it. However, there is a dilemma here, because if we break the law openly and defiantly then we risk fines, imprisonment, bad publicity and homophobic attacks. If, on the other hand, we break the law and try not to get caught, then the action so often goes unnoticed. Often the most potentially dangerous action is the most effective.

It was 4 a.m. when we planned to hang the banners. Stepping out of the car, which was parked just over the bridge for a quick getaway, I felt strangely excited and suitably justified in my action. It was only when I spotted the uniformed policeman in an unmarked car that I realised I was scared too. Lorries roared under the bridge as we squeezed the plump banners under the protective iron railings. Then, stretching our arms as far out over the ledge of the bridge as possible, we eased the banners over the edge.

Driving back down Highgate Hill at breakneck speed, back round to Archway Road and under the bridge, our faces dropped on discovering that one of the banners had got caught up in the rope and was hanging uselessly a third of the way down from the bridge. The other banner was back to front. I suddenly felt very stupid for not checking which way round the banner was before we hung it. There was only one thing for it: we had to go back and do it all again.

This time two of us decided to keep watch while the

High Risk Lives

other two sorted out the mess. I started to think of home: warm, safe, comfortable. Why was I out here in the cold risking getting caught when I could be tucked up in bed? But then I remembered the number of lesbians who had tried to kill themselves, perhaps by throwing themselves from bridges like the one I was standing on, and how sometimes in order to feel like a whole person it is necessary to stand up and fight.

We turned the banner round the right way and were just retrieving it when we heard a muffled shout warning us of another police car approaching. Quickly we struggled to our feet and started chatting, pretending to be on our way back from a great party as the van cruised past ... quarter to five on a Tuesday morning and vanloads of police out and about, and people moan about ratepayers' money being spent on lesbians and gays!

Back to the second banner. We heaved it over the ledge of the bridge and untangled it, then threw it back and cleared out of there fast. Driving under the bridge we felt dismayed to find the second banner had still not been disentangled. The first banner looked brilliant — 'Stop Clause 28', twenty-one-foot long, could not be missed by people going to work that day. We decided to make one more attempt at correcting the other banner. This time the car was driven onto the bridge and two of us got out while the other two stayed in the car. I pretended to be giving instructions to the people in our getaway car as the police drove past again. They didn't even notice us! Quickly we reassured ourselves as we tugged and strained at the banner. Hours of work had gone into each one and we knew that they would not be up there for long. They just had to be effective, Fate had to be on our side. This time as I got back into the car I knew it was for the last time. I was not going back to that bridge anymore: besides, I could feel the dawn coming soon.

Under the bridge we went again, only to find that the second banner was *still* tangled. We caught glimpses of the words when the wind blew at it, so after taking photos of our work we started home. I sank into my seat feeling a

Louder Than Words

huge sense of relief mixed with pride. I had taken my first real and worthwhile step in overcoming the ifs and buts of doing something. Even though it isn't considered proper, acceptable, on the right side of the law, it felt like an appropriate response to the prospect of the Clause.

We slept all the next day, and by the time anyone had the energy to go back to that by now very familiar place, the banners had been removed, leaving nothing as a reminder of all the hours of planning and action — not to mention the amount of thought as to the possible consequences. Even the photos didn't come out. But in the end the banners and the photographs were only symbols of what four women did one late night in March. What mattered most in the end was knowing that I could take action, that I could say *no* in my own way.

Sometimes it is very easy to forget the action that has been taken by ordinary lesbians like me. It is all too easy to forget us because we have too few images of ourselves as lesbians in this fight. Many of our voices will be lost in the historians' anxiety to record what they consider to be the more important events, the demos and the spectacular stunts. Those of us licking envelopes and decorating the walls with graffiti go unnoticed or noticed only by the police. We must not be forgotten, because it is we who will continue the struggle into the future. What we learn now and what we are taught will be all we have to carry on with, and if there is one thing I have discovered this year, it is the meaning of that old saying, 'actions speak louder than words'.

Michelle Butler

I have been involved in the political movement for the past three years. In that time my views have changed. At first I thought that as lesbians and gay men were an oppressed group they would be more aware of other people's struggles to overcome oppression, but as a young black lesbian I have encountered racism, sexism and ageism within the lesbian and gay communities. In meetings it is usually left to black lesbians and gays to challenge racism, women to challenge sexism, and so on.

So I attended the first meeting of LAGYAG (Lesbian And Gay Youth Action Group) knowing it was aimed at young lesbians and gays campaigning against the Clause, but really expecting just another gay group. How wrong I was. I was surprised at the vast amount of energy and commitment in the group, though very disappointed at the lack of gay men attending. We spent our first two meetings getting to know each other, choosing a name and, most importantly, brainstorming for an action we could all take part in. We achieved all our aims.

Tuesday, 5th January, 1988
That early evening Jo and I prepared an endless amount of sandwiches, filled our flasks with coffee, and checked our rucksacks to make sure we had packed all the necessities for a night out. (The only thing we didn't pack was the kitchen sink, though we were tempted!) Armed with our survival kits we made our way to Harrods in Knightsbridge. We had planned this action for the past few weeks in reaction to the Clause.

The plan was to camp outside Harrods disguised as bargain hunters, waiting for the day of their infamous annual sale which is covered by the national and international media. We had hoped to be at the front of the queue in order to gain publicity about the effects of the Clause, and at the end of the day to shock the local residents. Little did we know how well it would work.

10.30 p.m. approached as we trudged through the biting wind towards Harrods. We were pleased to see a small band of lesbians and one gay man gathered outside the main entrance. As the night wore on people joined and left us, until a group of twelve lesbians were left to hold the fort — our token gay man had also left us. We wondered where our gay brothers were but soon gave up hope of seeing a gay man that night.

The night brought the wind and rain, driving us to

Louder Than Words

take shelter beneath the main entrance and behind cardboard bodes which someone had kindly left on the other side of the road. The banners were used as blankets as we settled down to see the night through.

Before too long a taxi drove up and parked while an American tourist hobbled out on her crutches to take a photo of us. Fame at last! The banners and placards were whipped out of their hiding places and proudly displayed. As the taxi disappeared in the distance a security guard arrived to question us on our reasons for being there. We kept up the disguise and joked about all the bargains we wanted to pick up. He soon revealed the reasons why he had joined us as he asked about the banners and placards. In reply we shrugged our shoulders and smiled sweetly as we in return asked how did he know about them. He pointed at the hidden camera and we thanked him silently for telling us.

In order to keep awake and active we toured the area in groups of four, finding loads of graffiti and slogans like 'Lesbians Are Everywhere!', 'Stop The Clause' and 'We're Out And Staying Out'. The first group trotted back to the camp to share the experience as the other groups eagerly set out to see the sights for themselves.

By early morning we were all tired and cold. Bags as big as bin-liners hung from our eyes. Our first positive visitors were a small group of American tourists who later came back with breakfast for us! Reporters soon began to arrive as the queue grew, but they tended to avoid or ignore us completely, although we were at the head of the queue proudly holding the banners and placards. Though a few reporters reluctantly talked to us, or us to them, the event was never published except for a paragraph in *The Pink Paper*.

It was not a wasted night, though. The action was quite an experience for all of us. We learnt a little more about ourselves and each other. It's not something you'd forget. Doing action as a group, we all had to trust and rely on each other.

Anna Tan

Chapter 3
Meetings, Management and Leadership

Jonathan Louw

The lesbian and gay movement is traditionally good at political rhetoric, a mixed bag when it comes to analysis, and desperately underskilled in its management of human and material resources.

As the Stop The Clause campaign fades into memory, it is time to examine our organisational processes with a sense of the past, a knowledge of present weaknesses and strengths and, above all, with a feeling of urgency about our aims in the future. In particular this article reflects on the structures and methods we deploy to channel and unleash lesbian and gay political energies, and the exciting possibilities for change thrown up by the campaign against Clause 28.

There is no one way of organising effectively, yet the lesbian and gay movement seems at times to be stuck in the worst patterns of labour movement activism. We espouse collective action for the common good, yet sabotage ourselves with lack of imagination and punitive practices. We rely on depressingly familiar ways of organising meetings, marches, petitions — which produce equally depressing outcomes. We are slow to learn from the organisational ingenuity shown by parts of the women's and other social protest movements, both here and abroad. In general, the movement has not been able to find lasting ways of stimulating and harnessing people's creative energy into politically effective and personally enriching action.

The lesbian and gay movement gives little attention to the way it uses and abuses those it draws into its fold. How much is taken for granted, sometimes from so few. How little praise and thanks are given to our activists, working as we do within structures which dissipate energy, create frustration, alienate many and burn out others. There is almost no individual blame to be attached to these observations, for many of us are simply caught up in notions and traditions of organising which go unquestioned but which are, frankly, scandalously wasteful of human potential.

My observations are drawn mainly from experience of organising in London. Discussions with activists around Britain do, however, indicate a level of shared experience, suggesting that concerns voiced here may transcend geographical boundaries.

The London Effect

At the outset of the London Stop The Clause campaign it was envisaged that weekly general meetings would be the focus for policy making and accountability, and that these would be complemented by a range of 'special interest' groups such as the Arts Lobby, Trade Unionists Against The Clause, and the International Group. Within weeks, however, these special interest groups had moved centre stage to become a central organising feature of the campaign, while the general meetings foundered.

Very early on, the main weekly meetings became fractious and increasingly taken up with arguments on political direction and strategy, to the extent that only the loudest and most articulate were heard. Little time was left for determining and allocating necessary tasks, and the notional 'central forum' became ever more divorced from the driving seat of the campaign. Sub-groups gradually gave up reporting — or even attending — the weekly meetings, which became less and less effective. The only work carried out in this forum was the planning for the April 30th demo, and much of this was actually undertaken by a small and dedicated group who took little or no part in the weekly decision meetings. By the time April 30th came and went, just four months into the campaign, there was in no sense a centrally co-ordinated campaign against Clause 28 in London.

In early May a discussion meeting to determine future strategy disintegrated into a bitter wrangle over the role of heterosexuals as decision-makers within the campaign. Subsequent weekly meetings attracted no more than ten to fifteen people. Sub-groups continued to meet, but with little or no reference to one another. The strengths of devolved planning and decision-making had been undermined by organisational incoherence at the centre.

There are many lessons to be learned from the London campaign's failures. It could be argued, for instance, that these divisions and lack of co-ordination could have been predicted when, within the first month, a major split developed between those who wished to establish an autonomous Stop The Clause Campaign, and those who wanted closer alignment with the newly emerged Organisation for Lesbian and Gay Action, OLGA. Those within OLGA saw Clause 28 as a prime example of the need for a national organisation, which OLGA had just been set up to be! Those outside (in some cases erstwhile supporters of the notion of a national organisation) saw much of OLGA's work as political opportunism and the product of personal ambition. Poorly consulted decisions made by OLGA during the first frenetic weeks of the campaign were used to discredit the organisation.

Six weeks into the action it was clear that the majority speaking out at the weekly Stop The Clause meetings wanted a separate campaign, but this acrimonious debate set the tone for the following meetings. Many groups and individuals felt deeply alienated by the atmosphere at meetings — and so stayed away. It also led to a loss of

Meetings, Management and Leadership

support for OLGA in London at a critical time in that organisation's growth, a loss from which it has never recovered.

Some will say that analyses of organisational practice inevitably neglect the underlying political issues. This is only partly true, as can be illustrated by the case of the Stop The Clause campaign.

Lying behind many of the disputes were objections from labour movement-identified groups to a broad-based organisation (OLGA) taking a central role in the co-ordination of a single issue campaign. At least one of these groups, the Labour Campaign for Lesbian and Gay Rights (LCLGR), had in fact helped initiate the Legislation for Lesbian and Gay Rights Conference just a few months before. It was this conference, broadly based and non-party aligned, which gave birth to OLGA. LCLGR's original position of qualified support, derived from the recognition that there is no general lesbian and gay consensus on the way forward, swiftly became an entrenched point of principled opposition. What to the outsider might seem like a difference of strategy, which need not preclude effective collaboration and constructive debate, instead became a focus of highly personalised political division.

Exemplified here is our movement's failure to deal with legitimate difference, its failure to profit from differing perspectives and contributions, and thus its tendency to self-destruct. How, it may be asked, can any group with a limited constituency believe that amidst the political uncertainties of modern Britain — in which every social movement is struggling for a sense of the future — it alone knows how to achieve lesbian and gay equality? Yet this is how so many of us are taught to think by the political ideologies we have inherited or grown into, and have never been prepared to question.

The personality issues which surfaced so strongly and so negatively in the London Stop The Clause campaign point to a more general confusion around the question of leadership. The lesbian and gay Left is so suspicious of public political leadership that it abdicates this role to film, theatre and soap opera stars! The people we end up relying on to present our public face are not necessarily those best qualified to speak for us. Those that might be, the political activists, find themselves sniped at by other lesbians and gays as soon as they succeed in gaining wider media or political attention. Their smallest faults, as they struggle against media distortion and abuse, are seized on as indications of political treachery. Failed dialogue within the movement results in wider failure as activists with good communication skills are constantly undermined and unappreciated by their 'comrades' — with no acknowledgement given to the often considerable personal cost involved. A debate in the movement about leadership, accountability and charisma is long overdue.

The Problems

The impact of a political campaign is often dependent on the creation of a collective consciousness and will: this creates a special responsibility to use all public forums to best effect. Gatherings have to be crafted to involve and *inspire* — especially once the first flushes of anger that generate any campaign begin to fade, and new ways must be found to maintain momentum.

Yet most lesbian and gay campaigning meetings are far from inspirational. The reasons for this are not hard to find. For a start, meetings are time-consuming and rarely planned around childcare and access needs. Those who do attend are a relatively select few, therefore, or else are there at great personal cost. Either way, they are there as a statement of commitment and this commitment needs nurturing.

But lack of management skills and personal/political rivalries all too often make collective activity an alienating experience. The tasks in hand always seem too enormous for the activists, yet at the same time groups are often too big to be effective. Working in large groups (arguably anything more than twenty strong) is more often than not self-defeating. Those who do want to contribute are frustrated by the demands of democracy, so that when they do get the floor they tend to declaim rather than enter into a learning dialogue. Meanwhile the more reticent are put off by the size of the group and the often aggressive environment, as grievances are aired which, though often legitimate, serve to heighten confrontation.

Meetings tend to be over-ambitious, aiming to achieve so much more than the realistically attainable that all sense of direction is lost. Understanding of goals becomes more diffuse, the inspiration which brought people to the meeting is dulled, hopelessness begins to set in. The issues are too big after all, someone/something out there does have the upper hand over all of us, we are more divided than united. A sense of power is lost — and that is a tragic loss, because we as lesbians and gays have, above all, to believe in our power to change a world which shows no signs of changing of its own accord.

How many meetings have we attended where rhetoric has flowed so freely that people have left with nothing to do other than put the next meeting in their diaries? Such an outcome is nothing but mismanagement. We owe it to ourselves collectively to manage our time, energy, learning capacity and commitment with the greatest care.

On the Positive Side

Meetings, management of limited human resources, leadership — the list could go on. But space forbids further critique of the frequent poverty of our organisational practice. And little justice would be done to the extent and effectiveness of lesbian and gay organising during and since the Clause 28 campaign if the above observations were to stand alone.

Our successes deserve at least a little examination.

Encouragingly, areas of the Stop The Clause campaign were able to create maximum public impact at minimum organisational cost. The media's attention was caught by the audacity of small groups of highly organised people, as well as by the sheer size of our protests. Significantly, those at the forefront of the most imaginative actions have often been women and young people.

Organising has been partially liberated from its previous straitjacket by a dawning realisation that carefully planned direct action really can work. All the millions of hours of work that went into the big demonstrations in Manchester and London in February and April 1988 could not begin to match, in terms of public impact, the effectiveness of the relatively few hours of effort which made the House of Lords abseiling affair and the BBC Six O'Clock News incident such worldwide dramas. This is not to knock the big demos — although at worst they can be a miserable waste of collective potential, at their best they can succeed in giving participants an exhilarating sense of strength and togetherness. But it does recognise that affecting public consciousness often means manipulating the media and symbolic institutions to one's advantage.

The prime-time coverage of both these episodes granted the protagonists the legitimacy of news makers. The incidents were too sensational to be ignored — and in a real sense they demanded coverage in their own terms rather than the media's. What greater achievement could there be when every other piece of news about lesbians and gays is systematically distorted and misrepresented, by a deeply prejudiced media acting in the name of the supposed value structures of the reading, watching public? Moreover, the events were resoundingly inspirational. The women concerned took their chances and got away with it — no charges were made in either case. The stuff that fantasies are made of actually happened before our very eyes, and the same impact could be made by dramatising the inequities perpetrated by other pillars of the homophobic establishment.

Imagine the effect of an occupation of Westminster Abbey in protest at the Anglican Church's refusal to validate lesbian and gay relationships!

To an unprecedented extent lesbians took centre stage in a campaign mounted by the mixed lesbian and gay movement. This was evident in public meetings, backstage organising, media work and, above all, in direct action. Drawing on the precedents set in parts of the women's movement, lesbians in their skill and flair showed gay men of the '80s how much they had yet to learn about political effectiveness. This is a lesson to be cherished, for in it could well lie the future of a movement so long beset with the problem of how to avoid male dominance in its structures and organising. Perhaps the increasingly eye-catching activities of women and men in ACTUP (AIDS Coalition To Unleash Power) in 1989 bear witness to lessons well learnt.

Going Forward

Such positive developments bode well. Yet the troubled organisational history of ACTUP in London, which has significantly undermined the group's impact, highlights two continuing problems. One, which will not be addressed here, is the gay movement's tardy political response to HIV and AIDS in this country. (The conspicuous failure of the Stop The Clause campaign to address in any way the politics of AIDS will, it may be confidently predicted, confound future historians.)

The second problem, and the main concern here, lies in the area of organisational practice. Movers and shakers in organisations like ACTUP still fail to attach enough priority to the development of personal skills and ways of working which maximise involvement and minimise conflict or alienation. Enthusiasm, motivation and a pressing cause are not sufficient to make a campaign effective.

A successful campaign is surely one in which all

voices are heard, one that is run with consideration for the value of what people say but without allowing offensive statements to go unchallenged, one that gives people a sense of being part of a larger whole, one that tries to set achievable goals and, finally, one that allows individuals to undertake manageable tasks to be completed by an agreed time. One that entrusts a few accountable people with the effective management of its activities and meetings, to ensure that all this happens.

Yes, we need Management. This has traditionally been such a dirty word in the annals of extra-parliamentary activity that its use here could be deeply offensive to some. But what else, in the political context of lesbian and gay liberation, is the effective co-ordination and directing of human and material resources other than good management? As voluntary sector collective workplaces seem to be discovering on a wide scale, it is time to reclaim the true possibilities of management, acquire the necessary skills, and apply them to our political organising.

Only when workshops on meeting management, team building, organisational effectiveness and democratic leadership are taken as seriously as seminars on sadomasochism, socialism and sexual politics, will we have begun to take our organising and our future as a movement seriously.

Chapter 4
Disabled Lesbians and Gays Are Here to Stay!

Kirsten Hearn

I write this in memory of Julian Salmon (Gay Men's Disabled Group) and Mandy Dee (GEMMA). Throughout their lives they struggled in their own ways for more acceptance and understanding of the needs of disabled lesbians and gays. Without them the fight is harder, but their example gives me power.

A Convergence of Cripples

On the weekend of 15-17 April, 1988, sixty disabled lesbians and gays converged on Manchester for the first National Conference for Lesbians and Gays with Disabilities ever to have been held in this country. The idea to hold such a conference came out of a very angry caucus meeting for disabled lesbians and gays at the Legislation for Lesbian and Gay Rights Conference held in London in May 1987.

Limited provision had been made for our participation. As usual, it simply wasn't good enough. Was this an able-bodied plot, we wondered, as we struggled around the labyrinthine building, or dug our way out from under piles of unintelligible printed paper? Clearly it was not possible to give all our energies to the issue at hand. We were diverted by the sheer difficulty of participating fully.

As moaning old cripples we certainly lived up to the able-bodied stereotype, that we have nothing to contribute other than what directly concerns us at the present moment.

We decided to hold our own conference, and set to organising regular meetings to plan the event, raise money and set up outreach initiatives. We came up against the immediate problem all disabled people face when trying to start a revolution: the practical difficulties of organising ourselves. Finding a meeting place that would pass political scrutiny and be fully accessible was very difficult. After a few initial meetings at the friendly but overcrowded, smoky and not totally accessible Fallen Angel pub in London, we retreated to a less friendly, uncomfortable, but more accessible community centre a mile or so down the road. Feeling dejected and marginalised, we huddled forlornly in the cold, bare main room, surrounded by piled-up tables and chairs. Shut away from the community we were trying to infiltrate, we got on with the mammoth task of planning.

In December, disaster struck. Clause 14 (soon to become Clause 27, 28 and finally Section 28) reared its ugly head. Here was a lesbian and gay community, which we were attempting to batter into co-operation, facing the most severe threat since before Stonewall. For a short moment our resolve wavered: was it right to fight for our conference in the face of such a catastrophe? Should all energies be put into fighting the Clause? We decided that whatever happened, ableism was rife in the lesbian and gay communities, and our fight must go on. Besides, the sudden cosmetic unity of the community would give us an excellent platform for our cause.

The severely able-bodied community and the straight disabled community virtually ignored our campaign. It was necessary, therefore, to make complete and utter nuisances of ourselves. The pink press shuffled with embarrassment and granted smidgeons of coverage. Despite an extensive leafletting and mailing campaign, by January only a paltry £300 had been raised: this was way

Disabled Lesbians and Gays Are Here to Stay!

short of the total £8,000 needed. We pruned the budget, contemplated turning to crime, picked up our collecting tins and limped, rolled and wobbled into the clubs.

We crashed our way around, knocking over punters' beers, and the money dropped steadily into our bucket. Playing on the nuisance and embarrassment factor, we did not care why the pennies appeared. We suspected some gave out of misplaced pity, and we knew others paid so that we would leave them in peace. All's fair in the fight against ableism, we thought, as we staggered penny-laden away — we could deal with their dubious attitudes later.

Having surveyed members of disabled lesbian and gay groups, we decided to hold the conference in Manchester. It would be a two-day event for disabled lesbians and gays only. Manchester being in the middle of Britain meant that those coming from Scotland would not have so far to travel. There was a large and active lesbian and gay community, and a lot of cheap and accessible venues. Most importantly, there was a newly emerging disabled lesbian and gay community.

Sixty of us turned up. All sections of the disability community were represented, with ages ranging from seventeen to sixty; women outnumbered men by two to one, and most geographic areas were represented, as well as a sizable delegation from Europe. There were a handful of lesbian mothers, but the black and minority ethnic communities were poorly represented. It was clear that the all-white organising group had not done enough to seek out and encourage under-represented communities to attend.

Workshops took place on a wide range of topics, including Clause 28; our experiences as disabled lesbians and gays in the able-bodied lesbian and gay community; challenging race, gender, class discrimination; access and access codes, and much more. There were also separate disability workshops, separate space for women, working-class lesbians and gays, lesbian mothers and so on. There were several joint sessions, a press conference (at which only two lesbian or gay publications were represented, and no disabled press), and a highly successful social event.

The conference made a number of discussions about future action, which included the following: LANGUID (Lesbians And Gays United In Disability) should become a communications system and umbrella group for the already existing disabled lesbian and gay organisations; we should compile contact lists and produce a regular mailing; we should help to get disabled lesbian and gay representation on local and national groups, and help set up local disabled lesbian and gay groups; information should be provided about our liberation for severely able-bodied groups; its existence should be publicised, along with that of the other already existing disabled lesbian and gay groups; we should make contact and build links with groups of people with AIDS, and encourage their participation in LANGUID and other disabled lesbian and gay groups; links should be forged with black and minority ethnic communities, and disabled lesbians and gays from these communities should be sought out and encouraged to join LANGUID and other disabled lesbian and gay groups; we should put together an anthology of writing by disabled lesbians and gays, or persuade someone else to organise it; in order to fight homophobia in the straight disabled community we should infiltrate their groups; we should give support to straight disabled people around our joint struggle for the right to be sexual; we should make links with all other oppressed groups; and finally, more events of this kind should be organised.

Our Absence Is Required

Since the conference, more disabled lesbians and gays have slowly come out of the closet. To some extent, our profile has been raised within the able-bodied lesbian and gay community: we have been in prominence on several

Disabled Lesbians and Gays Are Here to Stay!

marches and parades; we have had a highly successful social in London, and — for the first time — events for our community in the North London Lesbian Strength and Gay Pride Festival; a disabled gay men's group has been started at Manchester Gay Centre; a short television programme was made about the lives of disabled lesbians and gays, featuring LANGUID members.

One year later, LANGUID members are now asking the question 'What has materially changed for us since the conference?'. Have severely able-bodied lesbians and gays noticed anything different? Listening to the pink press, or going down the clubs, I find it hard to believe that the LANGUID conference, and all it meant and achieved, ever happened.

LANGUID's human resources and energies are scant. Activists do what we can by stealing hours from our work or spare time. There is a limit to how much can be achieved without moral, material and political support. Sadly, despite our efforts, none of these is forthcoming, and the issues that face disabled lesbians and gays are still at the bottom of the political agenda.

We know that we share last place with a variety of other sections of the lesbian and gay communities. The problem with disability being an afterthought is that this means we do not get services which may support our participation. These take time to organise, so by the time someone remembers our existence it is too late to book the sign language interpreter, do special mailshots, organise transport, tape or braille the information, and so on.

Issues of equality are not fashionable for the majority of the severely able-bodied, white, middle-class lesbian and gay communities. To them, our disabilities preclude us from having, or wishing to express, an independent sexuality. We are therefore not considered 'proper' lesbians or gays. Most of us do not look, act, move or communicate in what is considered to be a lesbian or gay way. We are outsiders in our own community, and no-one hesitates to let us know that. The message may be shrouded in patronage or ignorance, but we know exactly what is meant by the space created by our absence.

In some sections of the lesbian and gay communities the provision of facilities to support our participation is seeped in 'right on' sentiment. This generally happens at lesbian events (the gay male community usually do not bother to try), provision is last-minute and sometimes inappropriate — for example, in the choice of interpreters for sign-language. An interpreter may be booked for a meeting, after which the organisers sit back and wait for deaf lesbians and gays to turn up, having made no attempt to ensure they know about the meeting. When no deaf people appear the organisers get disheartened, declare all disabled people totally ungrateful, moan about the 'waste of money' and resolve never to bother again. What they have forgotten is that communicating with deaf people (who generally do not use 'English' as their first language) needs specific kinds of publicity and outreach. Often, it is enough to appear at Brothers and Sisters Gay Deaf Group armed with leaflets and someone with a reasonable standard of British Sign Language. This simple activity appears to be beyond most groups, and one is left wondering what they are frightened of.

The tokenism exhibited by the 'right on' section of the lesbian and gay community is not merely confined to providing facilities. There are new names for them now. Sign language interpreters are fashionably referred to as 'signers'. This word is not approved by the deaf community since it denies the validity of British Sign Language as a living language. BSL users and their cultural experiences have been systematically denied and repressed by their hearing-dominated world for hundreds of years. *City Limits* and other papers also often mis-spell the word, thus advertising the interesting and much needed facility 'singers for the deaf'.

Their linguistic imperialism is not confined to the facilities we need — we now also have new labels for ourselves. We are no longer just 'the disabled', we are now known as 'people with special needs', 'differently

Disabled Lesbians and Gays Are Here to Stay!

abled' or 'physically challenged' — pretty euphemisms which carefully avoid any mention of who and what we really are. No account is taken of what we want to be called (generally 'people with disabilities' or 'disabled people'). We may be 'different' and we are certainly 'challenged', but there ain't nothing special about us, baby! We are disabled by this society, thank you very much! The only special thing about us is that the severely able-bodied are bent on treating us like little green furry things from outer space (when not ignoring us altogether), sentimental attitudes which are born out of embarrassment and misplaced pity. Our image seems to be totally controlled by people who are severely able-bodied, or able-bodied people who suddenly announce a convenient disability as soon as they are confronted by an angry disabled person. This ceases to exist when the threat goes away.

Either way, these people do not have the confidence of the disability community, and they have not conceived of the idea of consulting disabled lesbians and gays. Witness various peculiar references to disability in the pink press, especially *The Pink Paper* (*Capital Gay* and the rest seem to have been residing in an exclusively able-bodied zone): recently they published an article on the Disabled Olympics which appeared to have no relevance to disabled lesbians and gays. The pages of this 'newspaper' had until then been relatively devoid of articles on disability — perhaps they thought any old article on disability would do. They could have filled the space with something about us, or they could have written about how the taped version of their publication managed to appear week after week, relatively on time, without any support from them. The same wonderful rag asked me to review television programmes; they thought a blind television reviewer would be interesting? Is this tokenism, or is it because *Capital Gay* don't have a blind television reviewer? One wonders.

Before AIDS stole its way into the gay community, pubs and clubs would hold regular fundraising activities for charity. The charities selected were often straight, able-bodied-controlled disability groups, whose services went mainly to white people. We objected to gay money going to straight disabled organisations, since they actively oppressed disabled lesbians and gays. The charities gratefully took the money whilst we, though a small section of the charities' clientele, received no benefit.

On a visit to a women's club in London during the height of LANGUID's fundraising campaign, I witnessed a raffle and collection taking place in aid of the Great Ormond Street Hospital. Noticing the sizable amount collected, I approached the proprietress to suggest she run a benefit raffle for LANGUID. My request was refused as we were a 'political' group and her club was not into politics. I sought leave to hand out my leaflets, which gave the address and bank account details for postal donations, and we were refused this, too. Apparently the appeal of sick children was safer than disabled adults. The image of disability in children can be made particularly pathetic and piteous — also, they cannot answer back so well. Adult versions, especially lesbian and gay ones, were obviously disgusting to her and her clientele. But then, we knew that anyway. The fact that we are trying to become part of the community served by such pubs and clubs was obviously irrelevant. The proprietress was not going to aid and abet us in our aim in case we started coming into her club 'in hoards'. It is clear to me that we are more than an embarrassment in such places. Quite apart from our exclusion by the lack of access, the attitudes of the club owners militate against our acceptance. Their feelings about us are clearly demonstrated at every fundraiser they hold for able-bodied-controlled disability charities.

These days, the pubs and clubs are collecting for AIDS organisations. The mainly white clientele has a definite sense that it is helping itself, but there is still a prevailing feeling of 'There but for the grace of Gay God go I'. Sometimes the events are done in consultation with

Disabled Lesbians and Gays Are Here to Stay!

people with AIDS, but they have not made their clubs any more accessible. Some of the beneficiaries can no longer climb the stairs, stand the smoke or handle the crush. Still, AIDS has an emotional appeal, and not just because it is close to home for many people in the clubs. Most members of the gay community know someone who has died, is dying, or who is threatened because of HIV. The disease is in danger of being romanticised, its 'victims' often pretty young men, once hale and hearty, now struck down — while disability is seen as ugly and contagious. Equally emotive is the fact that an act of love can leave such a legacy. It is right to want to respond, to find ways of counteracting that terrible feeling of helplessness, but at what cost, and at the sacrifice of whose dignity?

It could be said that disabled lesbians and gays have gained because of AIDS. It has forced the gay community to recognise human frailty, and to start living at a rate and in a manner that will include all of us. But there is still this 'It can't happen to me' attitude. Some ignore the terrible threat and go on boogeying at 120 beats per minute. Those who do recognise AIDS as the biggest threat faced by the gay community for many years may still not understand the relevance of positive action on the disability front. Like AIDS, disability can strike out of the blue. A car smash, a sudden illness, a knife attack or HIV — all can cause disability.

As more research is done into the cause and prevention of AIDS, people with the virus may have increased life expectations. Living with AIDS means periods of complete or semi-incapacity interspersed with times of comparative good health. What about their needs when they are ill? When people with AIDS are unable to climb stairs, they cannot get into the clubs. Although it is a temporary state of affairs, it is still a problem. People with disabilities have similar difficulties. Some of us may know times when stair-climbing is impossible, and times when it is not. Many of us are also living with progressive illnesses, and some of our lives are threatened by them.

But, sadly, the connections are not being made.

It seems the gay community is dead set against recognising issues around disability, and people with AIDS are denying the connections. Where is the sense in this separation when people with AIDS, and lesbians and gays with disabilities, have so much to learn from each other, so much to share? Sadly, too, the straight disability community refuses to recognise the significance of AIDS. Only disabled lesbians and gays, members of the Disability Sub Group of the Haringey Lesbian and Gay Sub Committee, have addressed the issue. They attempted to make connections and open up dialogue, writing a policy paper which was sent to AIDS organisations two years ago. There was no response. The only occasion on which we have worked together was during the dispute with Uranian Travel in 1988. Even here, disabled lesbians and gays found ourselves blocked out of negotiations which were being led by Frontliners, and the dispute was never resolved to our satisfaction.

If disabled lesbians and gays are ever to be accepted as full participants in the lesbian and gay communities, all these connections have to be made. Severely able-bodied lesbians and gays have to stop thinking of us as outside their community. The pink pound must be put to use to benefit us all, exactly in the way it is being used to support people with AIDS. Unless the community welcomes all of us, irrespective of our abilities and disabilities, irrespective of our race, gender, class, size or age, it will not be providing a safe and welcoming environment for those sections of the communities whose participation will be threatened because they have AIDS. Why penalise the person, when the disabling nature of the community can be changed? It is not just that 'ramps and lifts are rights not gifts', it is our right to live, love and be happy. If our absence is really required, why not be honest and say so — 'No cripples beyond this point'.

Disabled Lesbians and Gays Are Here to Stay!

Epilogue

Some of this article was written in 1989: there has since been some development in the relationship between AIDS organisations and disability groups. Disabled lesbians and gays are involved in ACTUP (AIDS Coalition To Unleash Power), and ACTUP members are involved in direct action disability groups. Disabled lesbians and gays are now working together in some disability organisations and making our presence felt in a new lesbian and gay disability organisation, currently known as 'Regard'. This has been set up to challenge homophobia in the disability community. Two working disability cabarets, one for lesbians, and a mixed lesbian and gay event, were organised as part of North London Lesbian Strength and Gay Pride 1990. The success of these events has prompted disability groups to organise more in the future. Pride '90 tried to provide full access to the carnival and failed, and intend to try harder next year. Slowly but surely, progress is being made, but there is still a long way to go.

Acknowledgements

I should like to thank Sharon Smith, Fiona Clark and Kate Beagane for help with proof-reading and ideas in this article.

Chapter 5
Nuremberg Revisited?

Clause 28 and the Spectre of Nazism

Tara Kaufmann

This article originally appeared, in a shortened form, in *Jewish Socialist* No.14, Autumn 1988.

In June 1988 a new law came into force which was widely greeted as proof that Thatcher's Britain is nothing less than a fascist police state. 'The road to Auschwitz is clearly signposted' warned *Capital Gay*, while *City Limits* claimed that this law 'has no precedent since the Nazis seized control in Germany.' The new law was, in fact, not a measure to enforce racial hygiene, or to legitimise the incarceration of millions of political prisoners. It was designed primarily to undermine local authorities and capitalise on the Labour Party's problems with its 'loony left' image. Hardly Nuremberg revisited.

This is not to deny that Clause 28 (now Section 2A) of the Local Government Act is a particularly vicious and bigoted piece of legislation, cynically singling out a sector of the population for scapegoat status, and whipping up fear and hysteria in a deliberate attempt to create moral panic. This tactic has many historical precedents, including (but not limited to) the portrayal of Jews, homosexuals and others as folk devils in Nazi Germany. That there are comparisons between Nazi Germany and

Nuremberg Revisited?

Thatcher's Britain which can be drawn with some validity is undeniable, unless one views Hitler as a historical aberration, a product of nothing but his own insanity.

My concern, though, is that the use of the spectre of Nazism in the Stop The Clause campaign has been so obsessive and so ahistoric that it has obscured our understanding of the complex issues involved. Further, it has diverted attention from more contemporary issues and alliances which need to be forged and which are currently neglected.

Echoes of Antisemitism

Clause 28 exploits the 'otherness' of lesbians and gays, and lends institutional affirmation to further discrimination and persecution against a group which is already marginalised and vulnerable under the law. Homophobia and antisemitism are distinct phenomena with different origins, functions and meanings: recent homophobic rhetoric, however, has become uncannily evocative of classic antisemitism, reflecting fears around sexuality and defilement which are deeply ingrained in Western society. Lesbians and gays are perceived as a corrupting influence, reservoirs of disease and degradation, as a conspiratorial clique intent on undermining Christian values. We are also witnessing the growth of a new paranoia about homosexual 'power': the tabloid press would have us believe that Labour Party policy favours compulsory homosexuality, and that all over Britain five-year-olds are receiving instruction in practical sodomy. In the same month that Clause 28 became law, the *Sunday Telegraph* ran a centre-spread article asking 'Is There A Homosexual Conspiracy?', and concluded that indeed there was.

Black Triangles and Other Myths

We do not need to look overseas for illustrations of how a government can gradually and systematically erode the civil rights of a sector of the population: precedents in British law include, for example, the treatment of immigrants. None, however, is as compelling as Nazism, one of the most potent cultural landmarks of our time. Its reification as the ultimate scenario of inhumanity has obscured understanding of both its specificity and its context in history. The Holocaust, in particular, has become mythologised in the popular consciousness into little more than a combination of war story and grisly atrocity tale, along the lines of Jack The Ripper. For many, the events of the Holocaust bear as little relation to a reality undergone by living people as cowboys-and-indians films bear to the experience of Native American communities. Small wonder that it becomes so easy to press it into the service of political opportunism, so difficult to resist fetishising Nazism as a kitschy yardstick for any form of human suffering.

The Clause 28 campaign, unfortunately, fell prey to this temptation. Very early on, the London-based Arts Lobby produced posters featuring Pastor Niemöller's famous poem, 'First they came for the Jews' (see page 53), and including the myth that he was murdered by the Nazis. This poster sparked off a number of reprints and almost became the anthem of the campaign. Given the fame and importance of his words, it is perhaps surprising that little interest was shown in Martin Niemöller himself, or the context for his poem. Commonly used to protest matters of social injustice ranging from the level of student grants to the price of milk, this poem was in fact a personal statement of regret that opposition to Hitler within the Christian establishment had been, on the whole, clandestine and inadequate, that the German Church had 'let God wait ten years'. Niemöller's opposition to Hitler earned him several years' incarceration in first Sachsenhausen and then Dachau, but it is simply not true that he was murdered by the Nazis. He died in 1983.

Even more interesting is the case of the Great Black Triangle Myth. The recent upsurge in popularity of black triangles as a symbol of lesbian resistance derives from the legend that lesbians suffered in the same way as gay men under Hitler, that they were forced to wear black triangles as a badge of their sexuality, as some kind of equivalent to the pink triangles that branded gay men in concentration camps. Life as a lesbian in Nazi Germany was not easy, of course, and some women were sent to camps as a direct result of their sexuality. Survivors have reported seeing lesbian inmates wearing black triangles, and Jewish lesbians branded with yellow and black triangles. Interestingly, it has been reported — but never confirmed — that there were women prisoners branded with pink triangles in Ravensbruck.

The black triangle, however, did not signify lesbianism, but 'asocials' — offenders against the volkisch sensibility. This category included sexual outlaws such as prostitutes and lesbians, but also alcoholics, malingerers and the mentally ill. Although lesbian clubs and papers were closed down, and individuals interned in psychiatric hospitals (many of whom were later murdered in the 'euthanasia programme'), or arrested by the secret police, persecution of lesbians as lesbians was relatively rare, and they were never targeted as a group in the way that gay men were. In fact, lesbianism was not illegal in Nazi Germany: as in modern Britain, women were controlled by a complex set of social and political forces, and to assume that lesbians suffered equivalent oppression to gay men is to ignore the very different meanings and threats of male and female homosexuality. Those who perpetuate this myth are, usually unwittingly, buying into a history which obscures and distorts the specific experience of women.

Identity Crisis

Why do myths like these gain credence? What is so attractive, so powerful, about evoking images of Nazism in our political activism? Do we somehow 'need' Pastor Niemöller to have been murdered by the Nazis? Do lesbians have to prove some historical 'equivalency' to gay oppression in order to get anti-lesbianism taken seriously? This tendency is caused, in part, by the meaning of Nazism in modern consciousness and its use in political rhetoric. It also arises from the current crisis in identity politics.

It is hard to conceive how feminism would have developed without its positing of personal identity and subjective experience as fundamental to our political understanding and activism. It has enabled women to examine and analyse their lives and name their experiences in the context of oppression, as opposed to individual failure and self-blame. For many of us it has facilitated exploration of our identities, integration of our subjective experience with our political analysis, and resistance to cultural assimilation. It has also given us a Women's Movement which genuinely attempts — though arguably with little real commitment or success — to reflect the diversity of women's lives.

Identity politics has long been attacked and ridiculed by Left activists, who have caricatured its proponents as being too busy knitting muesli to make revolution. Much of the time this criticism has been based not in a desire to advance the cause of women's liberation, but in a wish to discredit feminism and devalue its achievements. Recently, however, growing discontent has been evident among those who previously embraced identity politics, but are far from happy with its current manifestations.

This ideology, which has enriched our movement almost immeasurably, has also, paradoxically, become one of our greatest weaknesses and dangers, a Frankenstein's monster no longer entirely within our control. There is a backlash building against the misuse

Nuremberg Revisited?

and abuse of identity politics which has boiled over into bitter disputes over sexual practice, personal adornment, and the use of lesbian and gay 'space'. We have developed a political discourse which has mutated the concept of personal identity as being intrinsic to our politics, to one in which our personal identity is our politics. Far from educating us about diversity of experience, this has restricted — even fossilised — our perception of human reality. Individual negotiation with present reality is allowed little room: we have become no more than the sum total of our gender, sexuality, ethnicity, age and ability. These 'identities' are presented as credentials: not in order to inform, educate or invite discussion, but to assert moral and political authority and the right to define 'the truth': in short, to stifle debate.

Identity politics is now a cult of victim-worship, in which oppression has been glamourised and equated with virtue and access to some kind of higher truth. 'Oppression points' have become so linked with status, with validity as a human being, that we as individuals are put under enormous pressure to present our credentials as victims of oppression. We can do this by bracketing our identities and destinies with those of other victims, past and present. Co-opting the horrors of Nazism to boost victim-status is a particular temptation for lesbians and gay men, as our claims for political solidarity are often met with ridicule. It sometimes seems as though our oppression status does not stand on its own merits, but must be proved by association with others who have gained public validation for their suffering. This results in those painful and sordid squabbles over property rights in victimhood with which we are all familiar.

In the interests of challenging a written history distorted by heterosexism, lesbians and gays have become concerned with 'reclaiming hidden histories', uncovering both closeted and 'out' lesbians and gays back to Boadicea and beyond. This 'reclaiming', however, is often done in a way both crude and ahistoric. At its worst, 'gay history' has often imposed an essentially modern idea of lesbian and gay identity on a time when homosexuality had a completely different function and meaning. We should address the problem of the labelling process and its historical roots, and approach questions of sexuality with a little more enquiry and awareness of the construction of contemporary meanings. If knowing our history is important for the lesbian and gay communities — which it is — then it must also be important that our knowledge be accurate and questioning. We should ask ourselves why we need labels and victim-status to the extent that they become self-defeating, self-fulfilling prophecies. As Stephen Howe asserts:

> History is more than memory, more than the commemoration of tragedy, just as it is more than the assertion of moral stances. Any history which is insensitive to the claims of memory ... runs the risk of inhumanity.

Lessons for the Future

'Anyone who in an argument starts comparing their opponent to Hitler probably hasn't got a very good case' (Stephen Howe).

Scare-mongering as a political tactic can be useful in the short term. In the long term, it undermines credibility and increases confusion and fear. There is sometimes a fine line to be drawn between getting people worried enough to get mobilised, and spreading misunderstanding and panic (rarely a useful strategy in political activism). On reflection, I believe most of us in the Stop The Clause campaign did not give this issue sufficient consideration.

It is, of course, vital that we learn the lessons of the past. But memory is useless without understanding, and understanding is obscured by misuse of history. What I am criticising is the usage of simplistic references, to the neglect of important social and cultural links. And what I am advocating is active understanding and use of history, challenging conventional perceptions of the past in order to write our own history with new awareness. Let's remember that the Stop The Clause campaign was not a charity, but a political struggle against an unjust law which eroded the rights of all, whatever their sexuality. As such, we did not need to go begging for favours: we had a right to solidarity and support from fellow activists.

We can also use a better understanding of history to construct and assert personal identity in a more thoughtful, positive way than we do at present. The development and management of a viable identity is a dynamic, lifelong process requiring the individual to synthesize divergent and conflicting aspects of her social experience, including historical factors. This task can hold particular difficulties for lesbians and gays who have been isolated from the usual networks of community and support, but all of us have choice and responsibility in our negotiation with the past. Those of us who combine different ethnic, sexual or situational identities can interweave our history, our present and our choices into an exciting and creative challenge to the status quo, or we can fall back on the tired and restrictive model of 'double oppression'.

History can and should be used to improve our understanding of the present and enable us to move forward. It should never be used to fossilise our imagination, our understanding, our activism. If we can learn to do this, there need be no sacred cows, no untouchables. I suggest, for a start, that an appropriate use of Nazi history would be to think again about black triangles: who wore them and why? What was the threat posed by 'asocials'? What linked lesbians with the unemployed, with alcoholics, with prostitutes? Just as the 'asocial' category was widened constantly to create yet more 'heretics', so in Thatcher's Britain the concept of 'normality' is being ever tightened. A thoughtful examination of these links could provide us with analogies infinitely more useful and enlightening than those we are currently struggling with.

Chapter 6
Don't Break Our Arts

The Arts Lobby and Section 28

David Benedict, Sue Sanders and Carole Woddis

For many, the fight against Clause 28 was a horrifying conclusion to all the political battles lesbians and gays had been fighting since the 1967 Sexual Offences Act. Seen by opponents both then and now as opening the floodgates to permissiveness, the Act, far from legitimising homosexuality, merely decriminalised it between consenting males over the age of twenty-one, in private. Since then, alongside the growth of a vocal lesbian/gay community, there have been attacks both physical and legislative which have led to all kinds of political action. Simultaneously, lesbians and gays have been involved both as individuals and as recognised bodies in other campaigns; on issues of race, gender, disability, education, and so on. For all of those in the vanguard, there were countless others unwilling or unable to take such direct action, who were nonetheless anxious to be part of it, or at least to savour its success. For many, the route was via a burgeoning gay culture.

The arts remain essential and dangerous. At once a voice of criticism and a celebration of values, they are indicative of the moral health of a society whether existing as consoling fantasy or as an imaginative vision of reality. From the late sixties a voice, previously highly encoded, dying through neglect or frankly ignored, began to be heard. 'Gay Liberation' led to an informed and energised recognition of a cultural identity with a past and a potential. Lesbian and gay arts organisations gained confidence, strength and diversity, challenging the accepted concepts on the cultural, social and educational agendas in terms of what was being said, where and to whom. Following the examples of women's, ethnic and other groups reclaiming and creating their culture, *identification*, *affirmation* and *inspiration* proved to be controlling ideas through which history could be explored, ideas communicated and the future imagined.

Gradually, our effect upon the mainstream became more pronounced. New attitudes were being bred. People who had worked in lesbian and gay environments drew on the experience when going on to work with mixed companies. Others left the arts and moved into areas such as the voluntary sector and local government, to often highly significant effect. After years of self-exploitation, funding from areas other than within, whether financial or in terms of resources, slowly became available to arts groups. This in turn led to a widening of the debate. Our perspective on the world was being expressed and perceived, and to that extent Clause 28 can be seen as an (unwarranted) measure of our success.

There is a widely held belief that the arts world is a cosy little nest for lesbians and gays, and that our sexuality is no cause for concern. Our presence and thus our politics should, therefore, be easily assimilated. The reality of a business clearly concerned with image, literally and metaphorically, is somewhat different. The performing arts in particular have a long tradition of dealing in sexual stereotypes, such as the limp-wristed man, promulgated by performers who all the while busily promote their own heterosexuality. Lesbians have perhaps fewer theatrical stereotypes to demolish, for, as everywhere else, they are rendered virtually invisible. For those of us involved in the arts, whether as creators or performers, 'coming out' is still a courageous personal and political act; one that is seen as 'limiting' and 'career damaging', particularly for lesbians. As in many workplaces, such constraints have not silenced the voices.

The most important side-effect of the Clause, and one that cannot have been anticipated by its proponents, was the unanimity of those voices when the threat was first perceived at the end of 1987. Following the formation of the Stop The Clause campaign, Richard Sandells of Gay Sweatshop circulated a letter calling on all arts-workers to recognise the dangers. Over fifty individuals from all sections of the arts community — writers, actors, directors, musicians, dancers, administrators, designers, photographers — met on 3rd January 1988 in response to this initiative. Not surprisingly there were opinions from more than one side of the political spectrum, but all of those who continued within the campaign were unanimously and implacably opposed to the Clause in its entirety. Any work of art funded directly or indirectly by a local authority was potentially under threat, as the presentation of a positive image of homosexuality could be interpreted as 'promotion'. Such art extended from the performance of a play to the stocking of a library book. After all, much of the parliamentary debate centred around the actions of left-wing councils apparently abusing rate-payers and the public purse by daring to condone such 'anarchic' pieces of literature as *Jenny Lives with Eric and Martin*, fallaciously rumoured to be freely available to children in schools.

It was recognised that we were being accorded the status of second-class citizens (together with a tacit go-ahead for gay-baiting), and that state censorship was upon us. For many of us in the arts, the concept of censorship was nothing new; that it should be within reach of the statute books made it a matter of universal and urgent concern. It did, however, provide a point of access for those who would not recognise a supposedly 'gay issue' as having meaning for them. It was felt that y drawing attention to the implications for artistic freedom and civil liberties, allegiances with prominent people within the media could be made, thereby publicising the Clause in all its manifestations to our best advantage.

Vast numbers of contacts were made via mass mailings to individuals, to arts-related unions, to the press and media. Within days a poster was produced, based on Pastor Niemöller's testimony under Nazi Germany, urging people to realise just what was at stake:

> First they came for the Jews and I did not speak out — because I was not a Jew.
>
> Then they came for the communists and I did not speak out — because I was not a communist.
>
> Then they came for the trade unionists and I did not speak out — because I was not a trade unionist.
>
> Then they came for me — and there was no-one left to speak out for me.

As hoped for, the poster struck a chord and not just with lesbians and gays; its huge popularity obviously stemming from the uncomfortable parallels between Niemöller's vision and Thatcher's Britain.

In other quarters, however, opposition was growing:

(i) Not since the horrors of daily AIDS headlines in 1985 had the tabloid press had such a field day. The synonymous nature of gays and 'loony lefties' was far too good to resist. 'Screaming Gays bring Commons to Halt' screamed the *Sun*, in response to the spontaneous but short-lived cry from Richard Sandells on the night the Clause went through its second reading, 'It's our *lives* you're dealing with here.'

(ii) On December 28th Bernard Levin wrote in *The Times*: 'The legislation is not the worst or the most important item in the rising temperature of hate, except in so far as it will inevitably turn up the flame ... The test of any country wishing to be thought of as civilised is the way it treats its minorities. On the whole Britain has scored well. Are we to throw it away because the yahoos have scented blood? ... Are we really to go back to a time when homosexuals were not simply embarrassed or reluctant to disclose their sexual nature, but afraid to?'

(iii) Either side of this, *The Guardian* and *The Independent* ran similar expressions of outrage. However, although areas of the arts world were certainly sympathetic and appalled by the implications of the Clause in terms of artistic freedom, many were unwilling to lend their support for so-called 'gay sex lessons' in schools. (Ironically, at this point no-one realised that the 1986 Education Act had put sex education into the hands of school governors, thus rendering the educational content of the Clause null and void, a fact only made clear to Dame Jill Knight and others once it passed into law.)

Whether seasoned activist or zealous novice, those within the Arts Lobby recognised that time was frighteningly short, which in turn led to a sense of pragmatism. In order to maximise our impact upon the debates in the House of Lords, we enlisted the support of Lord Falkland. A peer with a long history of enlightened interest in the Arts, he gradually was made aware of the specific dangers of the bill, particularly those concerning 'pretended family relationships'. We also worked with Mark Fisher, Labour's Shadow Arts Minister, and others within the Labour Commons benches, together with all the organisations proposing amendments. While seeking total rejection of the Clause, it was recognised that this was going to prove impossible, particularly given the timetable. Damage limitation in the form of amendments — the art of the possible — was thus the fallback position.

A major press conference was organised to coincide with the vote in the Lords. By this time we had contacted and were joined by Ian McKellen, who immediately devoted his time and formidable energies to the cause. His contacts proved invaluable in further extending support beyond the gay community via endless media appearances. The press conference attracted over 100 members of the press, who together with a number of peers ferried from the House of Lords, witnessed anti-Clause statements from authors, artists, librarians,

Lords, composers, comedians, directors, dancers, actors, 'agony aunts', singers, songwriters, producers and publishers. Each of the speakers, gay or straight, showed some of the literally hundreds of cheques and letters of support that had flooded in from across the country. Many of the speakers chose to address specific issues, others attacked the very foundations of the legislation:

> 'I'm not sure whether the wideness with which this act was drawn up was due to stupidity or cunning. I'm inclined to favour cunning. It's important that we oppose it not just in its wider implications in the arts, but at the narrow heart of this clause, so that gay children will not be afraid of their sexuality.'
>
> Caryll Churchill, Playwright

> 'Many of my friends are homosexual, and as far as I can see, if a family is considered to be a loving, close relationship, many of their relationships are far from "pretended". If I said that after this Clause is passed and if this theatre were funded by a local council, I probably could be prosecuted, or rather the council could, that's an alarming thought. If one of my three daughters decides she is gay, I would like to think that she could go to a support group. If this Clause is passed, those support groups will collapse. I, frankly, don't want to belong to a society that does not care for its minorities. And quite frankly, your Lordships, I don't actually consider that my friends', my daughters' or my own sexuality is any of your business.'
>
> Sheila Hancock, Actress/Director

In the following days, with the bill at committee stage, anti-Clause commentary began appearing in the most unlikely quarters of the press. The Lobby was besieged with requests for speakers to appear on TV chat shows, give radio and press interviews, or speak at public meetings. The Lobby had become a facilitative body matching speakers with organisations who sought to address all aspects of the Clause. Interestingly, the newspapers tended to focus on the artistic/civil liberties angles, while a succession of highly acrimonious TV debates dealt almost exclusively with lesbian motherhood and education. Such programmes may simply have polarized the opinions of many, but they still served to publicise the issues. Representatives addressed the Women's TUC Conference, Equity AGM (where an Arts Lobby motion was passed), the Birmingham NUT, etc. — and provided advice and support to organisations under direct pressure. This included the engineering of the restoration of the grant to Clyde Unity Theatre, whose production of the play *Killing Me Softly* was put in jeopardy by the actions of the Liverpool City Council. After a particularly virulent anti-gay campaign by the staff at Leeds College of Music, they were forced to concede defeat with the re-instatement of the Lesbian and Gay Society following our intervention.

In the wake of the Clause passing into law, it is important to understand what happened in order to evaluate the present and the future. Despite much trumpeting by hot-headed opponents, at the time of writing (1990) no case has gone before the courts, yet this does not mean that the law is toothless. It is no exaggeration to say that a climate of fear has been created. Due to its imprecise wording, funders and artists fight shy of the issues with a resultant silence. In effect, what has happened is that images of homosexuality have been privatised. Private (i.e. public!) schools can 'promote' homosexuality; private galleries can exhibit lesbian photography; commercial managements and those untouched by local authority funding remain free to produce gay plays. For local authority subsidised organisations — be they theatres, galleries, libraries or council buildings — it is a different story. Arts funding has always been a precarious matter. A low priority for most, if not all local authorities, the securing of funds for an arts organisation is problematic enough without having to convince local councillors that the work does not contravene ill-defined Government legislation. Despite accusations of 'crying wolf', books have disappeared from library shelves, photographs have been banned and theatre companies have lost bookings. With nobody prepared to go to court over the issue, other excuses are given and nothing can be proved. When Kent County Council banned Glyndebourne Touring Opera's production of *Death in Venice* from schools, they disingenuously remarked that Section 28 had nothing to do with it, they merely deemed the work 'unsuitable' for schools. Both the Arts Council — whose amendment to the Clause was taken up in the Lords and fell to a smaller margin than any other — and the regional arts associations remain immune to the legislation. Pressure must be brought to bear upon them and others to continue the fight. We have already seen lesbian and gay groups fall foul of the prejudiced attitudes of local councillors, who usually blame lack of funds, but who more recently have begun to cite the Section. With the vagueness of the wording, such groups cannot begin to countenance the challenging of such a decision in the courts.

Even more insidious is what writer Jim Hiley described at the press conference:

> 'I'm here because I'm gay ... Clause 28 is about legislators invading the imagination of artists. And what will follow Clause 28? Will we be required to promote heterosexuality? Will there be an official "truth" about sexuality in this country that artists will be required to comply with?'

It is easy to list works that scandalise the prurient and end up banned. Indeed such an event lends notoriety to the work. What cannot be counted is the loss of positive images that artists grow too afraid to create. Not everyone can afford to spend months creating gay art only to have its possibly well-disposed exhibitor reject it, fighting shy of the possibility of losing their local authority funding. Not everyone is strong enough to fight all the battles.

Understanding the immensity of the freedoms at stake, within the Arts Lobby itself there were remarkably few fights. Previously separatist lesbians and gay men found a common ground long since thought lost. Shared experiences and new alliances proved invigorating and binding. Phyllida Shaw wrote of the Arts Lobby in *The*

New Democrat:

> There is little doubt that its forceful line of argument led to the tabling of the [Arts Council] amendment which the Lords eventually supported ... That the arts world is an articulate one in which many homosexuals happen to work is significant. A less vocal lobby might have had no impact at all and the Government could have had a far smoother ride towards the implementation of a thoroughly nonsensical piece of legislation.

In the two years since its arrival, Section 28 has produced a defiance in many lesbian and gay artists that refuses to go away. AIDS and Section 28, both of which seem to threaten us with extinction, have served, in the nightmare of anger and loss, to sharpen our minds and strengthen our determination.

Editors' note:

At the time of going to press, Gay Sweatshop, Britain's only lesbian and gay theatre company, is to close due to the financial crisis facing all theatres and worsened by Clause 28, which has made local councils reluctant to make bookings.

Chapter 7
Lifestyle or Practice?

A New Target for Legislation

Diane Hamer, Tara Kaufmann and Paul Lincoln

PL: Homophobic legislation now seems to be focusing on the gay lifestyle, rather than homosexual practice. Does this herald a new type of law?

DH: Examining Section 28 in detail, a number of important differences between it and previous legislation are evident. For the first time lesbians are included in legislation — not by specific reference but because within Section 28 'homosexuality' is not defined as specifically male. Secondly, the legislation is aimed not at homosexual *acts* — a specific set of sexual practices — but at *homosexuality* itself, a state of being, a way of life. Lastly, the wording of subsection (2), 'Nothing in (1) above shall be taken to ... ', makes clear that the conception of the Section occurred squarely within an AIDS climate. This subsection commits to law a popular historical slippage between homosexuality and disease (homosexuality *as* disease).

TK: The crucial issue is the concept of lifestyle. Hitherto, legislation has focused on sexual acts, which are easier to define and prohibit. Given the assumed sexual passivity of women, this has resulted in restrictions on gay men. It is simply too difficult to prohibit lesbian activity, which is, after all, only a small shift along the continuum from that platonic emotional and physical closeness between women which has been considered more socially acceptable than such closeness between men. In recent years lesbianism has become politicised, visible and a social threat. How do you discourage that? Inevitably Section 28 had to tackle the modern meaning of homosexuality, which is rather more to do with culture, politics, lifestyle. In discouraging the promotion of something quite abstract they were, in fact, responding to an agenda set by us.

DH: Historically, there have been no successful attempts to legislate against lesbian sexual practice in Britain. An amendment to the Criminal Law Amendment Act, introduced by Henry Labouchere in 1875, was the first piece of legislation which specifically criminalised male homosexual acts.[1] Although Labouchere's amendment reduced the penalty for sodomy it simultaneously broadened the definition of punishable acts if taking place between men. Under the amendment (which became known as the 'Blackmailers' Charter') it was made a punishable offence even to act as though one were a 'sodomite'.

In 1921 an attempt was made to bring lesbians within this same law, but was defeated in Parliament on the grounds that if such a vice existed (and many members doubted even this) then to legislate against what must surely be a minority practice could only serve to bring it to public attention, thereby alerting many innocent women to its existence.

Section 28 signals the entry of lesbianism into the legislature for the first time. I think what this indicates, ironically, is the success of feminism and of lesbian and gay liberation in forcing a visible and affirmative lesbian identity onto political agendas in Britain.

In the wording of the Section — 'homosexuality' rather than 'homosexual acts' — it is clear that we have successfully shifted social definitions of homosexuality. That definition now incorporates the notion of

Lifestyle or Practice?

homosexuality as a lifestyle and culture, above and beyond mere physical sexual acts. Section 28 does not, as previous legislation has, criminalise individual behaviour, but instead is aimed at prohibiting public and political manifestations of homosexuality as a lifestyle.

TK: The whole language of homophobia is changing rapidly. Even just ten, fifteen years ago, public perception of 'the homosexual' was of a lonely, isolated, rather pathetic figure, given to lurking round parks and public toilets. It was assumed that there were hardly any of them, and 'we' certainly didn't know any ... Now we have what can only be described as a kind of conspiracy theory, the rise of paranoia, fear of homosexuality as a social threat, that homosexuals form some kind of Fifth Column, running the (now defunct) Greater London Council, the BBC, the schools, conspiring to undermine society ... I'm particularly interested in how recent homophobic rhetoric is borrowing off traditional anti-Semitism: the idea of a malignant force, a reservoir of disease and corruption, an invisible enemy which has both power and choice over its level of visibility and assimilation. This was exemplified for me in the *Sunday Telegraph* article which was headlined 'Is There A Homosexual conspiracy?', and concluding that indeed there was.

DH: And so Section 28 railroaded our own agenda, that of feminism and gay liberation, by aiming to restrict lifestyle, visibility and choice. We, after all, were the ones who argued that being lesbian or gay was a positive and political choice, thus defiantly discarding the safety of the liberal defence of homosexuality as an inborn defect which must be tolerated as it cannot be cured.

TK: But the Stop The Clause campaign retreated to just those arguments: that it's not possible to promote homosexuality — and that even if it were, we wouldn't want to anyway. This was a total contradiction of what feminists had been saying for the past twenty years!

DH: Yes, the second wave of feminism has argued that women can choose to be lesbian, and often promoted homosexuality as both personally liberating and politically desirable. We have rejected the notion of lesbianism as a biological given, in favour of a more complex model of sexuality as a social construct, fluctuating, even reversible, and open to external influence.

PL: So our campaigning strategy was completely wrong? It was based on the assumption that we are not the social threat we were being depicted as. All our liberating arguments about being lesbian and gay were dumped in the panic to hold on to tactics which were apparently legitimate and acceptable, but fundamentally reactionary. The arguments we chose were those which could be easily used in the House of Lords, and translated into a language that was not our own. Once the pressure was on, we collectively sold out within a matter of days.

DH: The involvement of Michael Cashman in the campaign was a fascinating phenomenon. Both positive and incredibly negative. Positive in that we used the tool of representation against an attack on representation ... The involvement of Cashman, the actor, in the campaign played on his role as 'Colin', the gay character in the popular soap opera 'EastEnders', presents us, its viewing public, with a sympathetic representation of homosexuality, an 'ordinary homosexual' with whom audiences can sympathise and even identify. For Michael Cashman to step off the 'EastEnders' set and use his public profile as a fictional gay man to enter into political life was, I think, a very creative move and one which made invaluable connections between lesbian and gay politics and people's 'everyday lives'. I'd also say that of other soap opera actors, notably the rest of the cast of 'EastEnders' and most of 'Brookside' too.

But what was potentially very valuable about these links was the demonstrable breakdown of false, arbitrary

Lifestyle or Practice?

distinctions between the popular media and 'real life', when fictional characters took their place on the roll-call of Section 28's opponents.

But of course neither 'Colin' nor Cashman was a politician or activist, and it could not be expected of him that he represent gay (much less lesbian) politics in all its various and complex hues.

PL: On the other hand, he was neither John Inman nor Kenneth Williams. He presented himself as a conventional individual who wanted to lead a safe, gay lifestyle. He was not flaunting anything, he was not theatrical and he was not melodramatic. If the campaign had to be led by a soap opera star, then he was probably a good one to do it. Yet when he came on stage at the January 9th demo to rapturous applause, I was shocked that I was being represented by this man. Because, although his involvement achieved a lot in terms of publicity, it did keep the world of the gay lifestyle within the world of the theatrical. What was most worrying was that most of these people were not real. It is gratifying when people like Ken Livingstone or Chris Smith make supportive statements — what does it mean when the cast of 'EastEnders' offer their support whilst in character? They are not vulnerable and they are not people located in the real world taking any risks.

DH: I don't think I agree with Paul on this. I think, as I said earlier, that using popular representations to political ends was an incredibly creative move — and I do believe Michael Cashman, the actor, risked something in doing what he did. His and other soaps actors' involvement in the campaign raises questions about what is 'political' and what is 'real', and how the media constructs our 'real' lives. I watch soap operas regularly, and in a way 'EastEnders' or 'Brookside' is more real to me than any Labour Party conference, for instance. It would be nice if the Labour Party came out in support of lesbian and gay rights (and indeed some individual Labour MPs have been invaluable), but perhaps the deployment of soap opera characters indicates a broader and more sophisticated definition of politics; politics as the discourses of popular culture rather than the formal politics of the parliamentary parties, where the former has far greater purchase on the popular imagination than the latter.

TK: The impact made by Michael Cashman's involvement was tremendous, but it also tied in with a really reactionary trend in the campaign. We argued that you cannot teach children to be gay — which of course you can't, in the sense that you would teach them fractions — but for me at least one of the better arguments for positive images in schools is that you will get more young people coming out gay. We also spend a lot of time defending artists who were not under threat, like Shakespeare and Wilde. Did anybody really believe that library shelves would be cleared of Baldwin and Genet? Or were they just an easier focus for campaigning than, say, increased funding for lesbian feminist writing? Similarly, relying on the obvious usefulness of AIDS projects for the government did rather tend to leave projects like LESPOP [Lesbian Policing Project] and the Lesbian Archives out in the cold. I think our scaremongering and 'playing safe' lost the campaign a lot of credibility: no doubt these arguments represented a large strain of thought in the lesbian and gay communities, but for many others they were adopted for tactical advantage. The temptations of this are obvious, but I think, in the end, it backfired.

PL: The campaign basically said that the only way to defend ourselves was to portray ourselves as being in the same position as those who are discriminated against for an identity they cannot opt in or out of. If I have the disadvantage of homosexuality then maybe a local authority will offer me municipal support. We are then able to slot into a group of people to whom it is considered reasonable to be patronising. If, however, I say assertively that I have chosen to be gay or lesbian, or that I am experimenting with my sexuality, then I cannot

Lifestyle or Practice?

expect municipal support. In this sense the campaign represented a collective moment of self doubt, a retreat from lesbian and gay rights.

TK: With Michael Cashman as the sorry case of a basically decent guy who just couldn't help it?

PL: It's not surprising that people who feel like victims should use the language of victims. Those activists in the campaign perhaps realised that nothing had lingered from the period of gay liberation and the early WLM.

DH: Of course, the position taken up by the dominant voices within the campaign involved a denial of the feminist analysis of sexuality as socially constructed, a reneging on the politics of choice. Contemporary debates, those within feminism or cultural studies for example — which draw on psychoanalysis to argue for the fluidity of sexual identity — were jettisoned in favour of a kind of self-congratulatory political rhetoric carried on amongst a predominantly male cast of celebrities with Cashman and McKellen as figureheads. Not only did the political positions adopted by prominent individuals have very little to do with contemporary debates (note Cashman's regular declarations that just as no-one made him gay, it is not possible to 'make' a heterosexual into a homosexual), but it also negated the tremendous energy and activity of lesbians within the campaign.

TK: Clause 28 attacked us at the point at which we were weakened, in a time of crisis. It hit us on the nub of identity politics, an issue over which the lesbian community was in a state of civil war. There was no consensus among feminists over hierarchies, oppression, the use of disadvantage as a status symbol and political weapon. On the one hand we had a rather authoritarian, Big Sister strand of radical feminism — on the other hand, a dangerously libertarian backlash. Feminist activism is in a state of crisis over identity politics — and Clause 28 hit us where we were most vulnerable. Gay men, in the meantime, had to contend with the AIDS issue, and were tired, demoralised, depleted and on the defensive. AIDS emphasised the historic links between homosexuality and disease, and created a social climate which was ripe for Clause 28.

DH: So we got into the contradictory position of organising a campaign based around individual personalities which came to stand in for a whole set of historical debates within lesbian and gay politics about the nature of sexual identity.

PL: Which raised the issue of leadership. In the States this is not such a sensitive topic, and Robin Tyler assumed the leadership role very effectively for the Washington demo. Over here there has not been a sense of leadership for ten years: no-one wanted a leader, and any activist aspiring to that role was punished. So into the vacuum stepped two actors, who were not representative, or even necessarily well-informed, of current lesbian and gay thought.

DH: Their pre-eminent position as public figures was useful for the campaign as a way of drawing public attention and support, but there were no guarantees that, as public mouthpieces, they would necessarily represent the complexity of our political thought.

PL: Why did it all happen this way?

TK: Maybe we have achieved lowest common denominator politics: coalition work is vital, but does depend on at least a minimum level of shared ground on which to build a united front.

PL: Because so much of our politics and our identity is defined under threat. Homosexuality has always been defined by heterosexuals. If what we are faced with is the whole weight of politics and the House of Lords, then we start speaking the language of Parliament. We spend so much of our lives working within this marginalisation that we stand in the space. We have no training in being ourselves ... In fact, we are only being attacked in quite a

Lifestyle or Practice?

narrow range of ways. So much was expected of the House of Lords, yet those people have always betrayed us! How could we have been so naive? Perhaps that form of political action was quite comforting.

DH: To the extent that there were moments when we believed we were going to win ... What I think did happen in much of the rhetoric supporting the introduction of the Clause was that there was almost a tacit acknowledgement of a universal notion of homosexual desire. But also a very firm distinction was drawn by the Right between homosexual desire (which we all have the potential for) and actually acting on that desire (which was regarded as irresponsible or perverted). In public statements put out by supporters of the Clause, a common anxiety seems to be that if young boys of girls are exposed to these dangerous external homosexual influences (dangerous because tempting), their own internal homosexual potential will be ignited. The model of sexuality at play here seems to be one of mobility, fluidity, potentiality for experiencing myriad sets of desires. It is a model which I feel accurately expresses human sexual potential at its best.

What I don't agree with is the drawing of a line between this set of internal possibilities and the living out of them. The supporters of Section 28 seemed to be saying, 'Yes, homosexuality is a choice. But it is a choice one has a responsibility not to take up.'

The Clause, therefore, was not attacking homosexual desire, the existence of which it basically accepted, but lesbian and gay *identity*, the public expression of which it believed was morally wrong. What we needed to do in response was to defend lesbian and gay identities as *choices* — responsible, healthy, life-enhancing choices. Instead we took up an essentially apologist position ('we're sorry, but we can't help it'), which left us open to the charge that while our homosexual feelings may be inevitable, we ought to cease advertising ('promoting') them. Instead of defending our right to promote, we pretended we'd never intended that in the first place.

TK: It creates a dichotomy between 'good gays' and 'bad gays'. The Section highlighted a large strain of liberal thought which applauds 'discretion', and deplores the activists, the ones who 'make an issue of it' and 'bring it upon themselves'. We tried to win their support by arguing in terms of our right to quietly bring up our children and be like everyone else. That tactic is doomed to failure, because the clause does not prohibit 'discreet' homosexuality, but visible political and cultural identity.

DH: And in response we have taken refuge in apologetic notions of identity which are defeatist and which ultimately take us backwards in our social and political development.

PL: Interestingly, the Local Government Act brought in a number of other regressive and often racist measures — contract compliance, for example. Obscured by the uproar over Clause 28, the Government was quietly pushing through legislation which was actually far more pernicious. We conspicuously failed to campaign on those issues, to make common cause with others who were also badly affected.

TK: Yet we did not feel confident enough to demand political solidarity on our own behalf, but hitched onto every bandwagon from Shakespeare to Auschwitz.

DH: We tried to win support by showing what nice people we all are, rather than emphasising what was at the heart of the debate: repression of sexual choice. This repression of choice implicates every individual, not simply those of us who are lesbians and gay men, because it circumscribes the boundaries of sexual possibility. But because we fell back on a defence of lesbians and gay men as a 'minority', we lost sight of this broader perspective. We failed to use Section 28 as a vehicle by which to insist on our own radical agenda in the terrain of sexual politics, instead accepting the terms of reference

Lifestyle or Practice?

of our opposition.

Notes

1. Although sodomy had been punishable by death for centuries prior to the Labouchere amendment, first under church law and then secular law, sodomy was not regarded as a specifically homosexual crime nor its participants as homosexual men.

Chapter 8
The Moon is Shining as Bright as Day

Parents, Children and Section 28

Nicola Field

Sometimes I dream I am pregnant. There is no father for this baby — it has all happened as a surprise, by chance. I see my stomach swell up, then it subsides and there is no baby ... I am disappointed because I was looking forward to cuddling my infant. I am also relieved because of all the pain, work and trouble I have been saved. My life can carry on unchanged. In other dreams I have to take care of a child. This child is myself at four years old and I am acutely aware of its needs and vulnerabilities. Given the responsibility of comforting it, I know that I will never reassure it. In many other dreams I am the child: unable to control my surroundings, frustrated in great efforts to achieve, lying and outwitting others, trying to please people in authority.

In this chapter I want to explore the implications of the Anti-Section 28 campaign as they relate to experiences of childhood, parenthood, and the family. I am concerned that, during the campaign, spokespersons for the lesbian and gay communities sacrificed a vision of real change for an image of respectability, in their grand effort to use the mass media to gain popular support. I believe that popular support was *not* gained, and suggest that by trying to make ourselves acceptable to a perceived notion of the 'average person' we will deny the knowledge we have gained as children and as carers of children, and endanger our survival as lesbians and gay men.

By exploring what we mean by the term 'child', and how the figure of the child has developed culturally and politically through the perception of the past, I would like to suggest that the movement for lesbian and gay liberation must develop new ways of thinking about education, the family and reproduction. This piece therefore represents a journey through history and memory, undertaken with a commitment to confront fundamental links between adults and children, reproduction and social class, education and wealth.

False Economies

Many gay liberationists bemoaned Section 28 as a retrograde step. They regarded its properties and principles as coming from a bygone age — it was therefore taking us back to the dark ages before the 1967 Sexual Offences Act, when arguments about homosexuality centred on questions of normality, live-and-let-live, bribery and corruption. It is true that we were now fighting a new piece of legislation specifically aimed at repressing and controlling the lives of lesbian and gay people. However, we were not being taken back into pre-sixties, neo-Victorian repression, but forward into a new age of social control underpinned by technology and surveillance. Section 28 was not seeking to overthrow the right of the individual adult to have sex with the adult of their choice. Its primary aim was to inhibit the circulation of writings, art works, films and videos which explore homosexual lives and present them as fulfilling, exciting, enjoyable.

Specifically, homosexuality as a 'pretended family

relationship' or as an 'acceptable alternative to heterosexuality' was a new social anathema which had to be checked. Family life, that peaceful, wholesome tradition where you know what's what and who's who, had to be protected. This is reminiscent of pre-1967 when Mary Whitehouse rose to fame on the crest of her pro-family campaign, identifying the Royal Family as the ideal model for us all. But this time, in the late 1980s, with the family in a greater state of collapse, morality is functioning as a camouflage for social unrest. Royal weddings and babies, rather than setting a standard for sexual behaviour, take the front page so that information about tax cuts for the rich, benefit cuts for the poor, and industrial unrest, are relegated to the inside pages.

Since 1967 we have seen a growth of the pink economy: gay clubs, fashions, cultures have boomed and are now big business. Television, publishing and cinema participate in this new market. Although still on the sidelines, the lesbian and gay man who is 'out' is definitely visible through economic clout. Socially and politically we have become a dangerously visible group, but in reality little has changed. Middle-class film-makers, actors and writers have established a comfortable context for their work, but the lives of working-class lesbians and gay men have not improved although the tolerance and the comradeship which cushioned many working-class lesbians and gays in the past are still there. Class boundaries, racism, sexism and all the traditions which divide people continue to develop. Lesbians and gays still share the brutal experience of law enforcement, psychiatry and other forms of social control with many other groups and communities. We are still entrenched in capitalism: exploitation, imperialism, poverty.

Homosexuality *is* a threat to Thatcherism: arguing that lesbians and gays do not represent a threat, but just want to live out their private and home lives in peace, is a plea for a certain kind of lifestyle to be accepted. This plea operates on an impractical level — it says, 'Why can't we all be nice to one another? We're not hurting anyone so why hurt us?' Persecution, exploitation and discrimination are not signs of meanness, nastiness or impoliteness; they are weapons of domination which will not be given up without a struggle. Those with power will not gladly give up their evil ways for spiritual fulfilment and world peace. Many gay activists who argue for the 'nice' alternative to liberation are implicated in systems of oppression.

It is essential that the demands of *everyone* are fully articulated, and not just those who are all too ready to label issues of abortion, birth control, sexual/racial harassment and violence as 'secondary' or 'marginal'. It is misguided to believe that women, for instance, can be freed from anti-lesbianism one year, from sexism the next, and from racism the year after.

The public opposition to Section 28 was very defensive. It centred on the following arguments:

1. Homosexuality is not a threat to society but a great contribution to it. There are many lesbians and gay men who have attained the pinnacles of success and achievement, especially in the arts.

2. You cannot teach a child to be homosexual, yet many children are taught to be heterosexual.

3. The make-up of families can be variable and need not consist of mother, father and 2.2 children.

4. Lesbian and gay parents love and care for their children as well as heterosexuals do.

5. Homosexuals do not abuse children nearly as much as heterosexual men do.

These arguments do not take into account the realities of power relations in our society, realities which centre, to a great extent, on the following principles:

1. Homosexuality and heterosexuality are not interchangeable alternatives. Heterosexual monogamy (or the appearance of it) is essential for capitalism to

continue. It is a selective concept, which does not recognise the extended family or the divided migrant family. It expects that women will work unwaged in the home to care for children, disabled people and old folk. This reality dominates the everyday lives of working-class people, while the rich buy their way out of this practical nightmare with home-helps, nannies and private tutors.

2. The family is essentially a unit managed from within by one of its members, who receives instructions from outside. We usually recognise this leader as the 'father' and acknowledge his power by conceding to it. In 'gay families', who will be the head of the household?

3. Post-industrial Britain cannot sustain the family. Despite Conservative propaganda promoting the family, social and economic policies like the Poll Tax and social security legislation are putting intolerable pressure on poor families and making it difficult for them to stay together.

4. Children are subject to constant authority, institutionalisation and punishment. Arguing for the rights of lesbian and gay parents to exercise care and control (ownership) over their children does nothing to question the artificial power of adults over young people.

5. There is a traditional and quite illogical double-think about education and sexuality. Moralists and conservatives believe that heterosexuality is natural and normal. They also argue that children must be taught this nature (just in case it doesn't come naturally). Many gay activists argue that children cannot be taught to be gay, while emphasising that most children are compelled to learn to be heterosexual.

Section 28 had a special kind of logic in a Britain of self-righteousness and self-deception: it was intended to protect a 'vulnerable' group of people — children. The wording of the Clause expressed a deeply-felt horror that children were not learning the difference between Right (heterosexuality) and Wrong (homosexuality). The use of children to justify repression, censorship and social control is a fundamental characteristic of British law and culture. This principle underpins most aspects of our daily lives. During debates and in propaganda, both sides in the Section 28 war vociferously defended the rights of parents, especially mothers, to care for their children and influence the environment in which they are educated and entertained. The questions were, 'Which kind of adult is more suitable to take care and control of children?' or 'Should we all have this right regardless of political, moral or religious convictions and practices?'. At no point were any questions raised about the position of children within our 'civilised' society.

When I was seven and my sister was three my parents separated, and began proceedings for a divorce which was finalised over four years later. During that time a custody case was fought and I was passed back and forth between my mother and father, amidst scenes of violence and anguish in public and private. My father wanted me but not my sister; my mother wanted us both. She was awarded custody but I have no memory of the final transfer. Suddenly I was with mummy and there was no question about it. Four or five years later, during a row with my mother I screamed my usual litany, my ace card (children can be so cruel): "I'm going to live with daddy!" On this occasion my mother did not retreat in despairing tears — perhaps I was now considered old enough, or manipulative enough, to know the bitter truth. She turned on me, cold with anger and miserable triumph, saying, "Don't think he wants you! Why did he give you up? Because he couldn't cope!".

From the time we are born until we are eighteen years of age, we are offered little or no choice about the way we live our lives. Laws and social mores decree whether we may have sexual relationships, when and where they can happen, and with whom. While we are young our parents and guardians are given complete licence to dictate where we live, what we wear, what we eat, whom we meet. For eleven years we are forced to attend educational or reformatory institutions, where decisions are made about what we may recognise in ourselves as worthy of development, about which of our talents are valuable, which are superfluous, and which are downright undesirable. For many years we are not entitled to be in any way economically independent. In our culture there is no tradition of respecting the opinions or feelings of children; adults are free to do so or not, according to choice. On top of all this, children are born into countless expectations made of them in relation to their gender, class, race, physical and mental abilities — and sexual preferences. In their struggle to belong, children must choose from a continuum of survival tactics. They may succeed in fulfilling all expectations and become a model young person, an 'heir of sorrows', or they may reject everything and drop out of recognised society. Most of us try to do both, and end up nearer one end of the scale than the other.

The World Health Organisation decrees that all children have a right to food, warmth and safety from physical danger. Most children live or die with these rights unfulfilled, and yet we continue to believe that, universally, children are precious, innocent, and the guardians of the future.

Save the Children

>Not in entire forgetfulness,
>And not in utter nakedness,
>But trailing clouds of glory do we come
>From God who is our home:
>Heaven lies about us in our infancy!
>Shades of the prison-house begin to close
>Upon the growing Boy
>But He beholds the light, and whence it flows,
>He sees it in His joy;

The Moon is Shining as Bright as Day

> The Youth, who daily farther from the east
> Must travel, still is Nature's Priest,
> And by the vision splendid
> Is on his way attended;
> At length the Man perceives it die away,
> And fade into the light of common day.
> Wordsworth, *Intimations of Immortality*, 1803.

Who was Wordsworth's child? An emblem of innocence, untouched by the corruption and disillusion of the adult world. A godly being destined for unholiness. Nature's joy, gradually consumed by man's artifice: the City. At school we are taught that nineteenth-century Romanticism was a breath of fresh air, a breeze which blew through Europe's eighteenth-century cultural cynicism. The beautiful concept of nature-as-art: a benign force of goodness, fertility and justice. Things as they should be — the labourer in the field, the dairymaid with red cheeks at the butter-churn, the peasant urchin gathering sticks for his grandmother's fire. This fantasy has never left us as our towns and cities have grown outwards and upwards. In the 1980s, New Romanticism cut across the last vestiges of popular materialism; in the 1990s, New Age philosophy gives company directors mineral water and meditation skills to wash away the guilt of the exploiter. Like Wordsworth, we find the cities suspicious and fear that rolling hills, chirruping hedgerows and trickling streams will soon be absorbed into an inexorable concrete vice. We yearn for the countryside, the land and the landscape, or else it terrifies us with its open spaces, its unlit lanes, its three buses a week. But ultimately, we suspect, as we gaze towards Sellafield, over Orgreave, through the wire at Greenham Common, rural life contains our past and our destiny.

As modern capitalism exploded in Wordsworth's time, the cities (especially London, the trading centre of the world) became a new metaphor for original sin. Never mind the hellfire of medieval Christianity, the cities were hell on earth. Prostitution, homosexuality, sex between different races, child slavery, gangsterism, cocaine, morphia: it would seduce and swallow you up if you stayed too long.

All industrial nations produced their own versions of this Romanticism. Rivalling England was Germany, whose self-esteem also meant it had a lot to lose. Germany's National Socialism could be described as the greatest Romanticism of them all. The Nazis blamed the cities for the de-domestication of women (who were finding work and independence in shops and offices). They also blamed the cities for the breakdown of total Aryan racial purity, and for the corruption of their children. German supremacy meant national pride, national confidence, a contempt for the allure of cosmopolitan culture. Drawing on an ancient tradition of anti-Semitism, they blamed the Jews for creating and developing the values of the city, and therefore for all that had gone wrong with Germany. Exterminating Jews was only one part of the Nazi plan; men and boys had to be removed from the weakening and dulling influence of women and girls; good women had to be separated from Jews, evil career women, lesbians and childless women — and forced to reproduce the 'perfect' children of the Third Reich.

During the eighteenth and nineteenth centuries, a liberal critique took shape which reduced class struggle to individual tolerance. It haunts us today in our debates about race, class and sexuality ('We should all try to understand one another!'). This intellectual movement was unhappy with what it saw, but it could not bring itself to incriminate its own interests. It pined for freedom to fulfil its own desires: 'I want to be happy! I want everyone to be happy!'. The child was a suitable figure for popular Romantic poets to use in their fantasies. Influential, wealthy, widely read, educated, convinced of their own importance, these literary figures would not endanger their relationship with the establishment.

To speak about the child kept them on the right side of respectability while they moaned about industrial progress making the streets dirty, rather like the moralists of today who chorus, 'It's the children I feel sorry for!'. Their invective and rhetoric paved the way for the growth of philanthropy in the dark days of Queen Victoria. While British rule crushed civilisations and communities across the world, missionaries roamed uncontrollably, looking for poor children to save, bright sparks to educate, suffering sinners to pity. Disturbed by the massive incidence of poverty, disease, malnutrition and illiteracy, wealthy, kindly folk took to the streets of the town, not in protest but in the spirit of romance.

Thatcherism embraces the 'Victorian value' of children as 'seen and not heard'. Offspring of wealthy parents drinking weak tea in the nursery, wearing velvet knickerbockers and golden ringlets, learning to read 'children's' stories, singing 'children's' songs; sent to bed early for disrupting a soirée, given bread and water for playing in the mud with the village children, pocket money stopped for frightening the maid with a joke spider. Starving children, selling matches, sweeping chimneys — poor little mites. Sent to prison for stealing bread, hunted for picking pockets, taught to read and write for the peace of mind of a good Christian lady. Barbarisms were swept away by the efforts of the well-meaning rich as they spared little expense to save the unfortunate children of the lowest classes. In the 1990s, Britain's philanthropy is back with a vengeance, but there the similarity ends. Today's charity has been through the cold shower of social awareness, it has erupted into a fountain of public relations know-how as consortiums and multinationals compete for the image with the biggest heart.

> To suggest that British industry is suspended over an abyss by a slender thread of juvenile labour, which eight hours of continual education will snap, that after a century of scientific discovery and economic progress it is still upon the bent backs of children of fourteen that our industrial organisation and national prosperity, and that rare birth of time, the Federation of British Industries itself, repose — is not all this, after all, a little pitiful? After fifty years of practical experience of the

effort of raising the age of school attendance, the onus of proof rests upon those who allege that education will impede industry, not upon those who argue that education will stimulate all healthy national activities, and industry among them.

  R.H. Tawney, 'Keep The Workers' Children In Their Place' from *The Daily News*, 14th December 1918.

In the 1940s and '50s, emerging from two world wars and devastated by death and danger, the literate working-classes demanded equality. A new civil right — the right to learn — became a need as industry flourished and culture multiplied. Socialist ideas of free education, free housing and free health care were absorbed into the British Way of Life, quietly settling into the unchanged class system, masking the aftermath of post-imperialism as people from Africa, the West Indies and Asia arrived, invited to take a share of Britain's new Golden Age. Wealth had hardly shifted and the maxim of 'equality of opportunity', once a battle-cry, became a litany repeated and repeated to drown out the protests of those whose lives, cultures, beliefs and predicaments continued unrecognised by establishments and institutions.

My father left school at 14, in 1943, to work on the Post Office telephone lines. Determined to work his way out of the council estate and give his children more than he ever had, he lied his way into jobs, learning skills after hours, going to night-school so that he would be able to read and write confidently and rise into management. All the while he was spending Sundays at Speakers' Corner, heckling the bosses, campaigning for boycotts on South African produce. Once, soon after he had started working, a man molested him on the underground. The memory of this has haunted him all his life, fostering in him a fear of homosexuality which has exploded into obsessive homo-horror. Combined with a growing addiction to bourgeois pursuits, proportionate to his elevation to executive level, this terror dominates most of his everyday life. The

The Moon is Shining as Bright as Day

unspeakable is poverty and perversion.

> Just how completely parental rights and responsibilities ... can be submerged by sex educators, some of whom have little respect for the individuality of children and nothing but contempt for parents, was dramatically illustrated in November 1971, when in Exeter Magistrates Court the school attendance laws, framed for use against delinquent parents, were turned against a competent and caring parent who so far forgot himself as to reject the philosophy and moral code contained in the sex education booklet being used in the city's schools. Alerted by the assertion in the booklet that 'there is no such thing as right or wrong', Colin Knapman studied the rest of the publication carefully. It became quite obvious to him that the document was based on a rejection of religion as a basis of sexual morality — for this was linked throughout with 'dogmatism', 'scruples', 'prudery'. Teachers who might oppose the syllabus were categorised, in advance, as 'prejudiced'. Right and wrong were to be decided only according to consequences. Homosexual relationships were described as lasting and enriching experiences, and one of the grosser pieces of misinformation contained in the document was that those who do not masturbate never discover the function of their sexual organs! Facing a charge of failing to send his children back to school, Mr Knapman told the magistrates that he had withdrawn his daughters from school after previously warning the headmaster that he would do so if the school introduced the scheme of education in personal relationships, as written in the document. Mr Knapman was found guilty and fined. He still refused to send his children to a state school, and had them educated privately — at great personal sacrifice.
>
> Mary Whitehouse, *Whatever Happened to Sex?*, 1977.

Censorship is about withholding information. Sex education, like art education, should be a dynamic popular movement for self-discovery. So far it has been held back by constant debate about explicitness, morality and the innate innocence of children. In relation to Section 28 the argument is about equal opportunities. 'Adding' information about lesbian and gay relationships to education about sex merely reinforces the facile notion that homosexuality can be a happy alternative, and ignores the supremacy of penis/vagina penetration in our cultural life, our work, our history and our laws. The 'institutionalisation' of homosexuality would automatically mean *more* rules about sex and sexuality, not less.

> In this country a biased and bigoted judiciary rarely, if ever, awards custody of children to a mother who is overtly lesbian, or is 'proved' to be lesbian by the court. Whereas in most cases 90 per cent of the time custody is awarded to the mother, with lesbians the situation is reversed. So biased are our courts and legal processes, in fact, that children are even taken away from happy loving relationships with mothers who are lesbian and put into institutional care. Our sexuality is perceived as being so threatening. That phrase 'pretended family relationship' is a massive insult to those of us who have children, have parents and families whose very existence has been denied in the wording of this pernicious legislation.
> Maureen Oliver, *Lesbian Mothers — the Struggle for Equality*, 1988.

Born in 1960 I was deeply influenced by the permissive society. As I grew up in the Home Counties, I could see it on the TV. Endless debates about whether sex should be debated. Sex remained a complete mystery. It was something biological and yet cerebral. Only "common" people did it, but my parents knew about it. It couldn't be restrained but it should be hidden. How degrading for grown-ups that they didn't have a secret den with a secret door, and had to do it in a perfectly ordinary bedroom. What a shock the day I was told that people actually did it for pleasure and not just to have children.

Ever since the beginnings of worker's education (outside the original 'public' school system), education has been intended to produce an appropriate labour force. It has also operated to impart the principles of dominant ideology (for instance, Catholicism, Protestantism,

The Moon is Shining as Bright as Day

imperialism, trade unionism, monetarism) to the English working class and to the people of occupied countries. The middle classes gain social mobility from education; through self-improvement, the mastery of a 'science' or an 'arts' subject, they can make their mark in the professional world. For the ruling/upper classes, education has changed only in relation to the process of financial investment and public image; the shaping of an aristocrat involves imparting a code of supremacy. Most education, therefore, is constantly subject to regulation and limitation.

> 'This is what our education system has to encourage. It has to foster the social goals of living together, and working together, for the common good. It has to prepare our young people to play a dynamic and constructive part in the development of a society in which all members share fairly in the good or bad fortune of the group, and in which progress is measured in terms of human well-being, not prestige buildings, cars or other such things, whether privately or publicly owned ... [It] must emphasise co-operative endeavour, not individual advancement; it must stress concepts of equality and the responsibility to give service which goes with any special ability ... [It] must counteract the temptation to intellectual arrogance; for this leads to the well-educated despising those whose abilities are non-academic or who have no special abilities, but are just human beings. Such arrogance has no place in a society of equal citizens ... the free citizens of Tanzania will have to judge social issues for themselves; there neither is, nor will be, a political 'holy book' which purports to give all the answers to all the social, political and economic problems which will face our country in the future. There will be philosophies and policies approved by our society which citizens should consider and apply in the light of their own thinking and experience. But the educational system of Tanzania would not be serving the interests of a democratic socialist society if it tried to stop people from thinking about the teachings, policies or the beliefs of leaders, either past or present. Only free people conscious of their own worth and their equality can build a free society.'
> Julius Nyerere, *UJAMAA — Essays on Socialism*, OUP, 1968.

High Risk Lives

Even now, in Thatcher's Britain where redistributing wealth means tax cuts for the rich, progressive, campaigning charities like Age Concern and Shelter can hope for reasonable coverage in the right-wing media when they issue press-releases about the plight of children. Billboards, posters and colour supplements show us the face of the 'innocent victim', the thin, dirty, cute white child whose chance in life depends on the generous-and-comfortable classes taking out a charitable tax-covenant. Homelessness, poverty, malnutrition and inadequate health care are all supposed to be curable by voluntary donation. A television advertising campaign which exhorts young people to rise up, resist oppression and take what is rightfully theirs would be unthinkable. Unlike privatisation advertisements it would be 'political'.

Section 28 is *very* British. It strikes a massive and harmonious chord in hearts obsessed with two grand horrors: the exposure of children to reality, and the expression of anything honest about sex. The adult world is a mysterious, glorious existence of choice, intimacy, independence, power. Until we enter this world we are transfixed by its sophistication. In the days of the Industrial Revolution, children who worked six days a week in the factory attended Sunday Schools on their only day off. The object of this 'education' was to enable illiterate workers to read written instructions for new machinery. How many of us dream of our schooldays, fantasise a rebellion, rehearse a 'get stuffed' speech twenty years too late? With sexual knowledge comes our fall, a huge disappointment followed by a lifelong search to regain the sense of a mystery which never existed but which kept us well-distracted and well-occupied.

Who invented 'the child'? Powerful men (and a few women) protecting their power, their class, their race, their money, their status.

The child must not be exposed.
It cannot choose.

It is completely impressionable.
It is sensitive and vulnerable.
It needs to learn morals.
If it is given too many options it will have no self-discipline and therefore be disobedient.
Children must learn their place like women, servants, slaves, factory and other low-paid workers.

Censorship underlies the methods of all teaching institutions. It mirrors the obligatory secrecy which protects the privacy of the family. Like Daddy's work and salary, a teacher's personal life is regarded as sacrosanct from her/his pupil's prying eyes. The sanctity of the parents' bedroom is echoed in the seclusion of the staffroom and the forbidden stationery cupboard. At home and school we are presented with any number of temptations and potentials for transgression by adults' provision of privacy *for themselves*. We learn that illicit behaviour is linked to the invasion of space, or the privilege of privacy. If you have your own room where no-one can watch you, you can preserve your authority and credibility in the outside world. This is the ace card of the property-owning 'democracy'. If you are denied space you will sacrifice almost anything for the precious privilege of privacy.

Those who censor say, 'I can read, view and listen and not be corrupted. You are weak and so are likely to be corrupted. I am a custodian of virtue and propriety. But I do not wish you to know what I do or what I think as it may corrupt you.' What are the censors afraid of? And if they are adult, and no longer have the eyes of innocence, how can they presume to protect innocence anyway?

In 1921, the year of enforced partition in colonised Ireland, the British Board of Film Censors published its criteria for censorship. It banned:
* Relations of capital and labour.
* Scenes tending to disparage public characters and institutions.

* Incidents having a tendency to disparage our allies.
* Scenes holding up the king's uniform to contempt or to ridicule.
* Subjects dealing with India, in which British officers are seen in an odious light, and otherwise attempting to suggest the disloyalty of native states, or bringing into disrepute British prestige in the Empire.

The anti-Section 28 campaign did not confront the fact that the control of children through school, the law and the family is an important factor in the strict maintenance of class division, racist persecution and harassment, and the economic slavery of women.

Soothing the Savage Breast

Art seduces, corrupts and reveals. It makes you think too much, allows unnecessary knowledge. Pluralism, or knowledge, or diversity is dangerous. It can present genuine choices which are difficult to control. Art allows things to be said which are not easily expressed in a speech, a political tract, a rule or a policy. Art must therefore be supervised and authorised. It is crucial to 'civilisation'. When the Nazi Party took control in 1930s Germany, Hitler made sure that all 'unofficial' art was suppressed. Through open, direct censorship artists were banned, deported, persecuted, imprisoned. Many others changed their work so that it would appeal to Hitler and they would be able to go on working. They became the producers of official 'Nazi Art'. Unofficial artists yearned for the good old days of the Weimar Republic, when the government gave them money to live on, galleries to exhibit in and themes to work with. Now that only the rich can afford to study art, and galleries are usually too frightened to show shocking work (remember the embryo earrings, the Tate bricks?), how many of us hunger for the good old sixties and seventies when you could get a job as a community artist or be paid to be outrageous?

The Moon is Shining as Bright as Day

Nostalgia is a dangerous luxury. Art is always caught up in its time; it is the tip of the iceberg — it is our mythology for understanding the conditions of our lives. It cannot be any more subject to 'equal opportunities' than football players or film stars. It shapes history and is shaped by it.

Opponents of Section 28 argued that artwork by and about lesbians and gay men should be fostered because it provides 'positive images', and integrates the homosexual identity into mainstream culture. Is this what we really want? A community art 'system' which allocates 'space' to different groups? What happens if that 'space' is not enough?

> 'If a government wants original art, great art, it only has to pay a lot of cricketers and professors and broken-down screevers to talk Balls about art to a lot of innocent children, and teach them how to draw and paint so badly that their own mothers are ashamed of them; and beg them to go in for something more respectable like selling gold bricks or white slaves ... And so they gather at last in the graveyard and dig up some poor pauper with their teeth and claws and say 'Lo, he was a genius, starved to death by the government.' And so he may have been. Or perhaps not. Everybody makes mistakes. Even a nation devoured by worms at government expense. But unless you spend millions you don't even get mistakes — you have nothing at all. Just a lot of social economics lying about like army disposal after the war before last, or the war after next.'
>
> Joyce Carey, *The Horse's Mouth*, 1944.

> 'But surely lessons on homosexuality will interfere with my children's normal progress?'
>
> 'Firstly there is no intention to teach about sexual practices, either heterosexual or homosexual. Secondly, youngsters do not simply become something because they discuss it in a classroom setting. (Do children paint like Picasso after art class?) Lesbians and gays certainly didn't "learn" their orientation through schooling'."
>
> *People Like Us*, London Strategic Policy Unit, 1988.

Who copies who? How do children learn? How do children learn about reproduction? How do they learn to see reproduction as only possible through heterosexual intercourse? What is the teaching of 'sexual practices'?

> 'Hypersexuality also leads *faute de mieux* to homosexual intercourse (inmates of prisons, daughters of the higher classes of society who are guarded so very carefully in their relations with men, or are afraid of impregnation — this latter group is very numerous). Frequently female servants are the seducers, or lady friends with perverse sexual inclinations, and lady teachers in seminaries.'
> Havelock Ellis, *Psychopathia Sexualis*, 1906.

> 'As a teacher, the frigide wields considerable power over the unformed minds of her pupils. She rarely takes pains to examine the justice of her indictment of man, and her bias is obvious to those whom she instructs. Her prudery is often imitated by the girls she is able to influence.'
> W. Gallicham, *Sexual Apathy and Coldness in Women*, 1927.

> 'Those who can marry and do not are thus deliberately disregarding their biological duty to the race to which they belong. Those who would marry but cannot are supremely unfortunate. Both of them are a menace to the society in which they live ... Now I submit that the National Union of Women Teachers is dominated by such as are here described, and that the unrest exhibited by that organisation [demanding equal pay with men] is not caused by inadequate salaries, but by the morbid condition of its militant members.'
> Letter to *The Woman Teacher*, January 1920.

Happy Families

Lesbians and gays are as much influenced by their past histories as are heterosexuals. They are, therefore, just as likely to try to re-create a family life in which they may have suffered, but in which they feel artificially secure. This 'pretended family life' will be based on property, inheritance and investment in the future. (The desire to inherit, invest and bequeath is firmly grounded in the class system and in imperialism — and has been well-identified and exploited by Margaret Thatcher who has actually appeared to own the future.) In this way, the idea that you should provide for your own old age by

The Moon is Shining as Bright as Day

having children and a private pension is reproduced in the 'pretended family'. The family itself is a privatised unit, but not only for the cheap care of children, sick people, disabled people and old people. It is an agent of social entertainment, being the privatisation-in-action of pleasure, happiness and security. The family is the only widely accepted form of worthwhile existence. Acceptability is what everyone wants. The following statements are based on conversations with lesbians planning to have children, either by donor insemination or by adoption.

> 'The reason I want to have children is because I had such a happy childhood. My parents gave me such a strong environment of love and security. I want to recreate that. My lover is expecting her baby in a few months and then I will try to get pregnant after a year or so ... I haven't really thought about what the babies will call us ... What I want to hand on to them isn't so much material things, although I do own my own house which my parents never did, but I suppose I want them to learn tolerance, that everyone has the right to be different. My lover didn't check that her donor was HIV negative, I think that was because he was a personal friend. He wasn't a gay man.'

> 'I think that women should be given the chance to be good mothers. My mother brought three of us up on her own with no money and so she didn't really have a chance. She always thought it more important to spend money on books than food. I've bought a flat with my lover, although she took some persuading because, for her, work is the most important thing. I really want the experience of giving birth, though sometimes I wonder if the baby would only be a fashion accessory. My mother lives round the corner from me. At the moment getting pregnant is out of the question because I have anorexia and I don't have periods. But when I meet nice men, especially attractive ones, I sort of check them out as potential donors by going out to dinner with them.'

> 'My lover and I have been planning to have a child for several years. She was self-inseminating for quite a while but didn't get pregnant, and now she's glad she didn't because she's realised she's not ready to be a parent ... I've had a hysterectomy so we've applied to adopt. My

dream is to have a little girl all of my own. My mother never really loved me, so I want the chance to experience real closeness and affection.'

'I'm looking for a donor but no-one seems to want to do it. They've got to be HIV-negative or be willing to take the test. I don't mind if they are someone I know, but I don't really want them to have anything to do with the baby, or to have any claims on it. I've been in a stable relationship for three years now, after quite a few serious affairs, and now I want to have a baby with her and settle down together in the same flat.'

'I want to have a child in the next few years because I think I would make a really good mother. I really love children, they're the only people you can really trust.'

Homosexual identity has been produced by the tyranny of the family. Lesbians and gay men are 'produced' by 'normal' heterosexual relationships. The sense of self as 'other', as strange, as sick, as different is interminably debated as a personal and a political issue. What are we then, we liberationists? Survivors of pro-heterosexual propaganda? Sexual pioneers in a new age of pleasure and choice? Subversives who challenge the standards of 'acceptable' behaviour?

This elevation of the nuclear family to pre-eminence in the sphere of personal life is not accidental. Every society needs structures for reproduction and child-rearing, but the possibilities are not limited to the nuclear family. Yet the privatised family fits well with capitalist relations of production. Capitalism has socialised production while maintaining that the products of socialised labour belong to the owners of private property. In many ways, child-rearing has also been progressively socialised over the last two centuries, with schools, the media, peer groups, and employers taking over functions that once belonged to parents. Nevertheless, capitalist society maintains that reproduction and child-rearing are private tasks, that children 'belong' to parents, who exercise the rights of ownership. Ideologically, capitalism drives people into heterosexual families: each generation comes of age having internalised a heterosexist model of intimacy and personal relationships. Materially, capitalism weakens the bonds that once kept families together so that their members experience a growing instability in the place they have come to expect happiness and emotional security. Thus, while capitalism has knocked the material foundation away from family life, lesbians, gay men and heterosexual feminists have become the scapegoats for the social instability of the system,

John Emilio, 'Capitalism and Gay Identity' from *Desire, The Politics of Sexuality*, eds. Snitow, Stansell & Thompson, 1984.

Time and again the rhetoric of lesbian and gay rights turns to notions of 'equality'. This is an obsession which only reflects the interests of white middle-class gay men, and is very misleading because the very thing that this kind of campaigning completely ignores is *equality*. How can equality mean that lesbians and gays make good mothers and fathers when mothers and fathers themselves are unequal? Such a limited approach to change prevents discussion about inequality between men and women, bosses and workers, parents and nannies, rich and poor. It disguises the real problems.

Women are traditionally the 'caring' parents, conditioned to nurture: cook, clean, nurse, sacrifice, comfort, instil moral values. Lesbian women are not 'real' women; that is, they do not subordinate their own desires and interests and make them secondary to those of their men and children. How can they if they choose a woman partner for life and sex? The lesbian mother, in the eyes of society, has already made her choice. She has chosen to indulge herself and is therefore morally reprehensible. She has lost her case even before the custody hearing because her very existence defies the true state of motherhood. To then make a plea for the care and control of her children is a further indication of her greed. She wants to have her cake and eat it too.

A father is rarely awarded custody. He must be freed from the domestic trap of childcare so that he can earn maintenance for his deserted children. This frees the state from the responsibility of maintaining a woman and her child. Modern Social Security legislation rules that a single mother or mother-to-be must reveal the name and whereabouts of the father and her baby. She is ordered to hand over details, photographs and information so that the errant man can be forced to fulfil his responsibility, and the errant woman can be forced to play out her role of dependence and subservience. How long before 'unfit' (i.e. poor, black or disabled), expectant, single mothers are 'offered' abortions as an alternative to child benefit?

The monogamous lesbian couple choose parenthood. Together with the help of a sympathetic male friend, impregnation is achieved. Very, very rarely, a doctor will support the process of artificial insemination. Sometimes, in desperation after many failures, the parents resort to heterosexual intercourse. Eventually a baby is produced and the lesbian couple begin to pick their way through the minefield of maternity leave, nominated-carer leave, child benefit, state nursery provision, child-care licensing, school waiting-lists, health care dispensation, prescription charge exemption forms, and so on. The process is one of double indemnity — a choice often between getting one's rights and hiding the truth of one's life. The pattern of these lives bears a marked resemblance to that of the heterosexual nuclear family. The partner of the biological mother carries on working, whilst the mother stays at home with the baby and tries to get on with some housework between feeds and nappy-changes. In effect, the exchange-values of work outside and work inside the home remain unequal, and the experience of biological motherhood continues to be inseparable from domesticity.

Stretching the Social Fabric

Every so often I dream that I am looking after a child. The child is myself at four years old. She is upset, shy and so vulnerable-looking that I want to pick her up and tell her that there's no need to feel shy or afraid, that it doesn't matter. That the grown-ups are only making rules to make her feel bad because if she feels good about herself they won't be able to make her do anything. I can't really do anything except try to comfort her. The damage has already been done. The damage is me.

Much of our lives is taken up with lamenting the passing of childhood. So prevalent are the many myths surrounding the notion of family that we are constantly trying to 'put things right', 'not make the mistakes our parents made', lying awake at night cursing ourselves for not having been more considerate, more assertive, more compassionate, less selfish, more confident, more self-respecting. We yearn for the days when we did not have to worry about money, sex, *security*. Our memories lurch from sentimental to vindictive. We cast ourselves as the victims, searching the past for remembrances of our feeling 'the odd one out', so that we can put the blame for our unhappiness upon heterosexuality, or heterosexism — upon individual fathers and mothers, teachers religious and secular, doctors ... Meanwhile, subsequent generations of children are learning similar lessons, undergoing repressive regimentation which, year by year, grows more dangerous than we dare contemplate.

We must start to question where our attitudes were formed, and how our prejudices and fears are sustained. We have to begin to acknowledge that our own beliefs are as influenced by the past as are those of the establishment. We should therefore be vigilant and wary of ourselves. We should not be surprised or taken aback when our 'enemies' begin to appropriate our principles, our slogans and to distort our values. Because we have operated so much in reaction to the 'oppressors' our principles have always been conditioned and structured by the status quo. It is therefore not surprising that now, after the baby boom and in the baby slump, the Tory government is proposing to offer targeted training for women and 'ethnic minorities' because Britain is short of skilled labour. And a prominent member of the

Conservative Party can appear on television applauding a networked lesbian and gay TV programme because it is a sign of the potential for private enterprise. If you can get the backing — do what you want.

Time is running out. It is crucial that we start thinking about and discussing real potentials for equality. We cannot afford to pick and choose our priorities. We cannot have equality and property, we cannot have equality and profit, we cannot have equality and a ruling class which controls us by law. We cannot have equality and a police force. We cannot have equality and marriage. For many of us lesbian and gay liberationists, freedom might be unbearable.

We have to bring our hopes, dreams and fears out into the open. We have to educate ourselves in the utopias of our forbears who also dreamed of change, of reform, of revolution. We have to learn from the mistakes of the past in order to formulate our manifesto for the future.

The language of revolution has been criticised, ridiculed, intellectualised in the sophisticated second half of the twentieth century. However, it is a language which expresses imperatives and demands. A manifesto or programme of change is not a by-product of a 'mob mentality' but a collective expression of confidence and hope. As yet we have no other, better language in which to express our desire. As with the language of sex ('I want', 'I must have') the language of revolution claims us, it restores our impulses, it draws us in. We can ignore the urgency of desire, preferring fear to eat our souls. Or we can be imaginative about our own future; refusing to hand over our selves to abstract powers. This *is* a call to arms.

Chapter 9
The Making of a Radical Blackgay Man

Peter Nevins

Four hundred years of involuntary shifting around this planet have affected our responses to physical, emotional, political, geographical, sexual and social changes. The effects are many and varied, they are destructive, they are strengthening, they are enlightening, they are crushing. I suggest that there is at least one effect that is common to the vast majority of Black people across the diaspora, and that is adaptability. The ease with which Black people can adapt to their enforced (or chosen) changes of circumstance, be they good or bad, is a constant source of hope and strength to me. I dwell on it. I wonder at it. I marvel and enjoy my own ability to change positively and sincerely, to make the most out of enforced negative vicissitudes.

Blacklesbians and Blackgay men have a specific relation to this ability to change. Lesbianism and gayness can and do set you apart from the main body of the community, and the decision to 'come out' can alter that relation further. This does not presuppose that you are not a part of your community, nor imply that you cannot be respected by your community, but the difference is clear. Perspectives on life have an added dimension; that dimension which is the inclusion of thoughts about, and consequences for, your sexuality in your deliberations about life. So realizations about sexuality set us apart, incur changes of many kinds and in many ways. That ability to adapt to new circumstances, with or without ease, can be our most useful capability. We have a valuable resource. Let's see ...

The meaning of the word 'progressive' has a particular set of emotions attached to it. 'Satisfactory development or advance' is a particularly nice definition, one which I can clearly identify as appropriate to my perception of myself. I am thoroughly satisfied with my development over the past thirteen years. People who know me now, though not thirteen years ago, could not imagine the person I then was.

Black people in general, and my family in particular, operate with tight communal relations and expectations. These relations do not accommodate the lives, feelings, expectations, hopes or desires of the happy or sad homosexual. Coming to terms with this fact means that you have to change your relation to 'the family'. I changed mine quite drastically. I left it.

The decision to leave home at the tender age of seventeen does not come without great trepidation and confusion, and is certainly not an option or desire for everyone, no matter how painful the circumstances. To even say that the whole decision was mine is somewhat misleading. My father could no longer bear the thought of his homosexual son. He initially tried to convince himself and me that I had been corrupted by one of those perverts (white) who made a career out of corrupting young lads, at their most impressionable age, but I was not convinced. He could not bear the thought of my going out of his house to do these perverted things. He tried to call my bluff with an ultimatum: I had to change my ways or get out of his house. I left. Thus began the merry road to self-fulfilment, affirmation and respect.

It was a long road. I moved in with my white boyfriend and moved among his white friends. Race was not an issue, my parents had made sure of that. They had to. They knew too well the pains of racism. My mother is white and consequently as a young woman in the late 1950s was afforded little respect, and a lot of abuse, for her choice of partner. She knew about racism and she was going to make damn sure that her brown babies were washed cleaner, dressed and fed better than any of the other babies around. She was going to make damn sure that her brown toddlers were in a pre-school nursery, with perfectly stitched name-tags and mittens that everybody could admire. She was going to make sure that her brown teenagers never knew what she knew about racism because they were going to get the best of everything, and so she never mentioned it. Or so she thought.

No, race was not an issue for this young happy homosexual, protected for years by the denial of its importance. It never occurred to me that white gay men fancied me only because I was black. I assumed if they fancied me at all it was because they found me handsome, or that I had an endearing personality. Neither was my homosexuality a political issue, or so I thought. I was simply me, moving totally within a homosexual world of which I assumed myself to be a part. I never thought that the nasty comments levelled at women were entrenched misogyny, I just thought that it was plain rudeness. I was never the defender of political justice, I was just 'a nice guy' who wasn't rude. I had no political analysis for my own or anybody else's behaviour.

There were other black gay men around, and some of us acknowledged each other for that, or became friends, while some treated each other as if they were invisible. At best there was a soulless curiosity, drawn from the fact that at any given point there were only one or two of us out at any one time. None of us ever talked about racism, most of us had white boyfriends. It is clear that that was considered to be the norm and unquestionable. And how else could we see things? We had entered into the white gay world, or were forced into it by virtue of the implied denial of a Blackgay identity. Implied because our necessity to survive in this white gay world was dependent on our embracing the white gay scene. Same-race relationships between black men could only threaten that embrace and isolate us from the only gay community we knew. The white gay men who involved themselves with us made sure that that was the case. The few black gay men who made loving relationships with each other were derided and accused of divisiveness. The white men who made these accusations with the most venom were the very ones who slept with our blackness, which meant that the possibility of a black man wanting only to sleep with, or love, other black men was a threat to the property rights that they claimed over our bodies.

And did we need to justify the fact that we slept with white men? Well of course not, race was not an issue, was it? Except for those of us who only wanted to sleep with other black men. This racist situation was also partly sustained by our own subconscious, so that we did not have to deal with ever-present feelings of guilt, which stemmed from the fact that we had removed ourselves from our black straight friends and our families in favour of an all-white gay world.

My familial protection from any understanding of racism and my subsequent lack of political integrity afforded me no choices. The simplicity with which I viewed my world meant that my situation was merely a matter of consequence. I had a white boyfriend and that was just a matter of fact, not a matter of choice. Similarly, I lived in a homosexual world because I was gay and therefore had no choice. At that time it was inconceivable that my life would or could be any different. Even when I left my boyfriend after five years I was none the wiser as to the real reason for my unhappiness. I believed that I simply no longer loved him. I believed that I was sick of the fighting, but I made no attempt to analyse the reason behind the fights.

The decision to leave that man was the beginning of my growth. The racism implicit in the relationship, as in many other relationships, made sure I did not develop. Did not develop out of the dependent, naive, inoffensive young man that I was when we met, and that I did not develop into an independent, confident, self-aware Blackman.

I think it is important to point out that this lack of development need not necessarily be as pernicious as it seems. Often those who have no political awareness do not see the implications of their behaviour. That is probably why some people are astounded when accused of racism. The racist content of their behaviour is implicit in their responses, rather than an overt attempt to subjugate. But unfortunately there are also many relationships which are based solely on racist assumptions about black men, or a historically determined, colonial desire to dominate or demonstrate supremacy.

At twenty-one, young, hard-working, 'intentionally homeless' and lost, I had to start again, re-assess my feelings, needs and potential. I was free at last, but what was I going to do with my freedom? What were these feelings I had to assess? What were my needs? And, as for potential, what did that mean? And did I care? No. First and foremost I was free and I knew what that meant. It meant that I did not have to consider my partner, his feelings or his moods anymore. It simply meant that I could go out when I felt like it, wear what I liked and talk whatever I liked, without somebody telling me that I was stupid, or that I had delusions of grandeur, or that I always tried to put him down. Yes, that was clear, I did not have that anymore. But that was all I knew.

I enjoyed that freedom to excess. I was out and drunk each night, hung over and working each day. Getting up off someone else's floor or out of someone else's bed, unaware of the inevitable cost to my physical and mental health (consequences to health and mental health that such a regime could only lead to). Actually, I was not completely unaware. I knew that this was not what I really wanted; I just hid behind an increasing quantity of lager.

I had officially been staying at the flat of a mutual friend of mine and my ex-lover's. This was a good ten miles from work and the only social life I knew, the gay scene. So I was spending an increasing number of nights on the settee of a friend who I had known, through my ex-lover, for many years. He asked me to move in, without qualification, without any philanthropic soul-saving. He liked me. I liked him. So it seemed like the most logical solution. So I did.

We have remained the most soul-connected friends to this day. I was exposed to a whole new way of life, of thinking and relating to others. Until then I had been used to that acid, competitive and destructive lifestyle that still plagues the conventional gay scene today: the one that so easily accommodates racism, misogyny and a general disregard for differences of any sort; the one that demands you conform to the most insidious codes of conduct, dress, sex and unbelievable destruction of all human beings. The one that makes it quite plain that Blackgay men will only be tolerated to the extent that we divest ourselves of any self-determination, only tolerated to the extent that we give over our most obvious difference to them so that they can satisfy their sexual boredom.

On much of the conventional gay scene we are either ignored completely or sought after in the most offensive manner. This makes quite plain the intentions of the pursuer, more often than not someone you already know to have a particular interest in Blackmen. All this did not exist in this new environment. Difference here was cherished. I found myself amongst people; partying with people; eating with people; living with people of amazing diversity, who all had respect for each other's humanity, be they black, white, blacklesbian, blackgay, straight, gay, children, older people, or whatever. Who liked or disliked each other depending; who agreed or disagreed with each other depending. What this environment was devoid of, for the first time in my life, was threat. Equanimity was based on the certain knowledge that you could say or be whatever you liked, provided that it was not a threat to anyone else. We seldom were a threat, since it was the very desire to live in an unthreatening environment that brought us together and conditioned our responses.

Oppression works on the knowledge that the expression of particular behaviour, language or opinions contain a threat to your existence. The fear of this threat is what keeps your mouth shut, your clothes uniform and your sexuality rigid. This threat was removed in my new environment simply because our philosophy was based on regard for the person next to us. In this environment I could grow. My imagination was free to contemplate the wildest of notions. I discovered that many of these wild notions were actually achievable or at least open to trial. Fear of change was replaced with a desire for change. Desire to explore. Desire to re-examine old dreams that had been choked and stifled. It was the basis for a personal politics that I had thus far not recognised.

Work took on a whole new meaning. I was not, all of a sudden, destined to wait on tables in thankless restaurants for thankless people. I need not drudge for sixty unsociable hours each week, in undesirable bars for an unusable pittance. Which old, asphyxiated dreams lurked in the back of my mind, the unrealization of which ate away at my self-confidence? *Enter politics*. Yes, I was still unaware, at this point, of that pernicious dynamic which would throw me right back into the realm of self-doubt, back to perceptions of predestined drudgery, back to paranoia, at the stroke of a pen. *College — why not?* Yes, I could go to college. Something that my father had always wanted. But this time it was what I wanted. I was assured that I could — higher education was not just for those who stayed on at school and earned their place. It was not the case that I had forsaken, forever, the opportunity of a degree for a life of 'gay abandon', as my father had claimed so adamantly years before.

Several people I knew had decided to go to college, they were all of my age or older, and had all been given places on a DipHe (Diploma in Higher Education) course on the basis of one written essay. This inspired me to do the same. It was the late-comer's entry onto the road to a degree. It was especially designed for mature students, and as such did not require formal qualifications. There seemed no problem — until I was rejected.

Then it hit me: it was precisely because I was Black. What was I to do? I had developed a self-confidence about my opinions amongst these very same people who were about to start their respective courses. I assumed that I was their equal on all levels of thinking, living and loving. How could I not be good enough to go on this course? I had been assured I was. I wondered what I could have done wrong. Had I not put enough effort into that preliminary essay?

My flatmate knew exactly why, and he reminded me. He also reminded me that I need not let them get away with it. I was not wrong. I was not deficient. What was wrong was their malignant racism. I had to make them tell me exactly why they had rejected me; this would provide me with a measure of their gall, from which I could plan my next move. Their gall was immense. They told me that the course was full of its quota of mature students, they were only accepting 'A' Level students now. They said to me that I should try an access course, a course designed for black 'under-achievers', those who had not succeeded at high school, had five or so years life/work experience, and had decided that they wanted to go into higher education. This was their starting point, in elementary maths, English grammar and study skills. The admissions tutor's racism was clear — I was Black and 22, and therefore an 'under-achiever'. Whereas, in fact, I had written a perfectly acceptable essay, and had not under-achieved at school. Quite the opposite: until I chose to leave home and live with my boyfriend and get a job, I had been doing extremely well at school and was destined for medical school. My capacity to do the work was not in question, as I had previously been assured. My hard, anxious, resentful yet enlightening time at college presaged my thinking about my identity.

My identity did not prove to be a difficult issue for me. I was gay and had never thought or felt otherwise. Problems around this issue had been the problems of other people. It had never been an issue for me that I did not conform to the perceived normal sexual behaviour. Any concern about my gayness had always been of how to survive the hostility, or who it was safe to tell, where and when was it wiser to tone down the camp, or what the hell to do when the gay scene is so naff. Gradually, with age and experience, these questions had become easier to deal with. For one thing, I supposed that if my sexuality was made plain to all and sundry, then that would clear up a whole heap of difficulties for me, with the exception of being discriminated against, attacked, excluded and/or misunderstood. But being Black means that you have to deal with these things anyway and always. There are no options. You can fight or succumb or die, but you cannot avoid them. Age and experience has also taught me that the 'gay scene', conventional, commercial, alternative, political or otherwise, is not what constitutes my ideas of a Gaylife. In fact, it has been relocated from 'a place', 'a scene' or a series of associations to an actual idea I have of myself wherever and whatever I do. My existence constitutes a Gaylife, when I am in a room on my own, a meeting at work or at a party of presumably straight people. I do not go to it and participate in it as an extra to my life.

I feel that it is important sometimes in the face of an oppressive world to clearly attach myself, or create for myself, an identity which can also demonstrate precisely what I am not. What I am not is the embodiment of white, heterosexual, male, patriarchy. Nor am I a black copy. I need to make this point because there are many gay men whose conception of gayness is concentrated around the mimicking of the quintessential heterosexual male response. They seem to think that this is fine, since they are, after all, gay, and as such devoid of the responsibility for perpetuating the images of manhood which are the cause of every oppressive system on the planet. This point is put very clearly by Kobena Mercer:

> The 'gay scene' promotes a version of sexuality which says that what is needed to undo the history of homosexual repression is some kind of metropolitan gay savage whose sole purpose is to express his naturalness, his sexuality, for he is at his most natural when he is most sexual. Like the main character in the film *Taxi Zum Klo*, this gay savage promotes a sexualized political identity for gay men who will destroy bourgeois morality by fucking it to death; this is supposed to be the real liberation. No matter if the sexual campaign is conducted by reasserting 'macho' masculinity (viz. the clone, the stud, heavy leather imagery, etc.), since what makes the difference from 'straights' and makes it OK, is that gays are only 'playing' at being butch — so it doesn't really matter, it's just good fun.[1]

Our oppressors are the same as those who oppress women, blacks, the disabled, the old, the young, lesbians, gays. The same ones who destroy the resources of the planet. The same ones who create the conditions for devastating disease. The same ones who deny people the right to respond to their bodies in the way that they choose, after lying to you and pressuring you into pumping your body full of carcinogenic chemicals through the foods you eat. It is of no benefit to me or the world to mimic them.

Similarly, my identity as a Black man is understood in clear and simple terms. Whatever I do, and however I do it, it is as a Blackman. Regardless of the millions of influences that have informed or deformed my thinking I am a repository of experiences peculiar to a late twentieth-century, English-born Blackman. I sometimes think that maybe the concept of assimilation, whereby black people prefer to interpret what they do in terms of its affinity to whiteness, is a delusion, a problem of identity which has everything to do with racism and nothing to do with blackness. One can straighten one's hair, consume white written literature, philosophy or politics to any degree, but it only adds to and does not

The Making of a Radical Blackgay Man

replace one's particular experience as a black person. This does not reduce assimilation as an issue. For indeed it is a source of great consternation, both to those who believe that what they say and do is 'closer' to whiteness, and to those black people who have to deal with the consequences; consequences that affirm notions of white superiority and affirm the belief that black people can indeed become 'civilized'. It seems more of an affront to black people to suppose that what constitutes the black person can be assimilated away quite so easily. For we need to remember very clearly that their wish to 'civilize' us is secondary. We were never meant to survive (in the west) beyond the immediate economic purposes that brought our ancestors into western civilisation. It is partly due to fear that some people believe that 'assimilation' is going to threaten 'the race'. We must never forget what it is that threatens our existence, or where our anger should be directed.

In the white lesbian and gay community, racism is not only present, it is amplified. The vast majority do not question its repugnance at all, blinkered by the fact of their own sexual oppression. Those who do, assume that commonality of sexuality excludes the possibility of racism. For Blacklesbians and Blackgay men socializing in the white lesbian and gay community, there is, as a result of this, extreme pressure to search for and identify with that sameness, and play down the differences of their blackness. We are required to live and believe the delusion of assimilation. We are required to be blinkered by the fact of our sexual oppression. This is not assimilation but denial. The primary delusion, I think, is that a lesbian is a lesbian and a gay man is a gay man — in fact, a Blacklesbian is not a white lesbian, and a Blackgay man is not a white gay man.

The consequences of this for the mental wellbeing of black lesbians and gay men ought to be obvious. To be in a situation where we are required to deny a part of our being has a devastating affect upon our self-perception. The reduction of ourselves to a single element is tantamount to self-destruction. If we are forced to regard our blackness as of no importance in the functioning of our life, we are forced to deny our very existence, for it will not go away. It will plague us, strengthening feelings of paranoia about our worth.

Of course, many would deny that this is so and say that this is my opinion only, and I cannot help thinking of days gone by when I probably would have denied it too. But the necessity for me to regain my self-worth forced me to look at myself in relation to the world around me, and at how it relates to me. My creativity was stifled. I was unable to free myself from the day-to-day business of surviving long enough to examine what was happening. This is as true now for many Blacklesbians and Blackgay men as it was true for me, before I decided that I was worth something and had something to say. Not worth something in terms defined by the white lesbian and gay community, or the Black straight world or the Black Lesbian and Gay community, for that matter, but worth something because of the very fact of my being. And every inch of my being is determined and expressed through my racial and sexual identity.

Precisely because of racism, its amplification on the gay scene and its subsequent effect upon Blacklesbians and Blackgays, it is necessary that we turn to each other to regain or keep our self-respect. We must have this so that we can fight against racism in the world in general, and in the lesbian and gay community in particular, fight against homophobia in the world in general, and in our black communities in particular.

Moving to London provided that possibility for me. In London there is a thriving network of Blacklesbians and Blackgays, some politically active or conscious, others not. My introduction to this network was through the Black Lesbian and Gay Centre, a project which provides a focus and arena for the interests, desires, social/political needs of Blacklesbians and Blackgay men. I learnt that there was a large body of people who felt the same way as I did, and who worked with passion to protect their identities. I also learnt that there were a large number of people who were confused, torn apart, lonely, as a result of the same dynamic that controlled my early years. For some the pain was even greater, for they recognised the situation they were in but did not know of any means to express their feeling about it, or that there were other people with the same or similar feelings and experiences. Much of the work of the project is about dealing with these predicaments.

For as long as racism and sexism and homophobia are around to damage the quality of lives, this work will need to be done. The results of this work, however, are evidenced not merely by our existence, but by the fact that so many of us survive and grow to feel happy and confident about our identities. Through this network many of us have overcome isolation and other obstacles in our way, so that we can get together and support each other, and laugh with each other in ways that we alone understand. Most importantly, this collected strength and confidence has meant that others have not had to go through the same painful learning process that some of us went through. This network is not just a resource, it is food for life. It provides each person with the background certainty that they need not be going 'off their head'. This certainty comes from sharing experiences with others whose lives and attitudes may well be far removed from your own, but who share an experience of racism and homophobia. It is important to discover that feelings which you thought were peculiar to you alone, and were the result of some inner psychological deficiency, are, in fact, shared.

> Many of us assume second-class personhood for so long that we are comfortable on our knees.[2]

This, of course, can very often be the case within inter-racial relationships as well as in relation to the lesbian and gay community or political activity. It is important that we organise together, autonomously and openly, so that we can encourage each other to value our own, and each other's, viewpoint and experiences. We do not have to agree with one another. Sharing each other's experiences and lives helps educate us about the world — gay/straight/lesbian/black — and how it relates to us as an identifiable group of people. We cannot afford to be second-class people to a lesbian and gay community that cannot even appreciate the breadth of our political agenda. Some of us have to engage actively or consciously in the larger political arena. To quote Audre Lorde:

> We cannot forget that we are lesbian and gay people of color surviving in a country that defines human — when it concerns itself with the question — as straight and white. We are Gays and Lesbians of color at a time in this country's history when its domestic and international policies, as well as its posture toward those developing nations with which we share heritage, are so reactionary that self-preservation demands we involve ourselves actively in those policies and postures. And we must have some input and effect upon those policies, if we are ever to take a responsible place within the international community of people of color, a human community which includes two-thirds of the world's population. It is a time when the increase in conservatism upon every front affecting our lives as people of color is oppressively obvious ...[3]

This is spoken in the context of the USA, but it is no less true for Britain. For example, at the 1989 Tory Party Conference, Prime Minister Margaret Thatcher had the audacity to refer to the 'Third World' nations as responsible for the desert conditions of some of their land, through their 'primitive' and 'crude' farming methods. Three years previously, at a Commonwealth Heads of Government meeting, where representatives of the Eminent Persons Group were relaying their findings on South Africa, Margaret Thatcher reminded the meeting that Britain and the USA, along with the entire West, gave 250 million dollars to help the famine situation in Ethiopia, caused, she emphasised, partly by drought and partly *by the way of life of these people.*

The Making of a Radical Blackgay Man

At a time when AIDS is the scourge of the world and its origins are loudly claimed to come from darkest Africa, few people have heard of Chemically Acquired Immune Deficiency Syndrome (CAIDS). This industrial disease is caused by prolonged exposure to Trichlorethylene (TCE), a chemical in wholesale use in the electronic sweatshops of Sri Lanka, Malaysia, Mexico and the Philippines. Most of those affected by it are people of colour, and their condition has received no publicity. Again there is no-one as clear as Audre Lorde:

> 'It is a time when we, Lesbians and Gays of color, cannot ignore our position as citizens of a country that stands on the wrong side of every liberation struggle on this globe, a country that publicly condones and connives with the most vicious and systematic program for genocide since Nazi Germany — apartheid in South Africa.'[4]

The white lesbian and gay political scene, by and large, will not take these issues on board. For us it is not even a matter of choice. So we have to organise amongst ourselves; either to organise for play and pleasure, without the strain of restricted conversation, or to support each other through the inevitable dilemmas and uncertainties that arise from trying to formulate a response in isolation to a racist world. We need to organise active political responses to racism and homophobia. We need to be alone together — to be freer to brainstorm ideas — in response to how we deal with every aspect of our lives. The white political lesbian and gay movement, for the most part, does not share with us a conception of oppression or progression that goes beyond the 'liberation' of sexuality. There are many who have broadened their political responses to challenge the basis of all oppression, and the many ways in which it manifests itself. And this is our hope. There is a growing consciousness, what Alice Walker calls a New Tribalism, that is worldwide and converging. It consists of people who are politically or spiritually active in the common pursuit of the health of the planet, and the expression of their highest self. Those of us who care, begin to get a vision of a better reality and are automatically drawn to each other.

Notes

1. Issue in search of an agenda, from 'Race, Sexual Politics and Black Masculinity: A Dossier' by Kobena Mercer and Isaac Julian, in *Unwrapping Masculinity*, eds. Rowena Chapman and Jonathan Rutherford, Lawrence & Wishart, 1988.
2. See *Black/out*, Magazine of the Coalition of Black Lesbians and Gays, Vol.1, No.3/4, 1987, p.3; from 'The Truth of the Matter' by Renee McCoy, Executive Director.
3. Ibid, p.13; 'Turning the Beat Around' by Audre Lorde.
4. Ibid, p.14.

Chapter 10
Sells Papers, Ruins Lives

Homophobia and the Media

James Baaden

Clause 28 granted homophobia a visibility in the public consciousness which it had never hitherto enjoyed either as a word or a concept. Recalling the language and concepts which characterised popular writing (in the English-speaking world) about homosexuality twenty years ago — and gave us the term 'homophobia' — is a useful means of beginning any examination of homophobia, for we are immediately brought face to face with the ambiguities which the term embodies and the shifts in understanding of homosexuality which give rise to those ambiguities.

The term 'homophobia' was coined at the beginning of the 1970s by an American psychologist, George Weinberg, author of a number of books on homosexuality and society. Quite a few objections have been raised to the word on what might be called etymological grounds: that the Greek roots of the word require it to mean 'fear of the same'. This is a logical argument only if one insists on comprehending all words of classical derivation purely in line with their Greek and Latin origins, a truism which has never had any place in the evolution of the English language. On the other hand, it does point up the fact that 'phobia' does indeed mean 'fear' — both in Greek and, even more importantly, in current Anglo-American usage, where it has gained wide currency as a psychological term denoting a morbid, irrational fear.

Today, especially within the discourse surrounding Clause 28, homophobia has moved away from this emphasis on the notion of an excessive terror which can be identified as some sort of mental disorder: we have instead witnessed the emergence of homophobia as a political and social term, referring (broadly speaking) to organised anti-gay/lesbian agitation and sentiment. This is quite different from an irrational, morbid fear of 'homosexuals' or homosexuality, and it should be stressed that there is a considerable gap between these two usages and understandings of the word 'homophobia'. For instance, nearly all of the literature about homophobia belongs to the realm of psychology and takes no note of homophobia as an organised social phenomenon having its basis in political (rather than individual psychological) realities. An influential article by MacDonald and Games in the first edition (1974) of the *Journal of Homosexuality* set the scene for the development of the notion of homophobia for the next dozen or so years, by defining the term as 'an irrational, persistent fear or dread of homosexuals.' A substantial body of writing in psychological journals exemplifies this approach: by 1978, homophobia was being identified as a 'severe disturbance' in an article entitled 'Towards a Gay Psychology', and as a 'mental health issue of the first magnitude' by another widely-read American psychologist, Judd Marmor.

The understanding of homophobia as a psychological concept was very trenchantly criticised in an important article in the lesbian feminist journal *Gossip*, by Celia Kitzinger in 1987, just before Clause 28 was unveiled. Looking back over the development of the concept, Celia Kitzinger — arguing explicitly in line with 'radical feminist values' — effectively evokes the deficiencies of the psychological approach. A psychologist herself, she states that she is 'fully aware of how psychology oppresses women in general and lesbians in particular' (and here, agreeing with her, I would recall the oppression of gay men by psychology), and goes on to point out that the identification of homophobia as a sickness or 'personality disorder' does not challenge the underlying presumption of psychology, namely its claim to define who is healthy and who is sick. It is this very authority which Kitzinger dismantles, adding parenthetically that 'yesterday it was lesbians who were "sick", today it's homophobes, and tomorrow it might be lesbians again.' Not only does the emphasis on homophobia as a disorder uphold the tyranny of psychological processes, she says, it also 'depoliticises' oppression, suggesting that the oppression of lesbians, for instance, is caused by some 'diagnosable phobia' afflicting the oppressors, rather than having its origins in political facts.

In conjunction with this line of argument, Kitzinger also demolishes the repetitive identification of homophobia as *irrational* — an 'irrational fear', a 'morbid dread', and 'irrational intolerance', etc. Again, her arguments, though dealing solely with the situation of lesbian women, can in this case be applied to gay men: stressing definitions of homophobia as an 'irrational' phenomenon implies that there are no logical grounds on which anyone might fear lesbianism — thus hostility to lesbians is again effectively robbed of its true political significance and turned into the illogical obsession of a disturbed mind. Citing Adrienne Rich and Rita Mae Brown, she argues that lesbianism is a phenomenon which presents a very clear challenge to the 'heteropatriarchal' order, and therefore the representatives and upholders of that order have many sound, thoroughly rational reasons to fear it.

Celia Kitzinger's points are of great value in looking at the climate which produced and accompanied Clause 28, especially as represented by the popular mass media. The Clause was a political tool, an amendment to a bill before Parliament, and it was drafted by politicians for political reasons. It does not help lesbians or gay men to dismiss the creators of the Clause as mentally ill individuals, driven by a morbid personality disorder. The utterances and actions of those who devised the Clause, and their supporters, show clearly that the political and social evolution of gay and lesbian identities and communities during the past thirty years or so has been accompanied by the development of an organised body of anti-gay/lesbian activity which, despite the term's imperfections, I would call homophobia.

During the 1950s, images of homosexuality gradually infiltrated the media. Recognisable gay stereotypes were becoming visible in certain forms of popular culture in Britain. Comedians such as Sid Field, Max Miller, Frankie Howerd, Stanley Baxter and Dick Emery paraded flamboyant, stereo-typically effeminate impersonations as part of their acts; audiences laughed. Yet what did those audiences see? The effeminate male was and is a peculiarly prominent device in British comedy: in American popular culture of the same period, he is notably absent (Milton Berle probably got closest, but he was still far removed from the explicitly camp posturing of, say, Kenneth Williams). Partly the effeminate male character was a means by which men (irrespective of sexuality) could indulge in utterances and actions of the type usually described as 'outrageous', and certainly excluded from the vocabulary of conventional masculine behaviour; partly they built on the British predilection in humour for the absurd; partly they capitalised on misogynistic imagery; and partly, perhaps, they were an 'acceptable face of homosexuality', foreshadowing a growing and enduring public perception that gay men could be 'fun', and might therefore be tolerated in certain qualified contexts. Nevertheless, the gap between comic stereotypes and the everyday lives of real gay men was immense, as immense as the gap between camp and sexuality: the audiences of the 1950s did not draw any connection between the characters they laughed at and the men being sent to prison by the thousands every year. The performers themselves generally led very public heterosexual private lives, and as a group certainly made no contribution towards demanding change in society.

By the 1960s, further cases of known 'homosexual males' became public and the media began to tell readers what they looked like. Thus the *Sunday Mirror* in 1953 advised its readers on 'How to spot a possible homo'; telltale indicators included 'dropped eyes', 'shifty glances' and 'a fondness for the theatre'. At this point, the question of crime took centre stage: suddenly there were homosexual spies, homosexual murderers, homosexual victims. The *Evening Standard* intoned in 1962 that 'spectacular homosexual cases' excited 'horror and sympathy'. The 'problem', the paper said, had two aspects: 'One is blackmail. The other is: can science help to release the homosexual from his secret life sentence?'. This summary highlights the main features of the media's discussion of homosexuality at the time: women are ignored; there is a 'problem'; blackmail has something to do with it, and needs to be tidied out of the way; the person at the centre is a shadowy being called 'the homosexual'; his 'problem' is a ghastly burden akin to a prison sentence and one which must remain 'secret'; nonetheless, it seems to be the cause of a scientifically identifiable disorder of which he may yet be cured.

Accordingly, the *Standard* felt that a bill then before Parliament calling for the implementation of the Wolfenden Committee's reforms, made good sense because it made 'medical reports' on homosexual men 'obligatory' — and a process of medical 'screening' would help to isolate the potential homosexual 'psychopath' and thereby protect society. Homosexual men who were victims of murder, the press suggested, were — rather than being worthy of sympathy — further examples of the 'problem'. In a report on the murders of two gay men in early 1962 in the *News of the World*, Jack Miller set the scene in familiar terms: 'These are the twilight murders ... Two men, if you can call Norman Rickard and Alan Vigar men, lived in the twilight world of the homosexual ....' On television, 'This Week' underscored the twilight in starkly visual terms in 1964: the men who spoke were never fully visible on screen, hidden either in shadow or off-camera. The following year, 'This Week' featured a programme on lesbians: having been entirely invisible, suddenly lesbians became even more publicly accessible than gay men, for nearly all of the women on 'This Week' appeared full-face before the camera. Enraged by the prospect, the *Daily Express* ordered its readers to take their own steps to ensure continued lesbian invisibility: 'You still have time to keep this filth out of your living rooms!'.

Against the backdrop of this sort of reporting, the 1967 Sexual Offences Act was passed, to be followed by the June 1969 Stonewall riot in New York City. A new vocabulary and a new vision of lesbian and gay identity swept through the western world, replacing the pained terminology of penal law reform, abnormal psychology, mental illness, compassion, tolerance, isolation and anguish. Rights, liberty and equality came onto the agenda: lesbian and gay identity was celebrated: struggle and resistance replaced pleas for understanding.

Since then, gay and lesbian identities, cultures and communities have been constructed before the eyes of the world. Yet what can be traced during the same period is the development of a gathering homophobic current in Britain: and this trend reflects the progress of events within the lesbian/gay movements and communities. Thus, as illustrated above, the language and concerns of Clause 28's creators are far removed from the thinking of commentators on homosexuality — whether hostile or sympathetic — at the time of the Wolfenden debate thirty years ago. The landscape has changed, and homophobia has come into being — perhaps we should say, has been constructed — as an identifiable, organised feature within the new terrain.

The Clause came as the culmination of a process of homophobic agitation in politics and the media which had intensified throughout the course of the 1980s. It is clear that during this period various circles in the churches, the press and the political parties — principally but by no means solely the Conservative Party — noted the emergence of visible and organised lesbian and gay communities. Similarly visible and organised homophobic identities and communities began to emerge concomitantly. The only danger in this is that it overlooks the element of opportunism: those who have consistently poured forth homophobic invective may well be motivated by deeply-held Christian convictions, yet none have sponsored legislation prohibiting 'promotion of adultery', for example, and many — like libertarian MP Teresa Gorman — have supported abortion rights.

This has been especially obvious in the churches, where focusing on issues of sexual morality (to the neglect of business ethics, for example), has been deployed to draw attention away from the church's continuing decline, and to consolidate the power of various right-wing interest groups.

The opportunist exploitation of homophobia in the churches reached a zenith at the November 1987 General Synod of the Church of England, which not coincidentally convened only a few weeks before Clause 28 emerged. The entire proceedings of the synod were overwhelmed by a deafening campaign by synod members and large sectors of the popular press, demanding a thoroughgoing witch-hunt to root out gay and lesbian Christians: the *Sunday People* disclosed that gay vicars incarnated 'the Devil within', accompanying its proclamation with lurid 'investigations' of the private lives of individual priests, and the leader of the homophobic onslaught in the synod, the Reverend Tony Higton, warned in the *Independent* that his crusade would not allow itself to be hindered by objections from those who claimed that they knew gay men or lesbians who were good and decent people. For the Higtonite, sexual orientation was a badge of wickedness which entirely outweighed any other moral consideration, including the evidence of a lifetime of good deeds.

Of course, to trace the sequence of events which gathered steam and eventually led to the explosion of Clause 28, one must go back much further than the November 1987 meeting of the general synod, an event which is chiefly significant as a manifestation of the high-profile, well organised homophobic action within major social institutions which got underway in the late 1980s. The 1970s were a period during which the media and other institutions slowly and warily took note of the evolution of lesbian/gay identities and communities. The approach taken by notable sections of the press during the 1960s — emphasising 'the homosexual' as a tragic, sick individual beset by a 'secret problem' and susceptible to blackmail and kindred criminal entanglements — remained durable but was clearly no longer entirely relevant. People who defined themselves as homosexuals — or, to be more precise, as gay men and lesbians — were organising themselves, holding meetings, expressing demands. The response of the more right-wing sector of the British press, as a rule, was to ignore these developments. If they were commented on, they were noted as quaint or amusing. Explicit attacks on gay and lesbian people, on the other hand, were also nothing like as numerous as they were to become in the 1980s. In the *Guardian* and similar papers, 'homosexuals' and their concerns were occasionally noted — politely, but usually without any detailed discussion, although a particularly unpleasant and flippant *Guardian* report of the 1979 Gay Pride rally was the subject of a women's sit-in at the editor's offices.

The phenomenon of gay liberation was the subject of feature articles throughout the seventies: it was depicted very much as a note of colour, an interesting and rather curious minority diversion. Publicly visible 'out' gay and lesbian figures were absent; gay men and lesbians had not as yet begun to organise within unions, political parties and other influential institutions; there were no gay and lesbian working parties or committees in local government; protection of lesbian and gay workers' rights

Sells Papers, Ruins Lives

had not as yet found its way into employers' anti-discrimination policies. From the point of view of the press, gay and lesbian identity only related to the private sex lives of a small number of unknown — if perhaps 'colourful' — individuals in London.

In the late 1970s, certain events made a dent on the general public consciousness. The *Gay News* blasphemy trial made that paper's name well-known; and yet, though many voices were raised in its support and in protest against the editor's conviction on blasphemy charges in 1977, much of this sympathy originated not from concern on behalf of gay men and lesbians, but from conventional left-wing commitment to freedom of the press and general distaste at the behaviour of Mary Whitehouse, who had brought the prosecution (privately).

The announcement at around the same time by Labour MP Maureen Colquhoun that she was a lesbian also drew less response than one might have expected: she was the first British MP to come out as either lesbian or gay. During 1978 the Press Council had refused to accept her complaint that she had been harassed by Nigel Dempster, the gossip columnist of the *Daily Mail*; she thereby joined the long list of complainants who have found the Council unwilling to take seriously any responsibility it may have to help protect lesbians and gay men from harassment and abuse. Five readers who formally objected during the same year to the *London Evening Standard*'s hostile and sensationalist coverage of the use of AID (Artificial Insemination by Donor) by lesbian mother, likewise found their complaints ejected by the Press Council. It was not until 1990 that Terry Sanderson, a gay journalist who has indefatigably scrutinised media coverage of lesbian and gay issues for many years, was successful in convincing the Council to rule that the use by the *Sun* of the words 'poof' and 'poofter' was insulting and unacceptable; three years earlier in 1987, at the time of the explosively homophobic Church of England synod assembly, the Press Council had dismissed complaints arising from the *Sun*'s reference to 'pulpit poofs' in a front-page banner headline.

When Mr Sanderson began collecting press clippings for a monthly media survey in the early 1980s, the harvest was scarce; by the latter part of the decade it had turned into an almost unmanageable torrent of material. In many respects, the election in 1981 of a Greater London Council with a Labour majority expressly committed to the promotion of minority — including lesbian and gay — interests had served as the spark which ignited the voluminous kindling available in the shape of complex fears held by upholders of the heterosexist status quo. The actions of the GLC made public the existence of gay and lesbian communities in London with their own needs and aspirations: lesbians and gay men gained a particular form of visibility which they had never enjoyed before, provoking a cataract of media fury and mockery in inverse proportion to the tiny proportion of the GLC budget spent on projects serving gay and lesbian Londoners.

We may recognise the role played by the 'complex fears held by upholders of the heterosexist status quo' mentioned above, without making concessions to the psychological worldview which — as demonstrated by Celia Kitzinger — stigmatises 'phobias' and 'disorders'. The salient point in the rational nature of these fears: they are not the products of deluded minds. Instead they represent perceptions of threat, and they operate at both the individual level and the collective institutional level. There exists a heterosexist social order, and there are many who, for the most diverse reasons, have a vested interest in maintaining and promoting it, whether in their individual personal lives or within the structures of larger social institutions. The challenge embodied by visible lesbian and gay identities and communities is manifold.

In this light, it is worth considering to what degree a heterosexual identity and community may have been shaped at the same time that lesbian/gay identities and communities — and the social phenomenon of homophobia — were being constructed. The heterosexual identity and community are rarely known as such: they go by names such as 'parents', 'married couples', 'ordinary people' and 'the family'. Even cursory analysis of the usage of these terms shows that they signify strictly defined political interest groups: in an objective sense, after all, 'parents' and 'the family' would include huge numbers of persons who are in fact excluded from these identities — single parents, lesbian mothers, gay fathers, and so on. A range of political code words has sprung up to indicate specific interest groups committed to the maintenance of heterosexism. Certainly, the very fact of visible lesbian/gay identities and communities challenges this task of maintenance: accordingly, lesbians and gay men inspire the fear which any perceived threat prompts among those who see a threat to their power base, their security, their illusions, their dreams.

But beyond this, there are perhaps more alarming worries which come from within, for all is not well within the heterosexist household. The very period under consideration, the 1980s, witnessed a succession of events, trends, revelations and debates which pointed up the many ways in which the claims made on behalf of heterosexual convention are illusory. More than one in three marriages fails; sexual violence by men against women is widespread; substantial numbers of children are abused within the nuclear family; countless women — for whom conventional heterosexual family life is supposed to be fulfilment itself — are making clear that they are unconvinced, disenchanted, fed up.

Homophobic activity has become perhaps the prime social and political vehicle for the release of the complex individual and collective fears, at least in Britain. In fact, the UK has moved in a unique direction in this respect. In other countries, for instance, the eighties saw improvements in the situation of lesbian and gay citizens. Notable reforms took place in such diverse countries as Israel, Denmark, New Zealand and Eire. Even before the upheavals of the winter of 1989-90, the position of gay men and lesbians in various Eastern European states had improved markedly: lesbian and gay groups had been set up with official toleration in East Germany, Poland, Hungary and Czechoslovakia. Britain was one of the very few states in the world which in terms of public policy deliberately moved in a clearly negative direction: others included Iran, Cuba and (until the revolution of December 1989) Romania, though none of these went so far as to enact new anti-homosexual legislation — in this Britain stood alone.

The first half of the 1980s was quieter than the second. Hostile coverage in the British press concentrated on the GLC, though other events provided grist to the homophobic mill. In early 1981, the Archbishop of Canterbury, Dr Robert Runcie, told the Church of England General Synod that gay and lesbian people were 'disabled' and — evidently convinced that his listeners would be looking to Roman military history for enlightenment — included the following bizarre excursus in his address: 'Were all those hairy old toughs of centurions in Tacitus, clinging to one another and begging for last kisses when the Legion was breaking up — all pansies? If you can believe that, you can believe anything.'

During the following year, a manufactured sex scandal in the tabloid press forced the head of the Queen's bodyguard, Commander Trestrail, to resign — phraseology collected by *Gay News* journalist Keith Howes from reports of the Trestrail affair at the time included 'nasty little secret', 'amazing double life', 'forbidden love', 'sordid secret', 'seedy' and 'disgraced'. The *News of the World*, meanwhile, remained true to form: 'The twilight world of unhappy gays' was lamented in July 1982, echoing the laboured imagery which had characterised its reporting some twenty years earlier. Two years later, in 1984, there erupted the major cause célèbre in the lesbian/gay community before the Clause, namely the seizure by HM Customs and Excise of huge quantities of imported books destined for 'Gay's The Word' bookstore in London. The story was largely ignored in the general press; even the *Guardian*, usually vigilant against breaches of freedom of expression, gave it scant attention. Periodicals concerned with civil liberties were coaxed with difficulty into taking note of the implications of the case: thus the *Index on Censorship* at length produced a report. By and large the gay and lesbian community was left to get on with it.

In 1985-86, as the 'Gay's The Word' fight continued, the tabloid press discovered a new 'scandal' in the Danish book *Jenny Lives with Eric and Martin*, a gentle story of a little girl who spends a weekend with her gay father and his lover. It had been published in an English translation by Gay Men's Press and had been available in the UK for some years, when suddenly the *Islington Gazette*, a local paper which has made a speciality of over-the-top homophobic invective (this particular issue contained no less than thirteen items relating to homosexuality in one form or another), announced that an incensed Church of England primary school headmaster had discovered a copy in a teacher's library. The story was quickly regurgitated as an 'exclusive' by the *Sun*, and the saga had begun. Before long, indignant Christians and right-wing MPs were fulminating against 'gay sex lessons' in 'Islington schools' for 'tiny tots' (of course, Islington did not even have its own school system at the time, let alone sex lessons for the 'tots'), a prime instance of the homophobic legends which were later to be invoked by the creators of Clause 28.

Meanwhile, AIDS had appeared in the press — as the 'gay plague'. In this area, there has been more or less no change — Britain's leading popular papers have stuck to the 'gay plague' line through thick and thin, year after year — so it would be adequate simply to say that their reporting then was well-nigh identical to what it is now, and probably always will be. The tabloid papers were quick to take up the stories of some of the first gay men who contracted AIDS: their homes were invaded, their neighbours harassed, distressing photographs of faces scarred with Karposi's Sarcoma lesions published. When

High Risk Lives

a prison chaplain died of AIDS in early 1985, uproar ensued. Zealously egged on by the tabloids, ambulance workers, First Aid staff and firemen declared that they would not rescue gay men in emergency situations. In the summer of the same year, it was revealed that the American film actor Rock Hudson had AIDS; he died that October. His films had no doubt brought much pleasure to millions of readers of the *Sun*, the *Daily Express*, the *Daily Mail*, the *Sunday People*, and so on, but this amounted to dust even before he himself had died: suddenly he was an ogre of 'promiscuity' who had been deservedly stricken down as punishment for his 'evil' lifestyle. Thus the tabloids gloated over his final months.

Five years later, it remains the same. When the British actor Ian Charleson died in early 1990, Fiona Macdonald Hull of the *Sun* stormed: 'Ian died because he caught AIDS. And it is almost certain that he caught AIDS because he was a homosexual ... his death ... must make our gay community face up to the fact that AIDS is a homosexual, drug-related disease. It is not a heterosexual disease. It becomes a heterosexual disease *only* when gays or drug addicts become either blood donors or switch sides. It is time the homosexuals and drug addicts cleaned up their act. They, and they alone, are responsible for people dying from AIDS.' (It should be recorded that heterosexual instances of AIDS doubled in the UK in the course of a twelve-month period during which Ms Hull — and may other similar tabloid journalists — stoutly insisted on denying the possibility of heterosexual transmission of HIV.)

At the end of 1986, the Chief Constable of Manchester, James Anderton, began to intone: AIDS, he announced, was the 'creation of homosexuals and prostitutes ... swirling around in a human cesspit' of their own making. The tabloids cheered. The *Sun*'s leader-writer enthused: 'The *Sun* hopes Mr Anderton will treat those perverts with the contempt they deserve.' A writer in the *Daily Express* went into greater detail: 'The homosexuals who have brought this plague upon us should be locked up.

Burning is too good for them. Bury them in a pit and pour on quick lime.' The Reverend William Oddie applauded Chief Constable Anderton in the *Sunday Telegraph*, adding for good measure that AIDS 'follows disobeying God's instructions', whilst the *Sunday Express* thundered that 'James Anderton is right.' George Gale of the *Sunday Mirror* felt confirmed in his oft-repeated demands that AIDS be made a notifiable disease and 'buggery ... a criminal offence' (his headline, however — 'When being gay should be a crime' — suggested that Gale had a more wide-ranging criminalisation in mind). The acclaim was short-lived, however: soon the Chief Constable was indeed asserting that he was inspired by signals, not from Rome but directly from God, and the tabloids were suddenly ill at ease with Anderton's new claims of divine prophetic status.

December 1986 was also the month of Councillor Brownhill, Leader of South Staffordshire Council and probably a reader of the *Daily Express*: though he did not get round to the specifics of describing how their bodies should be buried in pits with quick lime, he did publicly demand that in order to tackle the AIDS crisis 90 per cent of gay men should be exterminated in gas chambers. When a group of young demonstrators peacefully protested outside his house in the village of Wombourne, they were all thrown into jail for a week — over the Christmas break — on the pretext that police were unable to verify their addresses. Charges against the twelve demonstrators were dropped later in 1987. In the meantime, most of the press had ignored the story. The elected leader of a local authority had publicly called for the gassing of a huge number of his fellow-citizens; and protesters who had peaceably demonstrated against these obscenities had been locked up on no grounds at all. The press looked elsewhere.

Since enactment of the Local Government Act in May 1988, no further homophobic legislative measures have — so far — been successful in Parliament. Two series of a lesbian/gay magazine programme, 'Out On Tuesday', have been shown on Channel 4 (1989 and 1990). *The Two Of Us*, a play about two teenage boys, one gay, the other uncertain about his orientation, was initially suppressed by the BBC, then shown late at night, then re-shown during viewing hours for school programmes. In early 1990 a three-part dramatisation by the BBC of Jeanette Winterson's *Oranges Are Not The Only Fruit* attracted rapturous reviews; oddly enough, though it contained a potentially volatile mix of lesbianism, teenage love and harshly delineated evangelical Christianity, it prompted hardly a breath of disapproval from the likely quarters: perhaps they were too busy vociferating against *The Two Of Us*.

'Out' lesbian and gay figures have become more numerous in the media since 1987, and coverage of gay/lesbian issues has expanded in the 'quality' press: the *Independent* earns an honourable mention here. Within the tabloid papers, it is business as usual. Homophobia, it has been judged, sells papers. Every conceivable form of abuse is ever-present: the homophobic verbiage which characterises the British popular press is undoubtedly a unique phenomenon in the world media. Signs that the Press Council would ever seek to curb it were scarce until Terry Sanderson's success in the spring of 1990.

Looking back from the vantage point of nearly three years later, we can see that the year preceding the introduction of Clause 28 in Parliament represented a period during which well organised, high profile homophobic action moved to the fore in a variety of powerful social institutions: at the same time, the water of public opinion was tested as one extreme measure after another was suggested. The institutions included established religion, the press, the parties, local government and Parliament itself. The proposals put on the public agenda embraced genocide, criminalisation of sexual acts, and withdrawal of access to health care. The media had indicated that the British public was, generally speaking, quite prepared to give these notions a hearing: gay and lesbian voices were heard in protest, but objections from other quarters were muted. The ground had been well prepared for Clause 28, which is now imprinted on the statute books of the United Kingdom, and the consciousness of its lesbians and gay men.

Chapter 11
Out of the Box

Caroline Spry

Broadcasting's first open discussion of homosexuality crackled through the black and white fog of our TV sets in 1954. The intervening years have seen the chip gradually replacing the cathode ray to provide us with the most pervasive and persuasive form of global mass communication. The location of control over television is of crucial importance, and one that will become increasingly so in the volatile arena of broadcasting — terrestrial and satellite — in the next few years.

The participation of society as a whole — and specifically of disadvantaged groups — in the process of cultural production must be a cornerstone of a democratic society. As a means of providing news, information and entertainment, television has an undoubtedly powerful role in both reflecting and reinforcing ideas. So is there cause for concern for lesbians and gay men? What images of homosexuality have appeared on television?

During the formative years of broadcasting it was cinema which produced the predominant images of lesbians and gay men. Time and again it has been cinema which has pushed forward the bounds of public acceptability of controversial images and ideas, to be followed by television rather slowly. The first televised discussion of homosexuality came in the 1954 BBC programme 'In The News', when Lord Boothby discussed

Out of the Box

his call for a Royal Commission on the subject.

Since then broadcasting has gradually opened up to the continuing debate over the place of homosexuality in British society, albeit confining it to a number of fairly distinct genres of drama and factual television. The most common area of representation in television has been in the broadcasting of feature films which have either explicit or implicit references to homosexuality. One of the earliest to be shown was the 1950 film *Caged*, screened on ITV in 1968: this featured Hope Emerson as a mannish, sadistic matron in a women's prison. Since then, most of the 'gay' movies, from *Victim* (1961, starring Dirk Bogarde) to *Desert Hearts* (1986, Donna Deitch) have — or soon will have — reached the small screen with little or no controversy.

The distinctive area of the single television play has produced a surprising number of allusions to homosexuality. As early as 1957 the ITV adaptation of *The Woman in White* included oblique references to lesbianism, and in 1961 both male homosexuality (in ITV's 'The Collection') and butch lesbianism (in BBC's '"A" For Andromeda') appeared on screen.

The appearance of an adventurous new channel, BBC2, brought a more overt portrayal of gay men in a 1967 play *Boa Constrictor*, which featured three couples including two gay men. The late sixties and seventies saw the continued sporadic appearance of gay characters in television plays, most notably John Hurt's 1975 portrayal of Quentin Crisp in *The Naked Civil Servant*.

Long-running drama series as diverse as 'Crown Court', 'Angels', 'Executive Suite', 'St Elsewhere' and 'Bergerac' have included gay characters, albeit obliquely and usually negatively. But far more numerous have been depictions in light entertainment shows: often with regular 'gay' characters: the suggestion of a relationship between Hugh Lloyd and Terry Scott in 'Hugh and I' (early sixties BBC1), and the John Inman character in 'Are You Being Served?' (BBC1, 1973). Neither representation could be described as positive, however, and it was left to America to develop more progressive portrayals of gay men in the innovative 'Soap' and later 'Brothers'. A 1976 Granada television comedy project, 'All The Queen's Men', featured an all-gay Army unit but never came to fruition. Appearances of lesbian characters have been extremely rare: notable exceptions include the US series 'Golden Girls' and 'Kate And Allie', both of which included positive, though slightly patronising, portrayals of lesbian encounters.

In recent years the soap genre has hosted a number of gay characters. Channel 4's 'Brookside' briefly flirted with a lesbian sub-plot based round a disorganised feminist printing collective which added spice to Heather and Nicholas's conjugal difficulties. The gay theme was developed with the 'coming out' of Gordon Collins, which allowed discussion of attitudes to homosexuality (in particular those of Gordon's parents) and, of course, of AIDS. Meanwhile Colin, played by Michael Cashman in BBC1's 'EastEnders', played a similar role, providing a peg on which to hang issues of sexuality. At the time of writing, however, there are no regular appearances of gay characters in British soaps.

Since 1954 some factual output has examined the place of homosexuality in society. The least coverage has been in the realm of news and current affairs, where until the recent AIDS and Clause 28 reportage gay stories have been given only very occasional attention. Most impervious of all has been the news, making only brief reference to items such as the 1967 Sexual Offences Act or the more recent Local Government Act. The occasional gay march has received mention, and the customs raid against Gays The Word bookshop drew brief comments, but little else has broken through. In 1982 BBC1's 'Nationwide' covered *Gay News*' tenth birthday, but in general the sharp end of factual programming has only given space to gay issues when they impinge on heterosexual concerns.

More attention has been paid to lesbians and gay men in regular feature slots. In 1962 the BBC 'Gallery' programme discussed homosexuality, though with a very male bias, and focused on the debates which informed the 1967 Wolfenden Report. This report, which culminated in the 1967 Sexual Offences Act, also gave rise to a two-part 'Man Alive' feature called 'Consenting Adults' (BBC), which dealt in separate weeks with men and women. A brief look at the content of the women's programme gives us a flavour of how homosexuality was represented: a good deal of time was devoted to an interview with Steve, a prospective female-to-male transsexual (displaying a common confusion with homosexuality and transsexuality). This was followed by Julie and Cynthia talking in their comfortable Wandsworth home, indistinguishable from thousands of homes owned by married couples — so indistinguishable that the two women are faced with such questions as, 'If you go out together for dinner, who pays the bill?', and 'How do you organise your domestic life together? Is one of you a sort of dominant figure — like the man?'

The Wolfenden Report also opened television up to the first openly gay programme, Granada's 1957 'Homosexuality and the Law, A Prologue to the Wolfenden Report'. This was followed years later by ATV's look at lesbians, 'The Important Thing Is Love' (1971): bizarre and reactionary it may have been, but at that time the mere presence of 'real lesbians' on TV was a revelation and lifeline for many women.

Common to many of these programmes, though, was a stance of the heterosexual norm questioning the validity of homosexuality, and the representation of homosexuality as predominantly male. This began to change by the late seventies, as liberalisation in definitions of sexuality began to show in programmes which questioned less the right to homosexual existence, preferring to concentrate on specific topics. In 1978 'Brass Tacks' (BBC) looked at lesbian use of Artificial Insemination by Donor, while 'Grapevine' (BBC) reported on a gay community centre in Birmingham, and the Gay Sweatshop Tour of Belfast.

A leap of imagination was made by London Weekend Television with the production of their 'Gay Life' series in 1980 and 1981. These modest programmes were basically interviews in which gay men and lesbians discussed their lives and experiences. The tone was worthy, but the programmes represented TV's first weekly series attempting to look at gay people.

One area of television where frequent reference has been made to homosexuality is in the arts programmes. Biographies and interviews with artists such as Christopher Isherwood, David Hockney, Tennessee Williams and so on have not hesitated to name their sexuality. Again, the spotlight has been on men — a reflection of the place of women in the arts as much as a marker of the unacceptability of lesbianism. It is notable that a BBC programme about Colette, 'The Gentle Libertine' (1967), was not transmitted.

Another area of factual programming is that of access television. Born out of the sixties and seventies notion of a democratic broadcasting network, television responded with the BBC's 'Open Door' series from the Community Programme Unit. Over the years a small number of programmes have come from lesbians and gay men: the Scottish Minorities Group's 'Glad To Be Gay' in 1976, and coverage of the Clause 28 debate.

Undeniably, though, the space allowed for lesbians and gays to represent themselves remains very small. In the absence of access to television and mainstream cinema, and from the climate of political struggle among minority groups in the sixties and seventies, independent film and video have flourished. Lesbians and gay men have worked to produce material reflecting their experience and culture, including films such as *Word Is Out* (US, Peter Adair *et al*) and *Nighthawk* (Ron Peck and Paul Hallam). Their audiences were found in independent cinemas and discussion groups: their relationship to broadcast television was at that time non-existent.

In many ways, then, we have made progress since the early fifties. The social climate has changed, and with it

Out of the Box

the limits of television courage, but there is still a great deal of implicit and overt censorship to be challenged. As with many decisions in television, it is difficult to ascertain the reasons behind non-transmission, but, for the record, Thames Television's 1976 'Sex In Our Time: For Queer Read Gay', and Southern Television's 1979/80 'Southern Report: Lesbians', never reached our screens. Possibly par for the course in television write-offs, but possibly not.

Are we better off now? There is considerable dissatisfaction among lesbians and gays at their lack of representation, or misrepresentation, on television. Evidence for their complaint was provided by the invaluable 1985 survey by the Gays and Broadcasting Project, the results of which were published in the pamphlet *Are We Being Served?*. A group of lesbians and gay men monitored 688 hours of national television and radio during one week, and found a depressing picture. The total time of lesbian and gay representation as a percentage of total television output was 3.38 per cent, plummeting to 0.32 per cent on radio. Lesbian representation accounted for just 0.06 per cent of total television and radio output — 25 minutes out of 688 hours of broadcasting. This small amount of coverage was overwhelmingly negative and stereotypical. A depressing picture, but nevertheless I would argue that there has been a marginal improvement over the years.

One of the reasons for this improvement was the radical shift in the status quo of broadcasting that took place in November 1982, when the new fourth channel went on the air. Established under the 1981 Broadcasting Act, Channel 4 had a statutory obligation to 'contain a suitable proportion of matter calculated to appeal to tastes and interests not generally catered for by ITV.' The lesbian and gay communities seized this opportunity to demand access to the airwaves, calling for more positive representation across the broad span of the schedule, and also for specific gay slots — in particular for a magazine-style programme.

It is worth pausing here to consider what the notion of gay broadcasting serving a lesbian and gay audience and community might mean. The terms 'audience' and 'community' suggest a homogenous collective consciousness with clearly defined needs and demands. But when we talk about the gay audience, do we mean the 50-year-old white male Tory voter living in Chelmsford, or the 21-year-old Asian dyke living in Hackney? Clearly societal distinctions also operate in the lesbian and gay communities. It is the imperatives of a coherent demand for representation together with common points of struggle that lead to the notion of a somehow definable gay audience.

What of gay broadcasting? This seems to have two facets: firstly, an integration of gay issues, concerns and images within the totality of broadcasting; and secondly, specifically gay-orientated programmes.

Arguments have raged, both inside and outside television, about whether 'ghetto' slots further marginalise minority communities and prevent their integration into the mainstream. These are powerful and important arguments, but they do not seem to translate into visible results. So, whilst the perils of specialist slots are very real, they cannot be relinquished *before* the mainstream becomes fully representative. These programmes should only be axed when they are redundant.

A further cause of marginalising such programmes is the problem of ghetto hours. Late-night scheduling has been a consistent feature of lesbian and gay programming, exploiting the gay audience's motivation to watch these programmes while keeping them on the edges of broadcasting. As one television executive put it: 'We do a few gay programmes, and will carry on doing them. They go out at carefully placed times, late in the evening when most people can easily avoid them.'

Some progress has been made in reducing negative stereotyping. The Gays and Broadcasting research confirmed that fictionalised images of the effeminate man and the predatory dyke are still common, as is the collapsing together of all forms of difference into the strange and the perverse. But more recent material has presented lesbians and gay men as nice respectable citizens — just like anyone else. Colin's role in 'EastEnders' followed this line, as has Gordon's in 'Brookside'. Welcome though it is to see such friendly typecasting, we should hope that the opening up of broadcasting to more gay representation will allow for greater diversity.

Channel 4 has gone some way to remedying this situation. From its earliest days it has been the target of media vilification for its gay programming. At New Year 1983 it screened the light-hearted 'One In Five': it has also shown the film *My Beautiful Laundrette*, the sitcom 'Cornerhouse', documentaries such as 'Veronica 4 Rose', 'Breaking The Silence' and 'Bright Eyes', and the fictional 'Domestic Bliss'.

This progress has a fraught history, however. Mary Whitehouse, representing the National Viewers and Listeners Association, has repeatedly criticised Channel 4 for suggesting that gay is normal 'in the light of ... an AIDS epidemic.' Although a planned gay film series (including *Mädchen in Uniform*, *Before Stonewall* and *The Life and Times of Harvey Milk*) went ahead, the series title 'In The Pink' was removed. High ratings and positive viewer response, however, ensured that a second season was broadcast the following year, this time without controversy.

The success of these films enabled the early screening of the experimental gay magazine series 'Out On Tuesday', first broadcast at 11 p.m. on Valentine's Day, 1989. The series, produced by a number of different production companies, was an important piece of television: unable to fulfil all expectations, nonetheless it covered a lot of ground in a thought-provoking and stylish manner. High viewing figures allowed a second series to be shown at the earlier time of 9 p.m., and there are plans for a third series to follow.

Television coverage of homosexuality in recent years has increased considerably as a result of AIDS and, more recently, Clause 28. Documentaries, news and current affairs programmes have produced a diversity of information and opinion about AIDS and its relationship to gay men: most of this occurred within the explosion of interest in AIDS in 1986/7, as a response to the growing concern about the threat of AIDS to heterosexuals. It is arguable that the increased visibility of gay men in television drama was a reflection of their dramatic potential as 'dangerous' characters, and their function in raising discussion of AIDS.

Television's response to the struggle around Clause 28 reflected the status the campaign achieved in the political arena. The involvement of influential people, including many heterosexuals, in all areas of public life; the high visibility of figures such as Ian McKellen and Michael Cashman; the size and nature of the demonstrations and direct actions made it great television material. For probably the first time since 1967, homosexuality was at the forefront of public debate, resulting in moments of real visibility and intervention. I recall one evening, during the early days of the campaign, when on three occasions on different channels (an arts programme and two awards ceremonies) public statements were made against the Clause. No special programmes, no journalistic mediation — simply raw protest.

This was an indication of those gay people who work at all levels of broadcasting. Most are still very much in the closet, however, and those who are more or less open about their sexuality rarely prioritise gay representation on their broadcasting agenda. Overt lesbian presence, certainly at any level of decision-making or control, is almost non-existent, reflecting the general lack of women in positions of power within broadcasting. Despite the equal opportunities policies of major broadcasters, there are no effective steps being taken by the industry to remedy this situation, nor possibly any significant recognition of a need to do so.

Out of the Box

In a society where lesbians and gay men are a small but significant minority, and where individuals experience various forms of oppression and discrimination because of their sexuality, fair representation is only likely to take place within some form of public service broadcasting. British television was created with this idea in its heart, and has continued to develop over the last fifty years with these ideals firmly at the forefront. As we have seen, however, gays have not been well served within this tradition. We now face a period of great change and uncertainty in broadcasting, and a considerable threat to its role as a public service.

The contradictory policies of the commercial deregulation of broadcasting and the greater regulation of programme content (as proposed in the Broadcasting Bill 1990) could have serious repercussions for the quality of programming, the range of representation, and the effectiveness of the unions. The battle for ratings will undoubtedly become increasingly influential on programme form and content, as the number of channels proliferates with the spread of satellite and the probability of a fifth terrestrial channel. The opening up of BBC and ITV to independent producers and the ending of closed shops is already undermining the power of those who work within broadcasting: this could affect their ability to influence content, and also the training and employment practices of the broadcasting institutions.

In contrast to this move to open up broadcasting to the free market, there is the desire to monitor and control output. In 1989 a Private Member's Bill attempted to bring television under the Obscene Publications Act, while widening the legal definition of obscenity. The Bill failed, but is likely to resurface as government legislation. The fact that one of the Bill's triggers was the Channel 4 Screening of Derek Jarman's *Sebastiane* gives us some indication of the possible threats to homosexual images on television. The extent of the powers of the Broadcasting Standards Council, headed by William Rees-Mogg, are still unclear, but with its target of 'sex and violence' on television, homosexuality could well be the bull's-eye.

The outlook is not encouraging, although there are still some indicators of hope. Television is very much a reflection and reinforcement of its society, and the history of gay representation on television is closely linked to events outside. The opening up of broadcasting has developed across thirty years, but we are still left with huge room for improvement. Demands for change will continue, but it is difficult to imagine substantial progress being made in the current climate, as broadcasting, and the media in general, becomes increasingly unaccountable to society as a whole.

Chapter 12
Approximations: Image, Desire and Lesbian Identity

'Fat' as the Antithesis of 'Erotic'

Heather Smith

> 'You just want to push somebody
> And a body won't let you
> Just want to move somebody
> And a body won't let you ...
> Who do you talk to ...
> When a body's in trouble?
>
> You just want to run somebody
> And a body won't let you
> Want to let somebody and a body won't let
> You want to kiss, feel, hear, ride
> Stop, start somebody and a body won't let you
> Who do you talk to ...
> Who?
> Who do you talk to ...
> When a body's in trouble,
> When a body's in trouble.'[1]

> 'The hardest part of being a fat person is that it's not just your imagination that tells you you don't count. In some ways you really don't. It is an act of courage for a fat woman to even go out in public. Every day you are told, "Go home. This isn't for you, the world isn't for you".'[2]

Existing divisions amongst lesbian feminists have been emphasised by contemporary debates about pornography, sadomasochism censorship and identity politics. Those socialist feminists whose contributions I find most exciting and challenging[3] have drawn back the curtains to expose the contradictions and complexity of desire. Their resistance to essentialist and idealistic definitions of lesbian sex has led to an examination of the role power, pleasure and fantasy play in our sexual choices and practices. Eroticism has been placed firmly on the feminist agenda, a challenge to the desexualisation of lesbianism which represented a significant strand of seventies' feminism. Lesbian history has been re-evaluated, and butch femme images have been reclaimed as one of many possible ways to signify erotic identity. Discussions about 'dress sense' have represented a move away from androgyny towards making more complex, overtly erotic fashion statements. Emphasising the social construction of gender and sexuality, these writers question the biological determinism implicit in the automatic equation of woman as powerless and man as powerful, which leaves little room for change. Similarly, they challenge the cultural imperialism of a politics which ignores the complex ways in which class and culture affect our sexualities. They suggest that, by focusing on pornography and sadomasochism, many lesbian feminists avoid addressing more general problems and concerns about sexuality.

Sex resists simple definitions. It is anarchic. It cannot be prescribed and controlled. Sexuality is open to intervention because it is socially constructed and located within ever-changing cultural and historical moments, but desire is a discourse which can be changed through exploration rather than by prohibition.

I welcome the space that has been created to discuss our sexual pleasures and problems, yet I feel that certain gaps remain. While putting sex back into politics,[4] there has been little recognition of how appearance affects the politics of sex. Debates about sexism have included feminist critiques of sexual objectification and sexual stereotyping, but have largely excluded investigation of how women whose appearance contravenes cultural 'norms' are negated and abused.

Approximations: Image, Desire and Lesbian Identity

Sex is assumed to be the property of a 'physical elite':[5] our sexual possibilities are significantly affected by our appearance. Desire is written across flesh which is eroticised in rigid and exclusive ways in Western cultures. Women whose bodies are defined as 'defective' are pushed to the erotic margins of this society. Eroticism is defined around absence — defined in relation to what can never be erotic — for the polarized, competitive structure of Western capitalism requires such division.

Feminists have not explored sufficiently how the cultural concept of 'woman' varies in cultural, class and aesthetic contexts. The writing across a woman's body changes as that body becomes fat or scarred or old. Images have multiple meanings and we play an active and unpredictable role in constructing and interpreting our cultural concepts and products. No uniform or universal meaning of 'erotic' or 'desirable' exists. In twentieth-century Western cultures, however, there is some consensus concerning which bodies are 'sexually attractive' and central to concepts of desire, and which bodies are 'repulsive' and marginal. Many women are excluded by current definitions of 'beauty', but this article focuses on how being fat affects our sexual choices, particularly within the lesbian communities. I hope to establish fat oppression and looksism as areas of concern for feminism.

Extracts From A Diary

SEXUAL ABSENCE 1
Nothing changes/feelings shift, move endlessly in circles/moths beating at glass endlessly/all that energy expended on nothing/no-one lets you in/desire and what can be desired are all fixed within strict parameters/ established as everything you're not/desire written against your body/encoded in all the spaces which are not you/contours which are not yours/you occupy the gap between desire and fulfilment/absence of choice/no

choice at all/why are moths nocturnal when so strongly attracted to light? Why is the erasure of desire so difficult? In moments of despair you hit hope on the head with a hammer, but she goes on breathing in dark, safe spaces, echoes and cobwebs/tatters of past desire, spent and perfect, swim through time towards you, reminding you of what was but is no more/splinters in the flesh/tiny mouths open and close and never get fed — not even scraps — nothing at all. They ache and burn like a bleeding throat.

Appearance matters. Images make complex statements about identity. Such statements are culturally and historically specific, and while their meanings are not fixed or static, in the twentieth century they are the products of capitalism, imperialism, and patriarchy. In many cultures women are the bearers of cultural myths and signifiers of status. Our bodies are defined and controlled in the interests of power and profit. We are taught to equate beauty with 'success', 'social mobility' and sexual desire. Those women who do not conform to constructed aesthetic ideals are punished and excluded. Western cultures, structured around polarity and hierarchy, promote competition and conformity. Concepts of 'superior' and 'inferior' are central to discourses on 'beauty'. Affirmation depends on negation: white is valued at the expense of black; youth acquires status through the devaluation of ageing. The positive value attributed to thin bodies is dependent on definitions of fat as disgusting and diseased: fear and hatred of fat pervades contemporary Western cultures; fat women are excluded from many activities and possibilities because of our size. Lesbian definitions of 'beauty' differ slightly from heterosexual ones, but the pressure to be thin remains. 'Acceptable' lesbian images may be slowly changing, but the 'ideal' body stays the same.

We exist in a society in which 'a woman must continually watch herself. She is almost continually accompanied by her own image of herself', and in which

'Men act. Women appear. Men look at women. Women watch themselves being looked at'.[6] Furthermore, Western cultures prioritise the visual over other sensual impressions.[7] Consequently, a woman's sense of self-worth is very bound up with her image.

Women are encouraged to spend a lot of time and money attempting to reach impossible and ever-changing images of 'perfection'. We are expected to make seasonal adjustments to change our clothes, make-up and even our bodies in accordance with fashion. The diet industry (via the media) sells the myth that a new body shape can be obtained as easily as a new haircut, provided you can afford their products and endure prolonged starvation. The media promotes an obsession with fat and how to get rid of it; most women's magazines regularly feature diets and exercise regimes aimed at erasing all 'spare' flesh from a woman's body. Yet 95 per cent of diets fail, and among the 5 per cent of women who do achieve permanent weight-loss, many have developed serious eating disorders such as anorexia nervosa and bulimia. The price of 'success' may involve constant anxiety about potential weight-gain, may lead to serious damage to our health, even to death. Most women never become replicas of their celluloid and paper dreams. We remain always just approximations.

The diet industry thrives on the promise of transformation and perfection always held tantalizingly just out of reach. Endless failure is linked to endless profit. We punish ourselves for 'failing' and believe that we cannot be loved, desired or respected unless we get thin; and punishment is also linked to profit. The penalties against fat women are so extreme that women continue to starve themselves and buy useless diet products rather than endure such humiliation and exclusion.

> 'Making people look the way you want them to is an important part of the colonial process. By taking away a people's culture and pride in their appearance, you literally change the way they see themselves.'[8]

The fat-hatred embedded in Western cultures has massive international repercussions because of cultural imperialism. Britain and the US export an increasingly 'thin' ideal. Extremely profitable multinational companies sell size 10 clothes along with diets, cosmetics, 'Dallas', beauty contests, gyms and junk food to First Nation/Third World cultures, where fat has been considered beautiful and healthy. The diet industry sells the medical myths and the promise of 'perfection' (Western aesthetics with their associations of wealth, glamour and success). This colonisation of the body is part of a general process of the worldwide imposition of Western values. Cultural imperialism emphasises difference in a way which enables those with power to define the 'ideal'. While promoting the erasure of fat people, Western culture also requires our existence as 'other', to warn women everywhere that those who fail to subscribe to the cult of thinness will face exclusion and hatred. The pressures of racism have led to black people using dangerous skin bleaches, and having plastic surgery to change their features; and to black children playing at miming peeling off their skin or pulling out their hair, in 'what I like/don't like about myself' games. Now in the 'beauty' arena, the body as well as the skin is under attack, and women all over the world bear the burden of Western marketing strategies.

SEXUAL ABSENCE 2
Bad air and you go on breathing. And desire is starving and its belly grows huge but its lungs continue to process air and it lights small fires everywhere. The world is diseased and dying. Desire flutters in an empty room. Trapped in a cruel flesh joke, desire burns holes so deep they can never be repaired. I'll be your friend but I'll never be your lover. No matter how much you have to offer, the body is between. Too much equals not enough. Always the same equation. Righteous in their lack of desire, the media-munching thin people dispose

of us like a dirty garment. They keep us in jars like dead insects and fail to perceive the pulse of desire. We're a dirty stain they don't want to be reminded of.

Fat and Sexuality

In many cultures, sexual relationships are regarded as a central source of support and pleasure. In the West, the media constructs sex as something reserved for those who are considered 'beautiful'. Women who approximate to this still have lovers, but the further you move away from 'beauty', the more inaccessible sex becomes.

Fat women are sexually taboo. In sex the body is central, and although in the end it is more than the body that is loved, the body is the beginning and fat women just cannot get started. Positive images of sexually active fat women are absent from both mainstream and alternative media. Even pornography which explores marginalised and taboo sexualities, covers fat only in specialist issues which eroticise not the 'beauty' of fat but its 'ugliness'. This fetishisation of disgust encodes fat women in pornographic representation as desperate, slobbering nymphomaniacs.

Fat women are defined as undesirable, asexual, maternal, sexually desperate, rampant or repressed. We are misrepresented as dirty, ugly, stupid, irresponsible, out of control, weak-willed and greedy. The stigma attached to fat means that we are low-status as lovers, thus people who are attracted to fat women may repress their desire because they risk ridicule and pity if they choose such a low-status lover. Those people who do transgress social and sexual boundaries in loving fat women may punish their fat lover with ambivalence (for example, by wanting to be with them privately but not in public). Some fat women have lovers who desire and respect them, but for many more sex means the absence of, or the scraps.

Some fat women are positive about their bodies and

consider themselves powerful, beautiful, sexual, voluptuous and juicy, but many more of us internalise all the negative messages we receive about fat (clumsy, defective, inferior) and hate our bodies. Whenever we move down a street, enter a pub, club or restaurant we risk being laughed at, sworn at, spat at. Such extreme abuse contributes to our feeling that we do not deserve to exist, let alone be sexually assertive. Some fat women do not define themselves sexually because they do not consider themselves sexually viable, and see no point in labelling themselves in a vacuum. Those of us who are sexually assertive still find that our confidence crumbles when we are ridiculed in public spaces.

SEXUAL ABSENCE 3
The language of desire is rich and complex. It excludes you. For you, desire is a mobile flung in all directions and getting nowhere. If only desire were a plum-stone, all dried and hard, but it is soft and juicy and luscious. It gets bruised but the fruit remains. Persistent clinging flesh and juices that stain.

Sexuality is an area of our lives which involves risk, vulnerability and exposure. It requires trust. Fat women risk so much more than thin women when starting a sexual relationship, because we are taught that we are not capable of inspiring love or lust: we have forfeited the right to be sexual because our bodies are incompatible with desire. Consequently, we may lack confidence and feel less able to risk rejection. Non-monogamy may be less possible for us, and we may stay in relationships longer than we should because we are scared of not being able to find a replacement. We are never presented as sexual subjects or objects, so we are less likely to trigger desire, and if we do not believe that we are desirable we will project this and create further obstacles. When we are not in a sexual relationship this can confirm our own negativity.

Approximations: Image, Desire and Lesbian Identity

SEXUAL ABSENCE 4

Your mum is thirty. She thinks she looks like Deanna Durbin. She sets her hair every night — it is black and shines like the moon on a wet pavement. She has smooth, soft skin which glows softly as though a candle were just below the surface. She makes herself beautiful clothes — she's fat, so she has to. She works in a factory, hard, repetitive work. 'Good' money. She lives with your Grandma, whom she supports financially and in other ways. They are immigrants and in a town full of bigots they keep themselves to themselves. Sometimes women at work call her a fat Irish pig. She is friendly towards them, but they are not people she can count on. She and her Mum go to the pictures often, and on Saturday nights they fry steak and listen to the radio, and talk until the last embers have faded to ash. She has no women friends in England, she doesn't go to dances, but there is one special dance organised by the factory that she decides to go to. She makes a special suit of blue and silver and buys blue shoes. Her Mum says she looks beautiful and this is how she feels. She goes to the dance alone. Women line the walls, like rows of tulips in buckets waiting to be bought. No-one asks her to dance. She sits there all evening and no-one even talks to her. They don't notice her new suit, she can't feel attention on her face like fingers. They don't see her at all. She is the funniest person you know, she is warm, generous and intelligent, her smile could melt ice. But she sits there all night flat as a shadow on the wall and there is music and celebration and other people dancing. Always other people. When she goes home she cries and cannot be comforted. She went to a dance alone with hope and a new set of clothes, but all they saw was a fat woman and no-one asked her to dance.

Still she wears corsets and girdles, tight and uncomfortable. She says they keep her back warm. She tells you being fat ruined her life — nobody likes you if you're fat, they're not attracted to you. She got a man nobody else wanted and so she knows what she's talking about. And you feel excluded by the lesbian communities. You've learned the same lessons in different ways, which are somehow the same.

Most women are involved in the never-ending struggle against 'excess' flesh. Fat lesbians and fat heterosexual women may experience fat oppression in different ways, but it is present for both. Feminist lesbians may question sexual objectification and rigid 'beauty norms' more than many heterosexual men do. However, lesbians are more likely than men to feel ambivalent about their own bodies and may feel it especially difficult to desire a fat woman who embodies their own fears. As part of a sexual minority, lesbians have a restricted choice of lovers, but the number of available lovers for fat women shrinks further. Some fat women are so grateful to be desired that they will take whatever sex is offered; others have very specific criteria for lovers, and even less choice.

In a recent 'Out On Tuesday' programme on Channel 4, Susan Hemmings observed how, in Britain, feminist lesbians in the seventies were expected to be attracted to a woman on the basis of her ideas rather than her appearance. This ethos contributed to the desexualisation of lesbianism and also ignored a whole range of inequalities which erode some lesbians' choice of lovers. No matter how 'good' the ideas of a fat or old or disabled woman, our sexual choices are limited. If a woman feels inspired by us, she can become our friend, but this is a particular problem for fat lesbians who can have any number of intense, close relationships which inevitably stop just short of sex.

Women are not only attracted to ideas or a sense of humour. Desire is played out across flesh. The map of desire is flat and smooth, it does not get dirty or sick or old, it is a neat, hard bourgeois space resistant to transgression. Being a lesbian requires some shifting away from sexual conformity, but this does not mean we necessarily question other 'sexual norms'. Women

Approximations: Image, Desire and Lesbian Identity

'police' other women's bodies because we know how important our appearance is in a society which objectifies us. Feminist lesbians reject the ideology but continue the practice, for fat women are excluded from current 'acceptable' images within the lesbian communities. A sporty, 'boyish' dyke image prevails, so lean hard bodies are preferred to abundant soft flesh, compelling many feminist lesbians to diet, weight train and jog obsessively in order to attain this 'athletic ideal'.

This lean, sporty, androgynous image is as limiting and as difficult to achieve as more conventional beauty ideals. The pressure to develop an 'acceptable' dyke image devalues diversity and negates other possible lesbian images, such as the much despised femme of seventies and early eighties feminism. Neither lesbian 'clone' nor femme-y images are easily available to fat lesbians, who are often stereotyped as 'earth mothers' or 'diesel dykes'. We are assumed to be failed heterosexuals, feeding into the myth that the lesbian communities accommodate fat more easily than their straight equivalents. There are many fat lesbians, but very few on 'the scene', because those fat women who do go to lesbian clubs and bars are always in a minority and thus feel noticeable. Considerable pressure to conform exists within the lesbian feminist communities, and those of us who conspicuously deviate from the norm either get stared at or are ignored.

Within the lesbian communities, appearance as a signifier of sexual roles/practices can be very problematic. 'Your sexy persona does not necessarily indicate what you imagine your sexy being doing in bed, nor does it indicate who you're attracted to.'[9] For fat women, there are additional problems. Some feminist psychotherapists have interpreted fat as a 'protection' against sexuality, such theories relying on definitions of fat as undesirable, contributing to the myth that fat people are asexual. Lesbian feminists may, therefore, interpret a fat body as making a 'don't touch me' statement.

There is considerable pressure within our community

to have a lover, or to be in the process of finding one.[10] There is no overt recognition that fat women do not have equal access to sexual relationships: however, if a fat woman's friends never ask her whether she is attracted to someone, they assume that she is single because she is fat and that she is likely to remain without a lover. This is negation, not support. When a fat lesbian's friends discuss diets or the bits of their (thin) bodies they dislike for being too big, they negate her.

Current debates on lesbian 'dress sense' are opening up more possibilities for experiment with image. For many lesbians the opportunity to wear 'feminine' clothes is a relief 'after all these years of dressing like men who dress badly'.[11] Increasing recognition of how oppositional images get incorporated and redefined in 'mainstream' fashion, coupled with an awareness that images do not have fixed meanings and can be subverted, has led to a re-evaluation of traditionally 'erotic' clothes. 'Mightn't a lacy bra or sheer stockings have erotic appeal less because they are symbols of female powerlessness and more because they are familiar symbols of female sexuality?'[12]

The popularity of lesbian Balls and Fancy-dress parties suggests that many of us enjoy playing with images and moving away from conformity, but there are gaps in this debate. Women do not all have equal control over their image: poor, working-class women cannot afford designer jeans, leather jackets and other symbols of urban lesbian chic. Black and working-class women are often stereotyped as sexually available and promiscuous; old women, women with disabilities and fat women are perceived as asexual. When making erotic statements with clothes we have to be aware of existing stereotypes. Fat women have to travel miles to buy underwear, and our choice of erotic, indeed all, clothing is minimal. Most clothes shops sell nothing we can wear, and specialist shops are expensive and offer a very limited range of images. The message we receive is that we are not attractive and will not be provided with props to make us

Approximations: Image, Desire and Lesbian Identity

so. Fat women may not feel confident about exposing their bodies in those ways traditionally associated with eroticism. Moreover, as fat is defined as the antithesis of erotic, 'erotic' clothes on a fat body may be interpreted as contradictory or ridiculous.

The image of the lesbian and gay communities presented by the Stop The Clause campaign and by the 'Out On Tuesday' series was predominantly young, white, English middle-class, urban, able-bodied and 'conventionally attractive'. Many of the participants in 'OOT' were London-based, 'trendy' and intellectual. Such images obscure the diversity of our communities. We must work towards a wider range of 'acceptable' lesbian and gay images, and stop colluding with restrictive definitions. We need a positive-images campaign which is positive about *all* our images.

SEXUAL ABSENCE 5
Wings beating against glass/a bleeding that never ends/desire is endless corridors leading nowhere. A plant you don't water, it droops but it does not die/your collection of erotic images is considerable but it's always happening to someone else. Desire is played across 'perfect' flesh in 'perfect' rooms/you lie in your perfect room alone/all around you night throbs with desire/people connecting in new and old ways emphasise your disconnection. You are a bulb in scorched fabric/an invisible flame/a perfume without scent. You grow and decay in this sexual solitude.

Possibilities for Change

Sexuality is a difficult area in which to achieve change. Fat women can work on developing sexual confidence, and on believing that they deserve, and are capable of inspiring, love and lust, but such self-esteem is difficult to achieve and maintain in a sexual void. We can demand respect and an end to abuse, but we cannot demand to be desired, for desire operates in complex, often unconscious ways. Centuries of promotion of a thin ideal inscribe it deep within individual and collective unconsciousness. However, erotic symbols and fantasies are socially constructed and alterable, and by examining how conscious we are of how and why we suppress or express desire, we will be able to establish how fixed our impulses and fantasies are. Eroticism is open to feminist intervention, but change cannot be achieved easily where the unconscious is concerned. We cannot decide to alter our psyches in the way we might decide not to wear high heels, just because they damage us and make us vulnerable. We can explore how and why certain symbols, clothing, body shapes and parts are eroticised, and whether new erotic symbols can be introduced. We can analyse the role of image and status in the choice of lovers. We cannot force desire to take a shape it resists, but perhaps we can slowly remould it.

> '... there is a resistance to identity which lies at the very heart of psychic life.'
>
> 'The unconscious constantly reveals the "failure" of identity. Because there is no continuity of psychic life, so there is no stability of sexual identity — no position for women (or men) which is ever simply achieved.'[1][3]

We have unstable social and sexual identities. Our unconscious reveals many contradictions, dislocations and gaps through dreams, slips of the tongue and 'taboo' desires,[1][4] so that we are never completely socialised into dominant ways of thinking and feeling. There is always the possibility of disruption. As lesbians we bear testimony to this resistance to socialisation. We have refused to repress our desires, in spite of enormous pressure to conform to heterosexual norms.

We can use psychoanalytic theories to explore fat and sexuality. Some women do resist the pressure to loathe fat, and we should consider why they refuse to collude with widely accepted definitions of sexual attractiveness. We can also explore the meaning of taboo for those of us

Approximations: Image, Desire and Lesbian Identity

(lesbians) who are already defined as taboo. Perhaps some positive aspects are contained within fat's designation as taboo; for instance, some people find fat attractive *because* it is forbidden and marginal: 'It may be that the forbidden is exciting because it is forbidden. But, as Freud pointed out, things are taboo precisely because they are exciting, otherwise they need not be prohibited.'[15]

SEXUAL ABSENCE 6
Trapped on the edges of desire, I'm sitting on a bus without a destination. It's been parked in the depot for years. Sexual absence. The sadness of a closing-off of part of myself. The loss of deep pleasure, of pushing intensity to its furthest edges. Long hours of physical exploration/emotional connection so deep like moving through layers of sea. An underwater world, new and exciting and richer than surface communication. Intense excitement/deep relaxation/kisses/caresses/ laughter/explosions. Such knowing like reaching through deep snow to the land beneath. Curled up to keep warm but still breathing. Missing the intimacy/the emotional expansion/the pushing against the edges of friendship/merging and pushing away of barriers/the freedom of sexual contact/the extension of knowing and being known/the growth and strengthening of trust.

Sexual relationships can be liberating and affirming, they can offer intimacy and support, an outlet for emotional intensity not permitted in most other close relationships. You can kiss a friend on the lips, but if you put your tongue in her mouth it becomes something else. Sex is about transgressing boundaries and revealing more of yourself than you would usually dare.

While celebrating the pleasures of sex, we need to explore those ways in which sex can be problematic. We should question the centrality of sex, as this has an adverse and marginalising effect on other relationships. Such revision could increase the value of friendships, autonomy and other forms of creativity, and open up discussion on the pleasures of celibacy, masturbation, shared sex. We should also question the pressure to be constantly seeking a lover, and the all-consuming, obsessive nature of much passionate love. Whilst ever sexual relationships are foregrounded and idealised, those of us without a lover will be made to feel inferior and excluded.

> 'Big women can be extremely imposing. A large woman who is not apologising for her size is certainly not a figure to invite the dominant meanings which our culture attaches to femininity. She is impressive in ways that our culture cannot tolerate.'[16]

As fat women we are punished for not conforming to conventional feminine ideals. As fat lesbians we are negated for deviating from alternative womanly ideals. We must continue to intervene in contemporary feminist debates on desire, pleasure, power and image. We must emphasise how and why existing 'erotic' and aesthetic criteria exclude us. We can argue for a redefinition of concepts such as 'sexually attractive' to include all those women currently negated. We can continue to expose the artificiality of masculinity and femininity. If we stop shaving we can demonstrate the fallacy of the equation of woman and hairlessness; if we stop dieting we can show that woman equals big as well as small. Most women are dissatisfied with their bodies and feel that they are only approximations. No-one belongs to the physical elite for long. Our intervention can create more erotic possibilities for all women.

Western cultures market desire. Under capitalism, anything can become a commodity. We should resist the manipulation of our desires and form a coalition with women internationally to resist the colonisation of our bodies. We should question the centrality of appearance to sex and suggest that lesbians no longer make snap assessments of each other on the basis of how we look. While urging for a change in the terms of the debate, in the short-term fat women must argue that to be both fat and beautiful is not a contradiction in terms, as part of the process of beginning to celebrate our sexuality. Fat women are campaigning against all forms of discrimination currently experienced. We are challenging the fashion industry to improve its provision, so that we can experiment with images and make more erotic statements with clothes. Fat lesbians are planning to stop hiding away and to make a *big* impression on the scene.

We must all assert that fat is not the antithesis of erotic. We must redefine fat, have confidence and take pleasure in our bodies. Forced to exist on the social and sexual margins of a society which hates us, we can break through this confinement and move centre-stage. It is our turn for a bite of the apple.

Acknowledgements

I would like to thank Tina Jenkins, Meena Patel, Julie Mallett and Ruby Smith for their support during the writing of this article. Thanks also to all the fat lesbians at the first national fat women's conference for sharing their experiences.

Notes

1. Mary Margaret O'Hara, 'Body's in Trouble' from the album Miss America, Virgin Records Ltd, 1988.
2. Wendy Chapkis, *Beauty Secrets; Women and the Politics of Appearance*, The Women's Press, London, 1986.
3. Alice Echols, 'The New Feminism of Yin and Yang' from *Desire: The Politics of Sexuality*, Eds. Ann Snitow, Christine Stansell and Sharon Thompson, Virago Press, London, 1987.
4. Referred to on 'Out on Tuesday', Channel 4 TV, 1989/90.

5. Wendy Chapkis, op.cit., p.146.
6. John Berger, *Ways of Seeing*, Penguin Books, London, 1972, pp.46, 47.
7. Rosalind Coward, *Female Desire: Women's Sexuality Today*, Paladin, London, 1984, p.75.
8. Wendy Chapkis, op.cit., p.69.
9. Wendy Chapkis, op.cit. In the chapter 'Skin Deep' there are similar associations.
10. Lorna Hardy, 'Exposure' from *Out the Other Side*, Eds. Christian McEwen and Sue O'Sullivan, 1988, p.77.
11. Wendy Chapkis, op.cit., p.139.
12. Ibid., p.133.
13. Jacqueline Rose, 'Femininity and its Discontents' from *Sexuality — A Reader*, Virago Press, London, 1987, p.184.
14. Ibid.
15. Jessica Benjamin, 'Master and Slave: The Fantasy of Erotic Domination' from *Desire: The Politics of Sexuality*, p.308.
16. Rosalind Coward, op.cit., p.41.

Chapter 13
The Limits of Tolerance?

Lesbian and gay rights and local government in the 1980s

Bob Cant

No-one ever thought it would be easy to achieve equality for lesbians and gays. Centuries of oppression could not just be wiped out by a legislative dictate. Attempts by some Labour-led councils in the 1980s to respond to the demands of the lesbian and gay movement and to reduce the impact of that oppression, led to one of those great hypocritical moral panics which are so characteristic of British public life. Now that the shouting is over and the most homophobic piece of legislation for over a century is on the statute books, lesbians and gays are picking themselves up and asking if our involvement with local government was really worth the effort.

Local government had been a much under-estimated sector since 1945. Voter turnout in local elections was frequently as low as 25 per cent, in contrast with over 70 per cent in national elections. Before 1945, however, local government had been a crucially contested political arena and major initiatives had taken place in relation to social policies, often in opposition to the government of the day. The London County Council had, for example, been innovative in its approach to the public provision of both education and housing for working-class people. While the election of an authoritarian central government in

1979 resulted in cut-backs for local councils, it also provided a further stimulus for more community-oriented municipal projects.

Many Labour councils recognized that the victory of the Conservative Party in 1979 reflected a loss of faith in the way that both the economy and the welfare state had been managed by successive governments since 1945. They endeavoured, on a number of levels, to make themselves more accountable than previous Labour councils had been. They looked to ways of organizing cheap, safe public transport, of generating socially useful employment and, particularly after the 1981 riots, of improving the quality of urban life. Their vision of society was collectivist, grass-roots oriented and utterly antithetical to the privatised and mortgaged paradise of Thatcherism.

One of the most controversial areas of intervention by these new-style Labour councils was Equal Opportunities. The 1960s and 1970s had seen the emergence of a number of social movements among oppressed groups. The issues that they raised about the institutionalized nature of their oppression could not be resolved by any one local council. But some councils acknowledged that their procedures contributed to the oppression and undertook to make changes in an attempt to improve the material conditions of people in those oppressed groups. Their approaches differed — they consulted with organizations from the oppressed groups; they set up new committee structures; they funded voluntary groups and made space available to them; they arranged awareness-training for their staff. They raised enormous expectations.

While progressive Labour councils declared their intentions to address the expectations of women, of black people and disabled people, it was by no means clear that they would do so in relation to lesbians and gays. The public invisibility and the self-policing that are so central to lesbian and gay oppression place us in quite a different position, socially and economically, from each of these other groups. But was this political climate of friendliness towards the oppressed one that lesbians and gays could afford to ignore? Would we ever again have such an opportunity?

By the early 1980s the euphoria of early Gay Liberation politics had worn off. There were those — particularly gay men — who argued that there was no need for any gay politics at all. Their lifestyles focused on the social networks around the pubs and clubs that had emerged in the wake of Gay Liberation. The politically active were divided among themselves — most lesbians were then working in women-only organizations; some groups continued to campaign for law reforms; some groups sought alliances as part of the process of bringing about revolutionary change. One feature, common to this diversity, was visibility. While not all individuals felt able to be out and visible all the time, the invisibility that had isolated lesbians and gays for decades and stifled their creativity had, to some extent, been lifted. There were now, albeit only for a minority, alternatives to invisibility.

Visibility was not without its problems. While there were more opportunities for lesbians and gays to meet one another, to make friendships, to form relationships, to have sex, this attracted a number of forms of hostility. The largest gay national publication, *Gay News*, was dragged through the courts in 1977-78 on a charge of blasphemy, for publishing a homoerotic poem about Christ. Lesbians who wished to become parents by artificial insemination found themselves pilloried by the media. A survey by London Gay Switchboard in 1980 of people looking for accommodation found that one in four was homeless on account of their sexuality.

The employment protection legislation of the 1970s was of no assistance to lesbians and gays. John Warburton, a teacher for the progressive Inner London Education Authority, refused to lie to his pupils and was sacked; Louise Boychuk, sacked for wearing a 'Lesbians Ignite' badge at her work as an insurance clerk, found that the Employment Appeal Tribunal agreed with her employers' right to sack her; John Saunders, who had never wished to tell anyone at work that he was gay, found that the E.A.T. and the Scottish Court of Session agreed that his employers' prejudice justified their sacking of him; Susan Shell was sacked from her job as a care assistant by Barking's Labour council, when it was discovered that she was lesbian and she refused to resign.

The movement may have been divided in this period, but these attacks did not take place without resistance and the value of collective action was learned. The *Gay News* Defence Campaign may not have won the case for the paper, but it helped the community maintain a sense of strength and it led to the setting up of the Gay Activists Alliance. The victimized workers may not have won their jobs back, but they and other workers learned about the value of self-organization at work as well as about strategies for relating to trade unions. Lesbian and gay trade union groups became increasingly common from 1974 onwards, and the Gay Rights At Work campaign played a prominent part in a number of defence campaigns for dismissed workers. Many public-sector trade union conferences, such as NALGO, NUPE, NATFHE and CPSA passed resolutions in support of the employment rights of lesbians and gay men, and their journals carried articles and correspondence on the issue.

The Scottish Trades Union Congress in 1981 passed a resolution after debate on the John Saunders case, and it included the following section:

> Congress recognizes that discrimination in employment is part of a wider pattern of discrimination against homosexual men and women in society as a whole, and that a campaign to achieve the objects (listed above in the resolution) will be more effective if this is taken into account and is conducted in association with gay rights and civil liberty organizations. It further calls for discussion within the trade union movement on this question, with a view to dispelling the myths that surround homosexuality.

It is a mistake to imagine that resolutions passed at trade

The Limits of Tolerance?

union conferences represent the most deeply held feelings of the entire membership. But these resolutions represent an important public statement by trade union activists about the nature of discrimination experienced by lesbians and gays at work. They also contributed to a growing consciousness of the value of collectivism and of alliances among sections of the lesbian and gay trade movement. They represent a considerable achievement on the part of the lesbian and gay trade union groups. The Labour movement might not be a home for lesbians and gays, but it was certainly no longer enemy territory.

A turning point in the relationship between the movements came in August 1981, when Ken Livingstone, the newly elected leader of the Greater London Council, accepted an invitation to speak at Harrow Gay Unity. He told a packed meeting that he was opposed to discrimination against lesbians and gay men, and, further, that he wanted to see homosexuality regarded as being equally as valid as heterosexuality. He has described the press response in the next few days as a 'lunatic uproar'. He was, it seems, familiar enough with the nature of lesbians and gay oppression not to be surprised or swayed by this, but many of his colleagues in the Labour Party were horrified. It was one thing to be opposed to discrimination (and many of them now began for the first time to say that they did, indeed, oppose it), but it was quite another thing to talk openly about equal validity of sexuality. This very outrageousness on Livingstone's part, however, struck a chord in the lesbian and gay communities. At last, there was a national politician who listened to lesbians and gays and spoke out for us in a way that was without fear, shame or embarrassment. The traditional wings of the Labour movement were afraid that Livingstone had unleashed a torrent — and they were right.

The GLC was not, in fact, the first council to give support to lesbian and gay projects. In the late 1970s both Islington and Manchester Councils had given funding to voluntary groups, such as Friend and

Switchboard. These councils' low-key approach had saved them from widespread media hostility, but it also meant that awareness of the funded projects was limited to those who were already, to some extent, part of lesbian and gay networks. The visibility issue was not part of those councils' briefs. Some argued and some still argue that a low profile was more effective in meeting existing, clearly identified needs than utopian declarations about equality.

The strategy decided by the GLC for lesbian and gay anti-discrimination work was to give support to existing groups and projects. London being traditionally a magnet for exiles of all kinds, had a large openly lesbian and gay population with a diversity of interest. Funding was given to groups such as Lesbian and Gay Employment Rights and the Stonewall Housing Association, both of which were engaged in the kind of work that most people in the Labour movement could easily identify with. The GLC also agreed to give funding to the Gay London Policing group (GALOP), a monitoring project, in keeping with their overall concern about police accountability; and to the September In The Pink Festival, in keeping with their policy of generating cheap, enjoyable cultural activities. (It was during this festival that Jimi Somerville emerged into the public eye.) They were also concerned that their Equal Opportunities policies should apply to all funded groups, and their awareness of the multi-faceted discrimination experienced by black lesbians and gays led them to fund the Black Lesbian and Gay Centre Project.

One of the most controversial areas of GLC activity (and this was picked up by the Tories in a party political broadcast as early as 1984), was the Gay Teenage Group which had been set up by gay young men in 1976. GLC funding made it possible for them to conduct a research project into the lives of young lesbians and gays. Widely attacked by homophobes as a threat to family life, the report, in places, makes chilling reading — 12 per cent beaten up at school because of their sexuality; 10 per cent sacked from work; 19 per cent admitting to attempted

The Limits of Tolerance?

suicide. Despite all this, and very probably contributing to it, schools had very largely not taken on board the issue of homosexuality, and 60 per cent of the sample said it had never been mentioned at all. It can only be deduced that most young people learn about homosexuality from the negative and misinformed images in the mainstream media.

While an enormous amount of energy and enthusiasm was expended on GLC-related projects, it would be a mistake to think that they were greeted with uncritical acclaim by all lesbians and gays. Many who belonged to the GLC traditions could see no reason to trust any institution of the local state, or to risk becoming dependent on it; they argued that independent self-organization was the only way to effect changes in our lives. London Lesbian and Gay Switchboard, for example, only applied for relatively small equipment grants, as opposed to paid workers, and has continued to flourish independently. Some lesbian feminists saw the GLC as just another patriarchal institution whose Equal Opportunities policies would entrap women in another form of male domination. Another argument was that the payment of lesbian and gay workers would create further divisions and hierarchies within the communities, and would place the workers in situations where they had to choose between their loyalty to the community and their loyalty to their funding body. And working-class dykes and queens whose whole identity is often a conscious political expression, continued to get on with their lives. While the GLC recognized that lesbians and gays were not one homogenous community, these differences testified to our political heterogeneity.

The London Lesbian and Gay Centre was to prove to be the focus of a major set-piece battle between different groups of lesbians and gays. The GLC had given high priority to funding this community centre as a space where lesbians and gays could manage their own social activities. Even before the doors were opened in the spring of 1985, an almighty row had developed over the usage of the centre by SM (sadomasochism) groups. Lesbians Against Sado Masochism claimed that the dress codes and imagery of members of the SM groups were offensive to black people, to Jews, to gypsies, as well as to many lesbians and gays. They also argued that the normalization of such images by SM groups acclimatized people to brutality and made them less percipient about the advent of 'real fascism'. A group called Sexual Fringe, who saw themselves as sexual outlaws, rose to defend the rights of people with proscribed sexualities to seek self-determination for their bodies. They protested that the labelling of SM as fascist trivialized the real fight against fascism, and condemned what they saw as the policing of sexual identity by LASM. In the end an Extraordinary General Meeting of the LLGC decided that SM groups could use the centre.

In retrospect, it is not in the least surprising that the provision of this space generated all kinds of questions about the nature of the 'lesbian and gay community'. Further questions about the rights of paedophiles, transsexuals and bisexuals in relation to the centre were mooted, but full-scale debates never materialized. The fact that such debates about sex could even be envisaged at all testifies to the growing strength of sexual politics. But it seems unlikely that many GLC councillors had foreseen such a public debate between different lesbian and gay 'communities of interest', when they approved the funding for the centre. Municipal socialism in Britain had always had a puritanical element to it, and debates about sexual choice were no part of this tradition. Such debates, it was feared, would lead to 'Sex on the Rates' headlines and could threaten Labour's electoral prospects. The traditionalists in the Labour Party, already concerned at the loss of some 'respectable' working-class voters over the Tory council-house purchase policy, were alarmed that even more of them would desert Labour over such close associations with homosexuality.

One of the concepts which gained new prominence in the mid-1980s, and which was to be of concern to Labour traditionalists, was that of 'heterosexism'. It had been popularized in lesbian feminist circles by the American writer, Adrienne Rich, and was taken up as a way of understanding the common ground between the very different oppressions experienced by lesbians and gay men of different classes, different ages, different races, etc. A group of officers at the GLC's Industry and Employment Branch produced a booklet called *Danger: Heterosexism At Work*, which defined heterosexism as:

> 'a system of ideas and practices based on a set of beliefs about heterosexuality being the normal and natural sexuality for both women and men, and all other sexual practices, in particular homosexuality, being deviant. Heterosexism lays down the rules and conditions under which all sexualities are valued or devalued in our society and penalties/benefits accordingly awarded. Under heterosexism, lesbians and gay men are particularly penalized.'

This theoretical attempt to explain the ideological, institutional and material aspects of our oppression rejected the biological/Third Sex/'born that way' view of homosexuality, and located it firmly within society's structures. It highlighted how there would be limits on the 'sexual choices' available to people according to their class, race, gender, etc. If, as the theory of heterosexism suggested, the origins of homosexual oppression are social, then the solution to that oppression will also be social. Lesbian and gay rights is not, therefore, a matter of winning tolerance for a permanent minority; it is a matter of making structural changes in society. Heterosexism was a theory that was increasingly attractive to lesbian and gay socialists, but in the mid-1980s it still carried little clout in the lesbian and gay communities as a whole.

The GLC's lesbian and gay anti-discrimination policies provided inspiration not just in London, but all over the rest of the country as well. Lesbian and gay activists learned from the GLC experience about the benefits and dangers of working with local councils; heterosexual members of the Labour Party and councillors became less afraid of lesbian and gay issues; lesbian and gay rights increasingly became part of the package offered by the new social-movement oriented, urban Left. The leader of the Islington Council, Margaret Hodge, questioned the direction of some of this development and, in London Labour Briefing No.37, said 'the class nature of gay politics is much more ambiguous [than black politics and anti-racism] ... activists in gay and lesbian politics come from a group whose social, occupational, educational and cultural background bears little resemblance to the population of the Inner City.' Ignoring the whole question of invisibility, which is particularly oppressive to working-class lesbians and gays, she nonetheless raised matters which were on the minds of many other heterosexual politicians. None of them showed any interest, however, in debating the matter with her or with us. As well as the changing climate in local government, 1984 also saw the pioneering work of Lesbians And Gays Support The Miners. It seemed like a sea change.

The GLC's strategy of funding voluntary groups was less appropriate in smaller cities, where the visible lesbian and gay communities were proportionally much smaller. Manchester City Council was, in 1984, the first council to appoint workers to deal specifically with lesbian and gay issues as part of their Equal Opportunities Unit. This new unit also had responsibility for issues relating to race, gender, disability. Would it be possible for any such unit of paid council employees to negotiate with the local state the demands and needs of the oppressed? Val Stephens, the Chair of the Equal Opportunities Committee, and the late Margaret Roff, the lesbian Vice-Chair, shared the concern of local activists about the dangers of bureaucratizing the struggle against oppression. They laid great emphasis on the value of a high level of participation by members of the lesbian and gay communities. Lesbian and Gay-Men's Sub-Committees were set up in such a way as to give a high level of representation to people from outside the council's structure, and to ensure that their voices could be heard. Their outreach programme went beyond this and held meetings in gay clubs where scores of gay men, including working-class gay men, were able to hear about the council's Equal Opportunities policies on their own ground, and to express their viewpoint about their experiences of service provision by the council.

The aspirations of lesbians and gay men were often different, and lesbians campaigned for space that was free not only of heterosexism, but also of gay men; funding for a Lesbian Centre was eventually provided in 1989. There have also been ongoing tensions in relation to the council's bureaucracy, the expectations attached to the activists-turned-officers, and the question of prioritizing the needs of different oppressed groups. But, on the whole, the Manchester experiment has been an important breakthrough in the campaign to make the local state more accessible to its lesbian and gay citizens.

Councils in other parts of the country also adopted the Manchester approach and appointed workers or set up a unit. Nottingham City Council appointed a lesbian and a gay man on a job-share to assist the implementation of their policy. Some months before the 1983 council elections the Labour Campaign for Gay Rights group in Nottingham initiated a debate among the lesbian and gay groups in the city, resulting in the publication of a charter, 'A Fair Deal For Gays', which included proposals for council action around employment practices, housing, leisure services, etc. One of the members of the campaign, Richard McCance, stood as an openly gay candidate for Labour, winning with a 13 per cent swing a seat which the Tories had held for forty years. The strength of the local campaign was an important factor in the council's decision to commit funding to this area of work.

A number of Scottish councils adopted the kind of policies proposed by the 1981 STUC resolution, but none of them has set up a unit or appointed specific anti-discrimination workers. Some Scots activists argue that this is more effective in the context of the more collectivist Scottish political culture. It is certainly the case that Stirling Council has what is probably one of the most progressive same-sex-sharing tenancy policies in the country. In Scotland, the only way of gauging the effectiveness of this approach would be through a survey of the lesbian and gay community, but there, as in the rest of Britain, such expensive research is no longer a priority for hard-pressed local councils.

The lesbian and gay issue featured prominently in the Tory propaganda war against the GLC, although more on the level of rumour and innuendo than on the public level. As the date of abolition (April 1986) drew nearer, activists in London were determined that the momentum should not be lost in this area of local government work. Many more lesbians and gays were openly involved in their local Labour parties than would have been the case even five years previously, and they ensured that the Labour manifestos in the 1986 council elections included commitments to lesbian and gay work. The smaller size of the boroughs made the GLC-style financing of voluntary groups more difficult. A number of borough councils agreed to appoint workers with specific lesbian and gay responsibilities and, after long periods of consultation, Camden and Haringey agreed to set up their own lesbian and gay units. The Camden Unit had four workers and the Lesbian and Gay Committee was chaired by Sandra Plummer, a lesbian councillor; the Haringey Unit had six workers and the Sub-Committee was chaired by Vince Gillespie, a gay councillor. Activists in Haringey persuaded the council to suspend their commitment to go to full committee status, because a sub-committee could have a majority of non-councillors; this would facilitate greater participation by members of the lesbian and gay communities, particularly those who were black, disabled or unemployed.

The Haringey Lesbian and Gay Unit was established weeks before the 1986 council elections, and it featured prominently in the campaign. The Labour manifesto included many policy developments of the kind outlined in the GLC's Charter for Gay and Lesbian Rights in relation to housing, social services, education, community facilities, staff training and the needs of black lesbians and gays. It acknowledged the deep-rooted nature of heterosexism and made a commitment to fight that. It was a manifesto for change, and although it was given greater publicity by the Tories and the local press than by the Labour Party, it was with this manifesto that Labour increased its majority in Haringey.

One particularly significant result, against the trend in the rest of the borough, was the Tory capture of a predominantly white working-class ward in North Tottenham. Many of the voters there were the council-house tenants/potential home buyers who had been so important to Thatcher's electoral successes in southern England. The Tory campaign in this ward had begun by placing emphasis on everything that was deemed a threat to the mortgaged bliss of privatised nuclear family-life — gypsies, black muggers, Bernie Grant, the Lesbian and Gay Unit. As the campaign wore on, greater emphasis was placed on the lesbian and gay issue and the threat that Labour's policies posed to everything that was 'normal' and 'natural'. The Labour policy of 'ensuring that lesbianism and gayness are treated positively in the curriculum' was raised in such a way as to play on parents' fears for the safety of their children. Against the backdrop of the media's homophobic and moralistic coverage of AIDS, a panic was generated to suggest that the positive-images policy would lead to AIDS.

The Labour Women's Manifesto was subject to constant attack and deliberate confusion created between the terms 'heterosexism' and 'heterosexuality'. Labour, we were assured, would abolish heterosexuality! Such was the potency of this issue that the Tories took the unprecedented step of having their leaflets on heterosexism translated into Greek, to appeal to the Labour-voting Cypriot voters. They had realized that we were saying that lesbian and gay sexual relationships were as good as heterosexual relationships; they had realized the panic that this issue could generate. No-one in their right minds would have believed that Labour wanted to abolish heterosexuality or promote AIDS, but such was the level of fear and ignorance about homosexuality that these ideas could be aired. This election campaign was, apart from anything else, a good advertisement for the need for a positive-images policy to dispel, maybe not the hatred, but certainly the fear and the ignorance about homosexuality.

In the wake of the election in Haringey, an allegedly independent campaign, the Parents' Rights Group, was set up and led largely by working-class women. Their primary aim was to oppose positive images of lesbians and gays in education, and they soon had a high profile throughout Haringey. Petitions were circulated; schools were picketed; demonstrations were organized; books were burned. They claimed to speak for traditional family values and found support from various fundamentalists — Orthodox Jewish, Roman Catholic, Baptist — in an attempt both to broaden their appeal among Haringey's multiracial population and to strengthen their message that homosexuality was 'unnatural' in all cultures. Their allegations about what they called 'gay lessons' were reported in the national media and debated in Parliament.

The New Right had been showing an interest in Labour's support for lesbian and gay rights for some time, and a number of organizations such as the National Front, the New Patriotic Movement, the Moonies and the Campaign for a Free Britain, offered support to the PRG's campaign. More important than these political links, however, was the shift which the PRG campaign managed to generate in the public discourse about what was 'normal' and 'natural' in the family. The fact that educational policies, such as positive images, might attempt to reflect the social reality of an increasingly diverse society and to address the needs of individual children, was greatly undermined by this whole campaign. Patriarchal power in education was coming back in a big way, and was endorsed in the 1986 Education Act's stipulation that sex education should be taught within a moral framework and with due regard to family life. As far as the New Right was concerned, that was only a beginning.

The main resistance to the Parents' Rights Group campaign did not come from the council, where the Labour group effectively factionalized themselves — and their Public Relations Department — into silence. Council leaflets explaining their lesbian and gay education policies appeared months after the initial uproar, by which time opinions were more firmly set. A more immediate and effective resistance was organized by Positive Images, a local group set up by lesbian and gay activists and members of most of the Left groups. A mixed group, many of whose members showed little respect for the principle of lesbian and gay self-organization, it soon became a sectarian battlefield and did little to organize lesbians and gays with no previous political experience. But whatever their short-comings, Positive Images was the only group of people who were prepared to speak out and take action in the face of this backlash. In the short term it did sterling work in organizing petitions, counter-demonstrations and, most significantly, a mass lobby of Haringey Council in October, 1986, when the Labour councillors reaffirmed their commitment to all aspects of their lesbian and gay rights policy.

In a way that is all too typical of both the English Left and the English lesbian and gay movement, Positive Images failed to draw on the parallel developments around local government funding of lesbian and gay projects in the USA. Both San Francisco and New York had seen similar coalitions of inner-city white working-class groups in this scenario. The Labour Party in Haringey was terrified of the electoral implications of splits in the black communities, and made no statement at all about the increasing intimidation experienced by black lesbians and gays in this period. These fears were exacerbated when the Haringey West Indian Leadership Council passed a resolution which referred to homosexuality's 'roots in a morally decadent white and European society.' Haringey Black Action was then set up to oppose such reactionary politics, and, together with Positive Images, organized a successful demonstration through the centre of Haringey and through North Tottenham in defence of black lesbians and gays, and against racism and bigotry.

In retrospect, the Positive Images campaign succeeded to the extent that Haringey Council did not abandon its lesbian and gay rights policies, or disband its Lesbian and Gay Unit. In that year, Haringey's Labour councillors learned more about heterosexism than they would ever have believed possible, and they have become far more articulate in their defence of lesbian and gay rights than they were at the time of their election. The council's curriculum working-party on lesbian and gay issues in education produced a thoughtful and well-researched document, *Mirrors Round The Walls — Reflecting Diversity*, which received none of the media interest experienced by the earlier misinformation. But what Positive Images might have done, but did not do, was to generate any Left consensus on the family and relationships. The Left had discovered that more was being expected of them than tolerance, but while the PRG had succeeded in setting an agenda based on fear, hatred and ignorance, Positive Images failed to popularize our own agenda of equality, choice and resistance to oppression. It never really got to grips with the issues of childhood, innocence and learning about sexuality. It never made any links with the next 'sex and local government' moral panic about child abuse in Cleveland in the late eighties. The implications of both Haringey and Cleveland as indicators of the meaning of family life and sexual choice at that time have yet to be explored.

Easy though it is to criticize Positive Images' theoretical short-comings, the fact is that this was almost the only group in the country that was addressing these

The Limits of Tolerance?

issues at all. The rest of the Labour Left was certainly silent. The fascistic overtones of the PRG's campaign and the attack on Councillor Vince Gillespie went largely unreported in the Left media. Publications such as *Marxism Today*, *New Statesman*, *New Socialist* or *Tribune* hardly commented at all on the local government funding of lesbian and gay projects, the Haringey backlash or the debate around heterosexism. The only sources of information were tabloid hysteria, diatribes from the New Right in the 'quality' press and, most important of all, rumour. When in the spring of 1987 Lord Halsbury introduced a bill in the House of Lords to ban the promotion of homosexuality by local authorities, that too went unreported and undiscussed. Silence can be very powerful.

The public silence was broken early in 1987 by *Marxism Today*, who can seldom resist a bandwagon, even if they often fall under the wheels in the process; and the particular bandwagon they joined on this occasion was the one about what the Tories had labelled 'Loony Left' councils. They now proceeded to criticize a number of left-wing Labour councils for their management of particular policies. The hidden agenda — and there always seems to be one when the Left discusses lesbian and gay rights — was *Marxism Today*'s distrust of the 'Trots' who controlled these councils. There was no reason at all why these councils should have been regarded as above criticism, but in the context of that period when local government was under renewed attack from Thatcherism, the publication of sectarian, ill-researched articles in the magazine that likes to see itself as a broad-based forum of progressive ideas, was nothing less than destructive. Statements to the effect that, in relation to lesbian and gay rights, there had been no 'public work in the civil society' were simply mendacious.

Within the next few months the silence in the Left media was further broken by articles criticizing councils such as Haringey for 'moralism', suggesting that anti-heterosexist policies were undermining Labour's traditional family-based support, and advocating psychoanalytic theory as the road to lesbian and gay liberation. All of these are interesting concepts, worthy of discussion, but the context in which articles are published can be as important as the content of the articles themselves. None of these articles referred to the activities of the Parents' Rights Group, to the joblessness and homelessness that had caused lesbians and gays to seek support from councils in the first place, to the findings of the Gay Teenage Group survey about the intimidation and isolation of lesbian and gay teenagers in state schools, to the menace of fundamentalism — or to any other feature of our oppression. Any backlash problem which there might be seemed to relate not to the nature of our oppression, but to problems of management and presentation by these left-wing councils. The fact that there was no sense of any history of lesbian and gay struggle in any of these articles made it seem incomprehensible why any council would have adopted any policy or set up any unit to serve the needs of lesbians and gays. I thought about writing a science fiction short story entitled 'Haringey Lesbian And Gay Unit: It Came From Outer Space'.

Shortly after the appearance of the article in *Marxism Today*, Labour lost a by-election in Greenwich. Those of us who had been drawn towards Labour as a party of change now received a sharp reminder that whatever else it was at local level, it was at national level still essentially an electoral machine. We were reminded that before he became party leader, Neil Kinnock had said, in relation to Peter Tatchell, 'I am not in favour of witch-hunts but I do not mistake bloody witches for fairies.' The inquest into the Greenwich defeat was not to be a debate about the future direction of socialism in multi-cultural inner-city areas; it was to be an appeal to homophobia. A letter was leaked from Neil Kinnock's press office which said, among other things, 'The "Loony Labour Left" is taking its toll, the gays and lesbian issue is costing us dear among the pensioners; and fear of extremism is particularly prominent in the GLC area.' The author of this missive was Patricia Hewitt, who seemed determined to take on the mantle of Sara Barker, a notorious fixer and manipulator from the Labour Party of the fifties. The word had now gone out — the 'Loony Left' was to be bashed for the sake of the Party. To attack their anti-racist policies would have exposed Labour to (more) accusations of racism; far easier to attack the much less extensive lesbian and gay policies; and if that meant abandoning lesbians and gays to isolation and intimidation, so be it.

Isolated pockets of Labour support for lesbians and gays continued, but the rest of 1987 saw Labour silent in the face of renewed homophobic attacks by the Tories — the reference to the Positive Images issue in the 1987 election propaganda, the advocacy of traditional family values in the Department of Education and Science circular on sex education. When the Clause banning the promotion of homosexuality by local authorities was introduced into the Local Government Bill in December 1987, the Tories must have been confident of no Labour resistance; and with the honourable exception of Bernie Grant, now a Haringey MP, they were right. The resistance began when lesbians and gays organized themselves and made their voices heard throughout the country. We may not have been able to stop the legislation (although we did succeed in reducing its scope), but we let the world know that we remained strong and proud and shameless.

Inevitably, there has been an increased distrust of party politics in the lesbian and gay communities since the Clause debacle. Some have argued that by becoming involved in local government we had brought the whole disaster upon ourselves. Lesbian and gay activists are, once again, placing greater emphasis on independent self-organization, and the 1989 Gay Pride march, free of the possible taint of any local government subsidies, was the biggest ever. In their different ways, Neil Bartlett,

Clyde Unity Theatre and Square Peg are all heightening our awareness of the history of lesbian and gay lifestyles in Britain — whether it is in the nineteenth-century underworld networks, during 1930s Scotland, or at the Gateways Club. Politics, as an organized activity, is definitely out of favour and we can all gain from learning about the traditions of humour, resilience and survival of our own communities. Any community with a sense of its own history is stronger for that. But is that enough?

During the summer of 1988, just about the time when the Clause was becoming law, an English gay novel was published to widespread acclaim. *The Swimming Pool Library* by Alan Hollinghurst is a beautifully written, homoerotic novel set in the pre-AIDS gay male sub-culture of London in the early 1980s. Its central character is a rich young patrician gay man who becomes increasingly aware of previous generations of homosexual men in his class. His lovers and those of his antecedents are not themselves patricians — they are poor, they are working class, they are black, they lack his privileges; they are young and once their looks have gone they are expendable. A curious feature of the novel is the absence of women — particularly curious since family life and the inheritance principle are essential features of the central character's privilege. Women, even heterosexual women in his family, are given no real voice at all. The lifestyles in *The Swimming Pool Library* do not represent the entirety of the gay scene, but by locating the gay male scene so firmly within the traditional English class structure, Hollinghurst reminds us why the gay scene alone is not enough.

One of the things that those of us who were involved in local government campaigns were trying to do was to achieve some measure of redistribution in favour of all those lesbians and gays who do not belong to the charmed circles of *The Swimming Pool Library* — people who have no private income; people who depend on their jobs and would welcome job security; people who want council tenancies free of harassment, with friends and

The Limits of Tolerance?

lovers of their choice; people who want to meet others at venues which have disabled access, which are not commercially exploitative and which are run for the benefit of the community; people who want to display affection or consensual desire publicly without fear of violence or arrest; people who want to bring up children without intimidation from the courts or social workers; people who have survived the indoctrination of the education system but do not want to see the next generation of lesbians and gays subjected to the same process; people who wanted themselves and their lifestyles to be treated with respect by the health services. We did not believe that any of these should be the subject of charity or whim on the part of people more privileged than ourselves in this society. Since many of these services and facilities are, or were, wholly or partially within the remit of local government, it was only a matter of time before we focused our attention on local government for enhancement of such provision.

In an article in *Capital Gay* in February 1988, Paul Davies argued that lesbians and gays had made a mistake in allowing our politics 'to be colonized by the Left'. Although Neil Kinnock might disagree about who had colonized whom, the fact was that between 1984 and 1987 relations between left-wing urban Labour councils and the lesbian and gay movement became very close. Even without the Tory attacks on local government at that time, there are people who consider such close contact with any one political party a mistake. But what are the alternatives?

The Gay Business Association is probably the nearest that there is to a group holding a free-market-to-liberation point of view. Venues and services staffed by lesbians and gays are invaluable in maintaining a sense of community. Their involvement with parts of the Stop The Clause campaign, their support for AIDS-related benefits, their meetings with the Metropolitan Police, their re-vitalization of the financially flagging London Lesbian and Gay Centre, all testify to some commitment to the community.

Their commitment, however, does not really extend as far as promotion of Equal Opportunities; men-only nights greatly outnumber women-only nights in most venues; most lack disabled access; there is no policy of supporting anti-racist initiatives in either employment practices or customer relations. Prices are often excessively high and the lack of union bargaining rights at most venues does not lead one to believe that the profits are being re-distributed among the workforce. They may well claim that such commitments would result in bankruptcy, but if that were the case (and it seems unlikely), the case for a lesbian and gay politics that addresses problems in our social structures remains a strong one.

In the wake of the Clause, the Stonewall Trust was set up. It will be a lobbying organization and it deliberately eschews any party political association. It seems to aspire to the kind of role that the Child Poverty Action Group has — well-informed, articulate, independent. Its clean-cut image, it is hoped, may help it to make advances where the scruffier tendencies in lesbian and gay politics have failed. Any body which, by providing information and arguments to parliamentarians, can help to effect changes in our homophobic legal system is to be welcomed. But changes in legislation — like changes in local government provision — will only be as effective as society permits them to be. The Sex Disqualification (Removal) Act of 1919 paved the way for changes in women's employment rights, but the weakness of the Women's Movement in that period meant that the Act remained a dead letter. The conservatism of central and local government bureaucracy is only likely to be overcome if there is a strong, independent political movement keeping up the pressure for the legislation to be made meaningful.

Independent lesbian and gay self-organization remains central to any wider project that we become involved in. Issues relating to lesbians and gays may well arise in future campaigns relating to the environment, constitutional change, consumer protection, housing,

The Limits of Tolerance?

fundamentalism, and many other aspects of modern life. Involvement is one thing, but we should never make the mistake which we may have done in relation to local government, of appearing to focus all our energies in one direction. We need to be more tactical and not put all our eggs in one political basket. The increasingly pluralistic nature of our society means that politics are, in any case, undergoing fundamental transformation. Long-standing traditions and alliances in the Labour movement, in the Tory establishment and in the political centre have already undergone profound changes, and that process is not at an end. The long-term impact of the poll tax on the nature of local government itself is still unclear. The politics of nationalism in Scotland and Wales, as well as in Ireland, poses questions about the future of the United Kingdom. The Salman Rushdie affair has given a whole new meaning to both anti-racist and black community politics. The consensus politics of the post-1945 period in which so many of our demands were rooted is no more.

During a televised discussion of the Clause, Digby Anderson, one of the ideologues of the New Right, claimed that homosexuals had 'broken' some sort of unwritten agreement that homosexuality would be tolerated if family values were affirmed. By breaking that agreement, homosexuals 'got the backlash they asked for.' It is true that this 'agreement', or settlement as I would prefer to call it, had only been viable when lesbians and gays tolerated their own oppression, tolerated homophobic behaviour, tolerated heterosexist indoctrination, tolerated liberal tolerance. The upsurge in our activity and in our public demands in the mid-1980s represented a declaration that our tolerance was running out. It was time to re-draw the boundaries. While political organization among lesbians and gays may be taking a low profile, it is not true to say that the clocks have been turned back. Lesbians and gays are expressing themselves differently from the way they were before the Clause, but they are still saying as openly and as proudly as ever that they want the boundaries changed.

Lesbians and gays have never been and are not now a static, homogenous minority group to whom a finite set of civil rights can be 'granted'. Any future attempt to end our oppression or to re-draw the boundaries will, if it is to be more than tokenistic, have to touch on the question of how we learn our sexuality — or, as some of us see it, how we experience heterosexist socialization. We could do worse than try to reach some understanding in the lesbian and gay communities of what we mean by this question. We are unlikely to reach any definite agreement, but the debates will strengthen us for the next time, and weaken the impact of tangential arguments about policy presentation. The next time lesbians and gays are involved in any attempt to effect major change, we will be better served not by fitting on to the agenda of others, but by organizing independently and making alliances with other groups seeking progressive, structural, social changes. The local government campaign was one necessary part of the process of struggling to redistribute wealth and power, and to re-draw the boundaries of love.

Chapter 14
Labour and the Natural Order

Intentionally Promoting Heterosexuality

Sarah Roelofs

The Labour Party's initial official support for what became Section 28 of the 1988 Local Government Act, provoked fury and left a permanent residue of bitterness amongst lesbians and gay men. It took Labour nearly eight weeks to publicly oppose the Section in its entirety. When it did so, it was clearly only because of the enormous pressure of a mass lesbian and gay Stop The Clause campaign that involved soap-opera and Shakespearian actors. Even then there were sour comments from Labour's HQ that other important parts of the Local Government Bill were not receiving due attention because the Clause was hogging all the headlines.

Lesbian and gay bitterness was the more acute for a sense of betrayal, given the trail-blazing work of the Labour Greater London Council (GLC), subsequent lesbian and gay equality policies by a number of Labour local authorities, and the breakthroughs achieved by the Labour Campaign for Lesbian and Gay Rights — notably the 1985 Labour Annual Conference policy which was reaffirmed at the 1986 Annual Conference by a 79 per cent majority.

To dismiss what happened as the Labour Party merely showing its true colours, does not explain why Labour actually supported legislation which was immediately condemned by many who were considerably to the right of Labour's quite-right-enough Deputy Leader, Roy Hattersley. On 9th December 1987, the day after Labour first supported the Clause (when it was debated in Committee), *The Guardian* published an editorial that slammed Labour for its position. It said that 'there are fundamental issues of principle involved', but by December 1987 the only issue of principle for Labour was its electoral viability.

Nine months earlier, in March 1987 (just after the Greenwich by-election watershed), *The Sun* had published the infamous Hewitt letter. Highly confidential, but somewhat easily (deliberately?) leaked, this took the form of a memorandum from Labour Leader Neil Kinnock's Press Secretary, Patricia Hewitt, to London Labour MPs' Chair Frank Dobson. Commenting on the results of some private opinion polls commissioned by Labour, Ms Hewitt's letter contained the following historic comments: '... the "London effect" is now very noticeable. The "Loony Labour Left" is taking its toll, the gays and lesbian issue is costing us dear amongst the pensioners; and fear of extremism ... is particularly prominent in the GLC area.'

A clean-up campaign which would have put Domestos to shame was immediately launched in that supposed harbinger of the Rainbow revolution, the London Labour Party. By the autumn of 1987 a seminal document, *A Plan To Win*, had been produced and endorsed by London's Labour Executive. The document was signed by the Chair Glenys Thornton, the Secretary Terry Ashton, and the Treasurer Brian Nicholson. At the bottom of page one, at the end of paragraph 1.6, the last two sentences were divided by a crucial preposition — 'But': 'We have to reject completely any suggestion that we ditch or dilute any of our concerns about racial disadvantage, discrimination against women, against lesbians or gay men, or against people with disabilities. *But* at the same time we must never lose sight of our *over-riding duty to win elections*' (emphasis added).

The 'duty to win' is not the whole story, however, neither is it a recently acquired motto. In the last decade of the nineteenth century, as various socialist groups were moving towards establishing a Labour Party, an illuminating exchange took place between two Labour Movement figures. Edward Carpenter, a homosexual socialist radical, had recently published his book *Love's Coming Of Age*, which included discussion of homosexuality. The book caused Robert Blatchford, editor of the socialist newspaper *The Clarion*, to write to Mr Carpenter in some concern: economic change had to come first, said Mr Blatchford, and it would therefore be better not to mention sex until after socialism had been achieved. Mr Blatchford was especially concerned about the family — by which he meant the heterosexual, patriarchal family which he regarded as sacred in Labour's pantheon.

This is the crux of the matter. Opinion polls are taken as evidence of electoral viability; and winning elections — not lesbian and gay rights, or even socialism — is Labour's primary purpose. The Livingstonian GLC, even with its espousal of lesbian and gay rights, was electorally viable until Thatcher & Co., in the face of Labour defensiveness, managed to move the ideological goalposts. Post-GLC and with Third Term Thatcherism staring it in the face, Labour did, in a sense, revert to type. But that 'type' was not so much anti-lesbian and gay as pro-family. The Family, the bourgeois white, patriarchal, heterosexual family, wins elections — or so Labour believes — because Labour believes in The Family the way night follows day. It's 'natural'. When *The Sun* says lesbian mothers are unnatural, Labour instinctively agrees: would Labour back a lesbian mother standing as such to be an MP? Never — it would be electoral suicide. Labour opposes discrimination against lesbian mothers and has Annual Conference policy in support of lesbian mothers' custody rights, but this is quite separate from winning elections — which is what matters most.

By December 1987, having lost three successive general elections, plus some by-elections it thought it should have won, Labour was quite desperate. There were, it felt, lessons to be learnt, and by this stage it was somewhat obsessed with learning those lessons. It had knee-jerk reactions to the very mention of the words lesbian and gay. Faced with arguably the most reactionary piece of legislation this century, with its major implications for basic civil liberties and education, not to mention lesbians and gay men, Labour reduced it to being for or against the 'promotion' of homosexuality. No problem here — Labour was sure of the answer, and Front Bench spokesperson Dr John Cunningham was so pleased and relieved that this time Labour was going to get it right, that when he rose to speak on 8th December in Standing Committee A, he repeated Labour's position several times. Or maybe Dr Cunningham was feeling defensive — probably he was both pleased and defensive. Certainly he believed his action was right for the opinion polls. He said:

> 'I speak on behalf of the Labour Party when I say that it is not, and never has been, the duty or responsibility of either a local or education authority to promote homosexuality ... The Labour Party does not believe that councils or schools should promote homosexuality, and I hope that no-one in the Committee has any doubt about that ... I have made the position of the Labour Party clear. I repeat that it is not, and never has been, our policy to encourage local authorities or education authorities to promote homosexuality ... I shall vote for the amendment and I hope and expect that my honourable friends will do likewise.'

Dr Cunningham added, by way of a postscript:

> 'We may move an amendment on Report. But that amendment will do nothing to change the first part of the Clause ... We do not wish to change that in any way, shape or form, but we are anxious about the word "acceptability" later in the Clause' [A local authority shall not promote the teaching in any maintained school of the acceptability of homosexuality as a pretended family relationship].

And that was that. There were also some comments about homosexual authors and a few feeble attempts to refute allegations about Labour authorities — *not* that Labour authorities had not promoted homosexuality, but that only a few had and they had not spent millions of pounds doing it.

Dr Cunningham's views can be compared to those of Simon Hughes, delivering a swansong on behalf of the Liberal Party. Mr Hughes was also confident that he had it right — not for opinion polls necessarily, but right *per se*. This allowed him to go on the offensive, including on issues that Dr Cunningham devoutly wished would evaporate, like that *cause célèbre*, positive images of lesbians and gay men in education. Mr Hughes summarily dealt with opposition to such proposals: 'It is often necessary to counter negative images with positive images. That does not mean one is promoting that group's lifestyle, orientation or activity.' Simple.

Simon Hughes continued his dismissal with a swirl of dictionary arguments concerning the unacceptability of homosexual relationships as families. He had looked up 'family' in his dictionary before coming to the debate, and he reminded the Committee that it came from *familia*, meaning 'household', regardless of what the Government or the proposers of the new Clause might wish it to mean. Mr Hughes further argued that, 'Teaching that homosexuality is acceptable is perfectly proper ... If people say that it is wrong that teachers should be allowed, even encouraged, to tell pupils that it is acceptable to live in a household in a particular form of sexual relationship, that goes beyond what is a proper and a responsible training for life in society.' He accused the Government of outright discrimination and added that the 'banning of grant funding is highly undesirable'. His conclusion on behalf of the Liberal Party was that the new Clause was 'substantially defective', that if it was limited to 'prohibition on promoting homosexuality by teaching or by publishing material I would support it, but it is not, so I shall not support it.'

Dr Cunningham was Labour's official spokesperson, but he had a deputy, MP Allan Roberts, who was also on the Front Bench. Dr Cunningham was fixated on the potent effect of sex and socialism on Patricia Hewitt's homophobic pensioners, who were yet still ignorant of their imminent deliverance by Glenys Thornton's 'Plan To Win': Mr Roberts, though extremely mindful of Labour's Duty To Win, had had close working experience with the Labour Campaign for Lesbian and Gay Rights. He therefore tried to ride two horses, attempting to pad out Labour's newly acquired eleventh commandment, 'Thou shalt not promote homosexuality', with some points of principle. The effect, unfortunately, was a mite confused.

If this is what the new Clause meant, then Mr Roberts said he would support it; if it meant something else, he would not. The Clause was wrong if it meant schools could not have proper and adequate discussion, but if it meant that local authorities should not promote homosexuality then Mr Roberts would support it. What would matter was how the Clause was interpreted. 'It does not necessarily mean that people should not be told the truth in school about what happens in reality.' Accepting the reality of homosexuality does not promote it. Together with this unequivocal equivocation Mr Roberts did argue support for positive images, for freedom of the individual, for a wide definition of what constitutes a family, for civilised society; and he opposed discrimination in schools, the promotion of *any* kind of sexuality, and the introduction of paedophilia into the debate. He questioned the new Clause's sponsors' understanding of what was 'normal', and for good measure said that when he had visited the Soviet Union he had not liked it — there were no sex shops, a lot of censorship, and they denied that homosexuals existed.

It was during this discourse, however, that The Family made a fleeting, but telling, appearance. Mr Roberts, having been around lesbians and gay men, was aware of the million-dollar underlying issue: is the Heterosexual

Labour and the Natural Order

Family 'natural'? If heterosexuals are natural and normal, what are lesbians and gay men? Are lesbians and gay men born or made? These are crucial, fundamental questions. The Tories, Simon Hughes and Dr Cunningham simply ignored them, accepting the naturalness of the Heterosexual Family as read — though for different reasons. Allan Roberts raised the issue because he realised its importance for lesbian and gay liberation, but he then tried to dismiss it because he also realised that even to articulate the question ran counter to Labour's 'duty to win'. Becoming increasingly incoherent under the strain, he said:

> 'I do not know whether homosexuals are born homosexuals or acquire that trait because of the way in which they are brought up ... I do not know, but I do know that many homosexuals have not chosen to be homosexual but simply are that way. They exist, and society should not discriminate against them ... I do not believe that it is possible to make a heterosexual into a homosexual ... It is not a disease to be caught, and it cannot be taught ... All the evidence suggests that for 99.9 per cent of the population over the age of seven or eight homosexuality is determined.'

Interestingly, Parliament's only out-gay MP, Labour's Chris Smith, also raised the issue when the new Clause was first debated on the floor of the House of Commons a week later, on 15th December. He avoided Allan Roberts' fumblings, and simply stated his belief as fact:

> '... encouraging people to be homosexual ... is an absurd notion in any case. We are what we are. It is impossible to force or encourage someone into a different sexuality from that which pertains to them.'

What both Mr Roberts and Mr Smith were actually trying to do was get Labour off the 'promotion' hook. If people are born heterosexual or homosexual then the concept of 'promotion' is irrelevant. If, however, human beings are born with the capacity to be sexual — with a sexuality — but the manner in which that sexuality is expressed is socially constructed, then 'promotion' is possible.

Moreover, if within society one sexuality (i.e. heterosexuality) is presented, even promoted, as the single, normal, best sexuality, then the positive representation of another sexuality (i.e. homosexuality) as equally valid is problematic, to say the least. But does positive representation equal promotion? Can a positive image of lesbianism promote it? If all representations of lesbianism are negative (in line with society's presentation of heterosexuality as the only positive sexuality), then conceivably a positive image of lesbianism could have a promotional effect. It is this conundrum that lies at the very heart of the Section 28 debate — not to mention Labour's problems with it.

Of even more interest is the Tories' perception of all this. It would appear that they — unlike Labour — have an understanding that sexuality *is* socially constructed. Capitalism, being patriarchal, socially constructs sexuality within a heterosexual framework (the inter-relationship between capitalism, patriarchy and heterosexuality is outside the scope of this chapter, unfortunately, but is overdue for socialist analysis). It hardly needs to be said that Tories are capitalists, and therefore to a woman (Tory women playing a significant role in this) subscribe to the view that the dominance of heterosexuality, notably the White Heterosexual Family, is to be preserved come hell or high water. Tories know on which side their bread is buttered — the heterosexual side. At the very least, heterosexual *appearances* must, and will, be maintained. And so they are.

Back to Standing Committee A, considering new Clause 14 of the Local Government Bill on 8th December 1987. Far-right Tory MP David Wilshire proposed his amendment with arguments that, while miles wide of reality, were traditional and consistent with Law and Order Families. Nothing in the new Clause, he said, had anything to do with homosexuals. The activities singled out were to do with the use of ratepayers' money to promote certain ideas. These ideas were the 'promotion of homosexuality and its portrayal as a pretend family relationship', which 'seek to alter fundamentally the society in which we live.' Ealing Council had a policy of positive images of lesbians and gay men in the community and, Mr Wilshire stated, 'I contend that that is the promotion of homosexuality.' Given that in Mr Wilshire's view the promoters were seeking fundamental change in society by their actions, it was logical that he aimed to prohibit local authorities from teaching children 'about homosexual relationships as acceptable family relationships.' Mr Wilshire continued:

> 'The new clause is not anti-homosexuals. I believe that society needs to understand homosexuals and that homosexuals must not be discriminated against. Nevertheless I am certain that society has the right to prevent homosexuals encouraging others to be homosexual.'

Lesbian feminists have researched and analysed our society's intentional promotion of heterosexuality and described it as 'compulsory heterosexuality'. No-one gets any 'choice' — it's Jack and Jill (and in that order, too) from start till death do us part.

Since the victory of the Labour Campaign for Lesbian and Gay Rights at the Annual Labour Conference in the autumn of 1985, there had been some signposts to Labour's instincts on these matters. One, of course, was the Hewitt letter, but there were others that had occurred earlier. For example, in the spring of 1986 there was the Family Snaps Affair. In that April Labour won a by-election in Fulham, West London, with an ideal candidate in Nick Raynsford — he was white, heterosexual, middle-class, moderate, and he had a very nice family. Labour was euphoric. Criticism was made of his publicity leaflet, which featured a photograph not only of the candidate, but a Family Ensemble complete with children. The Executive's Lesbian and Gay Working Party made a number of points, primary of which was that a candidate's family — if indeed they had one — was irrelevant to an election campaign which ought to be about the candidate's political platform. Images are powerful and subliminal, and this one was quite discriminatory as it projected precisely that Family of which society so approves. What of single parents, black families, lesbian mothers, lesbian and gay couples, or those with no families? What about politics?

An unintended but fascinating postscript to this was the *New Statesman* editorial of 29th May 1987 — midway through the general election campaign. The opening sentence, beside the photograph of Husband and Wife Neil and Glenys Kinnock, stated: 'The Family is now a dominant, if implicit, theme in the election campaign.' The editorial continued: 'The family has been used, with spectacular success it seems, by the Labour Party for electoral purposes.' It was referring primarily to 'The Video', Labour's first party political broadcast of the campaign. Entitled 'Neil Kinnock — The Complete Picture', this was an extremely explicit projection of Neil Kinnock as the Happy Heterosexual Family Man. Extraordinarily, it ended not with the usual 'Vote Labour' or even 'Vote Kinnock', but merely 'Kinnock'.

The editorial also made reference to the use of 'infidelity' problems by the media against other politicians, namely David Steele and Roy Hattersley. It could also have mentioned another aspect of Labour's election advertising which, though more implicit than subliminal, was not at all lost on lesbians and gay men — or anybody not actively engaged in Happy Heterosexuality. This appeared in the press on 22nd May 1987 as a full-page photograph of a schoolboy (Jack?) and schoolgirl (Jill?), with him saying to her, 'Can I carry your books home from school?', and her replying glumly, 'No, I haven't got any.' — education cuts! Aside from the fact that Jill is quite capable of carrying her own books, her glumness could easily be due to being a young lesbian forced to suppress it and wishing Jack would take his stupid pick-up lines elsewhere.

The *New Statesman* editorial made an interesting comment: 'Labour's image-makers clearly thought family values had to be stressed to counteract ... alleged broadsides against heterosexism' (sic). The editorial made a number of remarkably pertinent points that were vindicatory for London Labour's Lesbian and Gay Working Party. It said that there was 'no empirical evidence for correlating a politician's effectiveness in office with his or her sexual orientation'; it was critical of 'a large reason for electing a party being because its leader is fortunate in his [sic] marriage'; it claimed that the family had been 'elevated into the status of party policy. If we are to vote for the family because it is good, warm and loving, what are we to do if it turns cold?'; it well-nigh accused Labour of giving 'a sharp twist to a competitive spiral of wholesome image making'; and it stated that the Tory Government must be defeated by 'the issues'.

However, the editorial's interpretation of this situation was that private life was being 'nationalised', and that there was an 'irrelevant and intrusive public discussion of personal matters.' The *New Statesman* was not saying that familial and sexual issues should not be discussed under any circumstances, but that the discussion had gone too far. It had become an 'invasion of privacy' (creation in the sixteenth and seventeenth centuries of 'bedrooms' was an important move in the development of sexual privacy, itself part of the development of a stable home unit appropriate to capitalism). At a glance this seems eminently reasonable — not least if it protects us from Family videos.

Deeper analysis, however, shows that flagging up 'Private — No Entry' neatly forecloses any discussion of causes as opposed to symptoms. The net result is that discussion of heterosexism — society's deliberate promotion of heterosexuality as the norm and superior — is prevented. Public debate of discrimination against lesbians and gay men is allowed, but not of its causes.

Labour has become trapped in this dynamic. Championing the symptoms, the rights of lesbians and gay men against discrimination, has led inexorably to demands that tackle the causes, for example positive images and assertions of homosexuality as equally valid with heterosexuality. However, strategies to tackle the causes have, even implicitly, to confront the injustice and inequality of the supremacy of the Heterosexual Family. It is an essential component of Labour's historical role of organising the working-class in the interests of capital, to ride tandem with the Tories on the issue of The Family. On the one hand this is easy, not to say natural, but the ride can become fraught with contradictions and potholes, such as what to do about Section 28.

These contradictions are not recent phenomena but are at least as old as the Labour Party itself. The seeds of Dr Cunningham's initial, somewhat grovelling support for Section 28, can be found in the early trade unions', and then the Labour Party leadership's, approach to family policy and women's rights. The contradictions are reflected in the political arguments — and political rows — between socialist feminists and the fledgling labour movement bureaucracy. And it did not take long for it all to boil down to that maxim — the Duty To Win. When the trade unions established the Labour Party as a parliamentary voice for organised labour, they likewise established the 'duty to win' — to achieve power in Parliament and then to hang on to that power come what may, or put more bluntly, regardless of socialist principle.

The specific reasons for this are to do with the development of the English Labour movement in relation to the development of British capitalism in the latter half of the nineteenth century. How feminism and sexual radicalism became increasingly a minority current in a labour movement dominated by economism, can be explained by examining the effect of the inter-relationship between patriarchy and British imperialism on the working class, but cannot be fully detailed here. Suffice it to say that a Labour bureaucracy developed that accepted some basic tenets of bourgeois ideology more wholly than the bourgeoisie itself. Socialism, then, was concerned with protecting and increasing working-class living standards, and not at all to do with fundamental change.

Labour and the Natural Order

Labour's socialism was therefore inherently hostile to sexual radicalism.

The exchange referred to earlier, between Robert Blatchford and Edward Carpenter, is an excellent illustration of Labour's early contradictions on these issues. In letters to Edward Carpenter written in December 1893 and January 1894, Robert Blatchford said: 'Perhaps I'm a prejudiced old Tory; but the whole subject is "nasty" to me ... if Socialists identify themselves with any sweeping changes in sexual relations the Industrial Change will be seriously retarded. The time is not ripe for Socialists, as Socialists, to meddle with the sexual question ... .' Patricia Hewitt could have appended the letters to her own, although hers was written some ninety years later.

Robert Blatchford's socialism became codified in Labour's founding policy statements and has become known as Labourism. The Labour Party as we know it was established in 1918. A new constitution was adopted transforming a loose federation of affiliated organisations into a centralised national political party. As well as the new constitution, the 1918 conference supported a policy manifesto, 'Labour and the New Order'. This document's vision was 'new' only insofar as it proposed rearrangements to the current 'social order'. It was less a programme for socialism than a commitment to social reform. The refounded Labour Party advocated State action to humanise private enterprise — welfare capitalism (or its modern term, market socialism).

Central to this was an affirmation of the traditional family with its concept of the 'family wage' and the dependent wife. Subsequently there developed 'welfare feminism' as opposed to the earlier 'equality feminism'. (This can be compared with the later debate between the anti-discriminatory lesbian and gay policy and that of homosexuality as an equally valid form of sexuality.) Welfare feminists were concerned with the health and welfare of working-class women, especially the relief of their poverty, rather than with pressing for changes in the role of women in the family.

One of the welfare feminists' main demands was for family endowment (later called family allowances). The Labour Party initially opposed such schemes as a weakening of family responsibilities and a threat to the family wage. However, it was then thought that additional family payments could remove most married women from the labour market, thus protecting men's jobs and strengthening the traditional family.

Another major example of early Labour's basic perception of The Family was its attitude to protective legislation for women. Welfare feminists vociferously supported protective legislation, and equality feminists vehemently opposed it. Labour, needless to say, was with the welfare feminists, viewing women workers as a threat to men's jobs and the male family wage — not to mention the sexual division of labour under capitalism.

Labour's illustrious memorial, the Welfare State, was — and is — fundamentally underpinned by these beliefs and attitudes. For Labour the traditional family has always been a moral absolute and not at all a changing social relationship, statistics on single-parent families notwithstanding — not to mention 'pretended families'.

It is a mistake, however, to view the Labour Party or the trade unions as ideologically homogenous. Just as many equality feminists opposed shoring up the traditional family at the beginning of the century, so present-day Labour has been challenged internally time and time again — and externally by the women's and lesbians and gay liberation movements — on its sexual politics. Even within the Parliamentary Labour Party in December 1987, faced with Section 28 many Labour MPs spoke immediately and forcefully against it. While Labour's official opposition to Section 28 — when it developed — was primarily based on civil liberties and tolerance, several MPs went further in their opposition.

Bernie Grant, representing Tottenham in the borough of Haringey and one of the first black MPs, was unequivocal and unambiguous in his opposition from the

Labour and the Natural Order

very start. He was the only MP to so oppose the new Clause in Standing Committee A on 8th December 1987. As ex-Leader of Haringey Council, and active in black politics for many years, Mr Grant was well acquainted with all the arguments about the alleged 'Loony Left' and threats to society as we know it. Blithely unworried by the implications of whether lesbians and gay men are born or bred, by whether one can or cannot promote, and by accusations of Labour promoting, Mr Grant boldly went where no labour leadership representative had dared to go. Using the wealth of material produced by Haringey Council to explain the whys and wherefores of lesbian and gay equality, Mr Grant stripped the new Clause bare of any respectable pretensions. Completely lacking in defensiveness, Mr Grant was able to make his view of the matter crystal clear:

> 'I oppose the amendments and I will vote against them irrespective of whether they come from the Government or from the honourable members whose names appear on the amendment paper, although a glance at these names makes my blood run cold ... The Government are being stampeded by a bunch of loony, rabid, right-wing fanatics. I recall a Tory councillor saying that all homosexuals should be exterminated ... The new Clause is dangerous. It covers the first item that I can think of to be prohibited from schools ... What else will they ban from schools? What else will local authorities be stopped from talking about? ... If the new Clause is accepted, it will be a signal to every fascist and everyone opposed to homosexuality that the Government are on their side.'

Bernie Grant also raised a pertinent point with regard to lesbian and gay equality with heterosexuals. If heterosexuality and homosexuality are equally valid, the one cannot stand in judgement on the other. He said:

> 'My difficulty is who will judge "promotion" and the "acceptability of homosexuality as a pretended family relationship". The people who will decide will all be heterosexuals. They will have a totally different interpretation of family life and of the so-called moral nature of the matter. Heterosexuals will decide what is the promotion of homosexuality and what a family is.'

When the new Clause was debated in the House of Commons on 5th December, Joan Ruddock was the only MP to attempt an amendment to delete it in its entirety. She also referred to 'the all-persuasive and all-pervasive culture of heterosexuality.' Mildred Gordon MP, formerly a teacher, said in her speech that 'far too often young children are presented, in schoolbooks and in pictures in school with the vision of the normal, acceptable, happy family as comprising a married, white middle-class man and woman, with two prissy children who are clean, neat and tidy, and yet the majority of children find that this does not relate to their households.'

When the Clause was debated in the House of Lords early in 1988, one Labour peer 'came out' as having been brought up by a 'pretended family'. Lord Rea revealed that his mother and her woman lover had brought him up. He was accused by the Tories of confusing friendship with a sexual relationship, which he strongly denied. Baroness Blackstone said, 'Families can take many forms. Young people know this. They live in many different forms of family. It is a pretense to set up a model of mother, father and children as the only acceptable form.' Lord Willis, who put several amendments to try and defeat the Clause, said in one of his speeches that 'It is curious that we do not hear too much about the heterosexuals and the way they flaunt themselves. I was recently at a film festival and you should have seen the heterosexuals flaunting themselves.' On the other hand, Labour fundamentalism was eloquently put by Lord Mason, formally Roy Mason and a Secretary of State for Northern Ireland. He said:

> 'There is great national concern that homosexuality is being financially promoted to the detriment of normal family relationships ... I am totally opposed to spending public money on promoting and encouraging homosexual and lesbian relationships, particularly as happy family units, thereby in the eyes of our young people making our proper established family institution look odd or queer.'

Labour and the Natural Order

While a few Labour MPs mentioned the born-or-bred question (Chris Smith, Ken Livingstone), it was always in relation to whether one can — and therefore whether Labour authorities could — 'promote' homosexuality. Allan Roberts repeated his prevarication of 8th December in his summing-up speech for Labour at the conclusion of the 9th March 1988 Parliamentary debate. No Labour MP matched the Tories' views as put by, for example, Tory peeress Baroness Strange, or Tory MP Nicholas Bennett. Baroness Strange said during the Lords' debate in February:

> 'I do not share Freud's belief that sexuality is fixed at birth ... circumstances and teaching have much to do with it. I speak for parents everywhere. We want our children to have the best possible chance of happiness ... the least possible chance of catching AIDS and dying prematurely ... We hope they will have children ... A human being is created by the love of a father and mother of a different sex. The basic principle is the family, on which all life and civilisation depend. We owe it to our forebears, to ourselves, to our children, and to God who created us, to keep it so.'

Nicholas Bennett, speaking in the final Commons debate in March, said:

> 'We want to encourage our young people wherever possible to be heterosexual ... That is the acceptable and proper way for our society to be preserved and maintained.'

Clearly the society, the life, and the civilisation referred to by Baroness Strange and Mr Bennett is synonymous with that of capitalist patriarchy. Labour hardly disagrees.

Labour promotes heterosexuality. Labour believes in heterosexuality, in the heterosexual family, as natural and normal. If some individuals happen to be homosexual then that is natural and normal too — for them. Labour does not believe in discrimination. But it is tied to the capitalist social order and therefore it cannot strategically deal with the causes of discrimination (this is as true of discrimination against women, against black people, against those with disabilities). It will attempt to tackle discrimination against lesbians and gay men, but it cannot tackle, can barely conceive of, the supremacist power relationship between heterosexuality and lesbians and gay men which causes the discrimination.

Moreover, Labour has a vocational mission. It has a 'duty to win'. As the presenter of a recent television programme analysing the Labour Party put it, 'Nothing is more sacred than getting Labour into power' (Fred Emery, 'Panorama', 5th September 1988). And nothing must threaten this sacred duty. Lesbian and gay liberation is perceived as doing so, because liberation, as opposed to rights, threatens the position of the heterosexual family. Section 28 hoisted Labour on the petard of its own contradictions.

Acknowledgement

Many thanks to Rebecca Flemming for her patient help with this article.

Sources
Hansard Parliamentary Debates, 8/12/87, 15/12/87, 11/1/88, 1/2/88, 2/2/88, 16/2/88, 9/3/88.
Faces of Feminism Olive Banks, Martin Robertson, 1981.
Parliamentary Socialism Ralph Milliband, Merlin, 1972.
Hidden From History Sheila Rowbotham, Pluto, 1974.
Socialism and the New Life Sheila Rowbotham and Jeffrey Weeks, Pluto, 1977.
Eve and the New Jerusalem Barbara Taylor, Virago, 1983.

Chapter 15
Living With HIV

Ian Fraser

In 1982 I had sex with three people, one of whom was an American. Two are still known to me and are not HIV+, as far as I know. By early 1983 my lymph glands were enlarged as a result of HIV, so it seems that the probable date of infection was October 1982.

I asked the VD clinic about the glands while on a routine checkup. They thought that it might be leukaemia. No test was available for HTLV3 (as it was then called), but an immunologist established that my immune system had abnormalities. The doctor wished to remove a lymph gland for examination, to verify HTLV3, but I refused to allow this despite considerable pressure and went instead to see a homeopath. She changed my entire perspective of the infection and it is to her, I believe, that I owe my current good health.

She began by assuring me that no disease is 100 per cent fatal. 'There are always survivors,' she said, and told me about cancer patients given six months to live by conventional doctors, whom she had sustained over several years. She spent time on finding out what sort of character I had, my history and any past diseases. This process in itself made me feel better, her calm reassurance so different from the doctor at the clinic, with his formal, polite and economical manner. Her credibility increased when she advised me that it did not really matter whether I believed in homeopathy or not. It might help if I did, but would still be effective if I did not. She explained its scientific basis and her whole approach was candid and open. The overall effect of this encounter was dramatic, because it was reassuring and put things in perspective.

While I was on holiday the clinic tested a blood sample without my permission and established that it was HIV positive. The young doctor in charge of my case insisted on telling my GP and wrote to him, but the letter was later withdrawn and suppressed by his superior at my request.

Since that time HIV has come to dominate gay life in this country. Organisations dealing with the infection include: Action Against AIDS, ACT-UP (AIDS Coalition To Unleash Power), Body Positive, Frontliners, Health Education Authorities, LAGER (Lesbian And Gay Employment Rights), Lambeth Lesbian and Gay Group, NALGO, Positively Healthy, and the Terrence Higgins Trust (THT). I have never actually used these for help or advice myself, as I was aware of my infection before they were formed and had by then come to terms with it. I once used Body Positive to put someone recently diagnosed in touch, and I once went to a THT Safe Sex talk out of interest, but the latter was like going to a CHE (Campaign for Homosexual Equality) meeting for the first time and did not tell me anything I did not already know. I found the format patronising and alienating, and felt that I did not belong. They were too 'posh' and refined, and not sufficiently down-to-earth for me.

I was a member of NALGO from 1979 until the GLC was abolished, when I ceased to be a member for a number of reasons: I could not afford it, and because the company for whom I worked was not a Local Authority, union membership was considered unacceptable. Efforts of NALGO's membership to develop policies for dealing with HIV infection and employment, and getting these converted into policy, have, however, led me to believe that NALGO membership is important not simply because of the wider political issues involved, but because HIV threatens employment security. Trades Unions have the expertise to deal with this, and to tackle employers in the event of such a case arising.

I have felt considerable moral pressure to take part in organisations helping people with AIDS/HIV, especially when I meet those apparently unaffected by the disease giving so much time and effort to those who are. I have avoided getting involved, however, because I believe the subject would become obsessive and I would become introspective. It is important that this does not happen. Also I dislike bureaucratic organisation, perhaps because of my early experience with CHE. Some people like committees and organising, others don't, and I am one of the latter. I would take part in a group which was run in a businesslike way, and which had realistic aims. However, so much that needs to be done requires professional lobbying and political change, and I question whether a well-meaning group of amateurs can do much beyond counselling and sharing information.

A good example of this is the Lambeth Lesbian and Gay Group which was set up a few years ago and whose meetings I attended three or four times. The initial meeting attracted more than a hundred local lesbians and gays full of enthusiasm and curiosity. Those with experience of Local Authority procedure, who perhaps enjoy it or enjoy showing off their knowledge of it, then started calling 'points of order' or complaining about issues not being on the agenda, of being taken out of sequence. The result was that the vast majority of those attending the initial meeting went home and stayed home, and the Group, as far as I am aware, achieved little. The most constructive move was when Linda Bellos stood up and announced that she thought that the group was a complete waste of time unless it had power, and to have power it would have to be a Council Committee with the right to interfere in all other committees.

I would never discourage someone from trying to start a group. Sometimes such initiatives lead to great things. I always donate to these organisations and have benefitted to the extent that organisations like THT, Body Positive and LAGER have made the general public aware of the infection and have made some employers take it into account. NALGO in particular has adopted very good policies, which makes my own employment more secure, and of all the organisations listed I would suggest that NALGO's contribution has probably been the greatest. LAGER, too, is trying to change the rules which govern employment, and I believe help would be available if I had to take action against an employer. It is not inconceivable that other organisations would become relevant in the future if I fell ill, but I like to assume that I am not going to fall seriously ill.

In the early seventies I canvassed for a Labour candidate, who, when elected, turned out to be anti-gay. It was the beginning of my disillusionment with the Labour Party. Now, I believe that a Labour Government holds more promise of greatly improving the lot of people with HIV/AIDS. It could mean legislation to prevent discrimination, dismissal, and also help with housing in the event of illness. The fundamental need is for statutory change involving protection by law.

ACT-UP is the organisation I should most like to be part of. High-profile action is the quickest way to force change. Their abseiling action involving condoms used as balloons over Wormwood Scrubs was another brilliant gesture. There is no such thing as bad publicity, and sometimes the only way to force change is to be anti-social and become a problem which eventually the authorities have to deal with. I know it is true, because I have to respond to public pressure daily in my job, and that is how issues become prominent and how spending priorities are established. If someone shouts loud enough, long enough, about an issue, money will eventually be found. This is the way in which Britain is run.

My main concern is what will happen if the worst takes place? While I have friends who would probably help me a great deal, there is no legal arrangement to deal with someone who has declining health because of

AIDS. The worst scenario is: illness, debilitation, absence from work, loss of job and income, loss of home, total dependency on friends, institutionalisation or homelessness. Ideally, someone with a terminal illness should at least have the right to work part-time as long as they are able. I view employment positively, because for me it is a routine which I enjoy and which keeps me going. I have one of the best jobs I could possibly hope for — a Landscape Architect involved in establishing wild-life habitats, public open spaces, playgrounds, planting areas and gardens, and in planning and urban design.

Building Societies, too, should be forced to address the problem of terminally ill mortgagees. They are strongly placed to agree a Code of Practice to protect those with HIV infection. The problem is going to get much larger, and it is not good enough simply to make money out of the rush to home ownership. Although a homeowner myself, I have always believed that communal ownership on a small scale would solve many problems associated with terminal illness or permanent disablement.

When I was at the GLC, Ken Livingstone was in charge and I thought it was the beginning of Utopia, so many wonderful things were happening at last. The way he has been treated by Kinnock has infuriated me, and Labour's failure to adopt strong gay policies is disastrous. I wrote to Neil Kinnock during the last election, asking him to withdraw the remark that gays and lesbians were losing votes on the doorsteps of the pensioners. I didn't get a reply before election day, so I voted Green; it arrived two days after the election, reassuring me that the Labour Party was committed to improving gay rights.

Over the last few years I have also complained to the Press Council on a number of occasions, about various newspapers using such terms as 'Gay Plague', or saying that the disease was spread by whispered conversations, or for exaggerating the amount of money spent by local authorities on gay issues. All adjudications took several months and none was successful. I reported the whole lot in a letter to the *Guardian* when the Press Council became a prominent issue, but it was never published. I have written several further letters to the *Independent* and the *Guardian* without success, one letter criticising the *Guardian*'s AIDS information which has always been about two years out of date.

The *Guardian* did publish an article about Insurance Assessors who thought that AIDS would have little effect on the heterosexual population. I pointed out that there was already a huge reservoir of infection amongst the 18 to 25-year-olds here and in the United States, simply because straight youths were not changing their habits. Anything from 70 to 90 per cent would not use condoms. My letter was ignored, yet an article (between 7th and 10th October 1989) said that there was a sudden alarming increase in heterosexual youth AIDS cases in the States! More recently there have been letters and articles predicting a world population of 15 billion, but no account has been taken of the fact that between 10 and 25 per cent could die of AIDS in the next twenty years, as is already happening in parts of Africa.

A couple of years ago ex-Bishop Montefiore suggested in the *Guardian* that spending money on AZT was wasteful, and that it should be spent on hip replacements instead. I was so angry that I wrote a furious letter to him accusing him of being un-Christian and ignorant, and also wrote to the Archbishop of Canterbury, whom I also regard as ineffectual. It led to a dialogue with Montefiore, with my telling him about my friend who has had AIDS now for six years and who, thanks to AZT, is still alive. I said that someone in Montefiore's position should check his facts before sounding off, and advised him to campaign for more resources all round instead of trying to trade one disadvantaged group off against another. I also suggested that he go and live in San Francisco for six months, where he might see for himself and in practice the ideal which Jesus Christ was talking about, which is far removed from anything the Church of England ever practises in this country. His reply was in part denial of the criticisms, and in part an attempt to change the issue or confuse the matter. The irritating thing was that he seemed to be unaware of the beneficial effects of AZT, or the creative potential of AIDS sufferers.

I have also written to various television channels about their coverage of AIDS, saying either 'thank you' because it was good, or criticising them if it was bad. Unlike newspapers they always acknowledge letters. I was even invited to appear on a TV programme, but declined because of the rough time friends had received, and because of the sloppy way previous programmes in that particular series had been presented. I complained to the BBC about Jonathan Dimbleby's failure to mention AIDS in his 'Review of the Year 1988'. They didn't bother to reply, so I wrote again. This was also ignored, so I wrote to Marmaduke Hussey and Sue Lawley, who had been inviting us, the viewers, to express our views about TV. That correspondence got no further and I have come to the conclusion that either they all recognise my name, or else there is a conspiracy!

I wrote to the *Sunday Correspondent* criticising a claim in their first issue that the recent flattening in the rise of the monthly AIDS figures is due to the Government's propaganda campaign of 1986. I pointed out that AIDS has an incubation period of 7-10 years, and that the results of the Government's efforts, if any, will not appear until 1993. I also suggested that any flattening in the rise in the AIDS figures is probably due to statistical methods, the way in which cause of death is defined, or political whims, rather than to any real changes.

I wrote to the Health Education Authority telling them that I didn't think their advertisements would affect lifestyles much, if at all. It seems that young heterosexuals still think the disease is something that happens to others. The only thing that will make them change their attitudes will be knowing someone with AIDS and watching them decline. I don't think gay men changed their habits because of advertisements; we did so, some of us, because we saw our friends dying of it and the horrible effect that it has. There was a time when we naively believed that it was caused by Immune Overload — too many stimulants and not enough rest and nutrition. It took a while to realise that it is a virus.

I have come to the same conclusion as many people who find that they have a potentially fatal disease. You value each day and each experience, and you don't put off projects which you want to tackle. Time may be short, so the quality of life goes up. I also realise the importance of having some sort of discipline and routine to hold on to. For some people this may be self-imposed; for me, my work forms part of it — it is something which I enjoy and from which I get considerable satisfaction. I have seen people deteriorate quickly when they give up a routine, believing that this is the right thing to do. I have seen it happen, for instance, to people at retirement.

Faced with a major risk to your health you become more assertive about your needs. You are not going to sacrifice sleep pretending you can catch up later. It may mean being anti-social at times, but that is too bad. I insist on eating properly and will not skimp, even if it means altering the social calendar to suit. Many may interpret such a self-centred approach as selfish or stand-offish — that is too bad. It is a question of survival.

Chapter 16
Caring, Campaigning and the Dehomosexualisation of AIDS

Christopher Scott

The history of AIDS campaigning is a short one. When 'Gay Related Immune Deficiency' first started decimating our community early in the 1980s, we reacted with fear and bewilderment. In the face of societal indifference — followed by outright hostility — we were forced into a frantic effort to meet the needs of those who were ill. In 1984 the Terrence Higgins Trust started its Safer Sex campaign — a year before the Health Education Authority took notice — and the gay community embarked on a process of rapid self-education.

In the few short years since AIDS came to dominate our lives, we have created a network of caring, service-providing charities, pioneered imaginative public health campaigns and pushed the government and medical profession to take the threat of AIDS seriously.

And yet I am not happy. It seems to me that this explosion of energy has been drained of its radical potential, diverted into areas of service provision which should be the State's concern. We have swallowed our anger, presented a respectable front, in our bid to gain public support. In return, we have been allowed the role of 'mother's little helper', and our services are being relied upon to support the public. Dehomosexualisation of AIDS has cost us dear, in both our caring and our campaigning.

Caring

Those who doubt the existence of a 'gay community' should note the extraordinary — and entirely voluntary — wave of health education undertaken in gay pubs and clubs, newsletters and social groups. Gay Switchboards have passed on information to every man who phoned in, self-help groups and caring services were set up, and — when there was time to breathe — attempts were made to persuade a reluctant government that the deaths of so many gay men was an issue worthy of their attention.

In the face of an epidemic which was sweeping away our friends and lovers, we sought help where we could. Political scruples about voluntary action subverting the role of the statutory sector suddenly seemed a luxury: we were in need, now.

Inevitably, many organisations have been created which effectively avoided confronting the government. Services which ideally should be provided by the statutory sector are instead being provided by voluntary agencies which are heavily dependent on fundraising and/or State aid. To be sure, this has enabled us to be more creative, flexible and sensitive in our caring than any statutory provision could be, but the contemporary role of the voluntary sector as a consistent challenger of government ethics is considerably limited: by tied funding or charity law, most voluntary groups are not allowed the luxury of political activity. Have we contributed to our own marginalisation? Has increased public sympathy cost us too dear?

This need to attract statutory funding and support has necessitated many compromises, one of which has been to 'straighten' our image. Many of those organisations which were dependent in their early days on the passion and commitment of lesbians and gay men are now run by heterosexual 'professionals'. Although gays continue to be present in these organisations in large numbers, it is interesting to see what price has been paid for continued government funding. HIV and AIDS organisations have been effectively dehomosexualised: many devoted workers have been left feeling devalued and exploited. They have seen their work taken on by people with different motivations and agendas, and fear that such disparity must weaken both impact and cohesion of purpose.

Connected with this has been a false glamourisation of AIDS work, and a masking of fear with macho posturing. People have wanted to prove they are not scared of AIDS work and have put themselves under enormous pressure to provide what may well be an impossible service.

Campaigning

Despite the flowering of services, the increasing activities of local authorities and the creation of many new and sympathetic organisations, public misconceptions about HIV and AIDS remain high. Rights to insurance, housing and employment remain limited, and the severe discrimination endured by PWAs (People With Aids) is as real as ever.

Gay energy has been taken up with service provision and public education: little has been left for meaningful activism, and our anger, fear and grief has been kept strictly privatised, so as not to exacerbate the hostility we face in the outside world, and so as not to risk funding.

We are the victims of a societal ethic that voluntary service provision should not be tainted by association with political activism. We are the inheritors of a political culture that does not have a history of mass street action: civil disobedience, yes, but never on the scale of the American civil rights movement. This has combined with a poor record on coalition building and activist management, a public perception of lesbian and gay politics as party political and a preserve of the Left, and a high level of internalised oppression expressed as apathy.

This has resulted in an AIDS activism which is limited and inaccessible, centred around those who are directly involved in caring for PWAs, those who gain prestige from that involvement. Inevitably, this is an environment of intense emotional conflicts: outsiders watch helplessly on the margins, excluded by the climate of anger, despair and jealousy. Accusations fly about the relevance of different forms of treatment, the value of colluding with the medical profession, the spectre of 'AIDS professionals' lining their nests, profiting from the miseries of others. Much AIDS activism has been initiated by those groups trying to concurrently provide a caring service. With the risk of public anger being taken out on the dying, frontline activism is simply a luxury we cannot afford.

This uneasy coexistence of agendas is highlighted by the position of women within AIDS culture. Although some lesbians exploited the opportunity to distance themselves from dirty, dangerous male sexuality, a vastly disproportionate number devoted themselves to AIDS work. Most of these women came from a political background of feminism, which has achieved far greater levels of activity than gay men ever managed. AIDS may well have taught gay men how to work with, as well as benefit from, the services of lesbians.

But with all the right-on posturing and good intentions in the world, AIDS service provision has been reactive, and so flawed. The needs of women with HIV and AIDS, and women carers, were not fully anticipated, have not been met. Despite the hard work invested in service provision for men, women have had to struggle every bit as hard as gay men a few years earlier, to carve out services for themselves. Another illustration of the same lesson: caring for others must not detract from caring for ourselves.

The Dehomosexualisation of AIDS

AIDS may be everybody's problem, but in Europe and North America it is still mainly a gay problem.

We must demand the same level of statutory care as

any other citizen, but that must not be bought with our anger and integrity. Who else will fight for our liberation? Who else will forge and strengthen links with the multiplicity of others with whom some creative collaboration could yield fruitful results — those affected by disability, chronic sickness, inadequate welfare provision, NHS reforms, prejudice?

There is room for organising in a non-party political way, and for the creation of umbrella organisations which bring together gay men or people with AIDS, representing not any attempt at service delivery, but a demand for government action.

The political activity around Clause 28 was one of the few occasions when lesbians and gay men have worked together and successfully expressed their anger. Whilst AIDS was not well included as an issue in the campaign, it was clearly at the back of every civil servant's mind as the details of the Clause were worked out. This campaign may have definitively proved that HIV and AIDS is not a specifically gay issue.

The experience of the last decade has demanded that we all talk openly about sexuality, disease and death, in order to curtail further unnecessary transmission of HIV. The challenge of AIDS involves more than individual sexual behaviour: it represents an opportunity to work through our commonest societal fears and taboos, to reach new understanding and evolve compassionate action. How to do that on the issue of AIDS, and with the efforts and talents of lesbians and gay men, is the question which must not now be avoided.

Chapter 17
Pulpits, Courts and Scandal

Savitri Hensman

Churchgoing Anglicans are a small minority of England's population. However, what happens in the Church of England can have a major impact on people outside it, as well as on regular church attenders, for a number of reasons. It is the religious body most closely linked with the State, which appoints its senior clergy and has representatives in the House of Lords. Tens of millions of people take part in its ceremonies from time to time, or have neighbours who do, and many of them rely on it to uphold and promote traditional English values. It has a sizable workforce. It is wealthy and owns numerous buildings, often made use of by other organisations (for instance for meetings, jumble sales or offices).

The human rights and relationships of lesbians and gays were recently the subject of heated debate — and legal action — in the Church of England. There was widespread interest. Newspaper headlines announced that 'pulpit poofs' could stay, but later 'Church "gays"' were 'forced out of HQ'. How did the furore start? What really happened? What are the immediate and long-term consequences?

Vacuum

In 1987 the Church of England's position on sexuality

Pulpits, Courts and Scandal

was confused. Some members still believed that the only rightful form of sex was between a dominant husband and obedient wife in a lifelong heterosexual marriage. But this had been increasingly called into question: women campaigned for equality, divorced people and unmarried parents became more assertive, and theologians showed that what had been claimed as universal truths often arose from particular cultures and societies.

In the 1950s the Church of England had called for reform of the law under which gay sex was illegal under all circumstances, though it still held the position that such acts were immoral. Few members dared to dissent in public. However, the joy and fulfilment which many had found in lesbian and gay relationships did not seem to fit the official pronouncements about sin!

Over the next three decades, many theologians took a fresh look at the whole subject of human sexuality. It has been argued persuasively that passages from the Bible which had been taken as prohibiting gay sex were either mistranslated or taken out of context; that, in any case, the Bible could not be read as a set of rules to be unthinkingly obeyed; that love and justice in sexual relationships mattered more than gender; and that homophobia itself was sinful. It has also been shown that blessings of lesbian and gay relationships have been celebrated by the Christian community since ancient times.

A working party of the Church of England's Board for Social Responsibility stated in 1979:

> 'We do not think it is possible to deny that there are circumstances in which individuals may justifiably choose to enter into a homosexual relationship ... [although] such a relationship could not be regarded as the moral or social equivalent of marriage.'

The Board refused to endorse this. The chairman at the time, Graham Leonard, was later to become the Bishop of London.

Lesbians and gays — an increasing number of whom

were at least halfway out of the closet — continued to take part in church activities. Gay clergy helped to keep congregations alive in areas where class snobbery and racism had alienated much of the population from the Church of England, and where many other ministers refused to work. *Faith In The City*, a report published by the Church of England in 1985, pointed out that there were:

> 'proportionately many more single clergy and Church workers in Urban Priority Areas than in other areas, and this has implications for pastoral support. Homosexual clergy also need appropriate pastoral support, even though in evidence to us they said that they often prefer to work in Urban Priority Areas because of the greater degree of acceptance and diversity of life-styles. Support needs to be given to them, not least in their ministry to other homosexuals, who tend to be drawn to the inner cities.'

The nature of this 'support' was soon to become clear.

Many other Anglicans were feeling confused. The simple guidelines on sexual morality which, when they were children, the Church of England and society as a whole had appeared to accept, were being challenged. Some council employees were forbidden to treat unmarried mothers, lesbians and gays less favourably than 'respectable' people. Partners in same-sex couples and remarried divorcees were accepted in positions of church leadership. Many people had struggled to adhere to a strict moral code for years (while others had worked hard at least to keep up appearances): some may have felt that their efforts were no longer appreciated.

Moreover, the so-called 'permissive society' was not protecting women from being treated as sex-objects: far from it; pornography flourished, kerb-crawlers harassed passers-by on the streets.

Regulating what adolescents knew about sex, and preventing them from going to bed with their girlfriends or boyfriends, had become difficult. Many mothers were upset because they feared for the safety of their children

— and because, for numerous women, control over young people had been one of the few ways to exercise power in society.

The safety of women and children in their own homes could not, of course, be guaranteed. Women's organisations had publicised the fact that wives were often assaulted (sometimes raped) by their husbands, and that numerous children were severely beaten or sexually abused by men in their families. Writers and broadcasters increasingly took up these issues. Many Anglicans had been brought up to revere 'the family', and felt that this publicity was damaging to the ideas they cherished; a number of men also had reason to fear that their own behaviour would be exposed. Some churchpeople fought hard to defend patriarchal values. Feminist and other Christian thinkers had written thought-provoking articles and books on sexuality. However, these were frequently in technical language and sold in only a few outlets; and many clergy were not concerned with encouraging the laity to grapple with complex issues.

For a number of reasons, then, there were numerous Anglicans ready to respond to the message of moral crusaders who campaigned on a range of issues, from telephone chatlines to abortion.

Meanwhile the Church of England was proving to be a nuisance to the government. With various motives — from the fear that the worst excesses of Thatcherism were making the existing social order less stable, to the belief that God was on the side of oppressed people seeking justice — its leaders spoke out against particularly inhumane State policies. The growing gap between rich and poor and the splitting up of black families through racist immigration laws and practices, for instance, were criticised. Values such as avarice and callousness were denounced.

MPs called on the Church to turn her attention to sexual morality rather than Tory politics, calls which seemed, at first, to have little success. However, the right-wing Christian Church was becoming increasingly active: for instance, the president of the National Council for Christian Standards in Society, the Earl of Halsbury, tried to make the 'promoting' of homosexuality in schools unlawful, but failed.

Falling Short of Ideals

In November 1987 Tony Higton, the rector of Hawkwell in Essex, put forward a motion to General Synod which reaffirmed the

> 'biblical standard, given for the well-being of society ...[that] fornication, adultery and homosexual acts are sinful in all circumstances ... [and that] Christian leaders are called on to be exemplary in all spheres of morality, including sexual morality, as a condition of being appointed to or remaining in office. [Those who had] fallen into sexual sin [should] repent and receive absolution.'

The private members' motions with the most signatures were discussed, including Higton's proposal that ministers in gay relationships should be sacked, and that lesbian and gay theological students who were not celibate and refused to fake heterosexuality should be denied ordination.

The Lesbian and Gay Christian Movement (LGCM), among others, took an active interest. LGCM had been set up in the 1970s; it rented a room in St Botolph's, Aldgate, a church well-known for work with single homeless people in London. The Movement brought together gays, lesbians and heterosexuals from various denominations (Anglicans, Methodists, Roman Catholics and others), who believed that 'human sexuality in all its richness is a gift of God gladly to be accepted, enjoyed and honoured, as a way of both expressing and growing in love, in accordance with the life and teaching of Jesus Christ.' It provided counselling, held meetings and conferences, coordinated local groups and distributed literature.

LGCM urged support for an amendment moved by

Malcolm Johnson (the rector of St Botolph's), which deleted almost all of Higton's wording and instead affirmed 'the essential of the biblical message that human love is a reflection of divine love and should be characterised by the permanency and commitment of relationships.' Stability and permanence were to be encouraged, young people and parents warned of 'the dangers, both spiritual and physical, of sexual promiscuity whether heterosexual or homosexual'.

Shortly before the debate, a sensational attack on lesbian and gay Christians was published by a national newspaper. Some clergymen had been approached by a journalist masquerading as a man in distress about his sexuality. They had tried to help him and, as a result, had lurid stories about their own sex-lives splashed across the newspaper's pages. Synod members were under pressure to crack down on gay clergy, who were portrayed as leading lives of wild abandon!

On 11th November, 1987, Synod was tense as Higton proposed his motion. He was appalled, he said, by clergy who 'blatantly' exhibited their homosexuality, for instance by going to gay pubs. He told of theological colleges where men were at risk of sexual advances, and expressed his scepticism about 'so-called' faithful and committed relationships between homosexuals. Synod, he argued, should speak clearly to nation and church. 'People who call themselves gay Christians' were undermining the gospel.

Johnson was one of the handful in the debate who spoke positively about lesbian and gay relationships. He pointed out that his amendment avoided being divisive, and criticised Higton's motion as a cowardly attack on gay clergy working courageously and effectively in inner cities. The amendment was defeated. Among those who voted against it were some closeted gays: if there was to be a purge, they did not wish to be among the victims.

However, the bishops (both heterosexual and gay) were not keen on being forced to harass priests, deacons and layworkers whom they liked and respected, and on whom they relied. Several spoke out against the harshly self-righteous tone of the original motion. The Bishop of Chester proposed an amendment which still condemned lesbian and gay sex but put no obligation on bishops to punish in any way people who took part in it. 'Fornication and adultery' were sins against the ideal that sex should only take place in 'a permanent married relationship', 'homosexual genital acts also fall short of this ideal', Christians were 'called to be exemplary in all spheres of morality, including sexual morality', and 'holiness of life is particularly required of Christian leaders'.

The wording was strange. What, for instance, is the difference between sinning and falling short? Christians are used to confessing their sins against God and against other humans, but is it really possible to sin against an ideal? Nevertheless, the amendment won a majority of votes.

After the debate, a number of bishops hastened to assure the mass media that they would not knowingly employ gay clergy, although one or two spoke out against homophobia. Higton had not succeeded completely, but Synod had indeed spoken clearly to the nation. Lesbians and gays, it had been implied, were irresponsible predators who did not deserve to be employed; those who insisted on equality were a threat.

By allowing innuendo, fear and bigotry to determine policy, Christians had managed to set a moral example to their neighbours. The following month, a new version of Halsbury's bill was introduced with government backing, obtained by MPs Jill Knight, a sponsor of the Conservative Family Campaign, and David Wilshire, also part of the increasingly influential Christian right-wing. This became Section 28.

Other unpleasant surprises were in store for lesbians and gays in the Church of England.

Law and Disgrace

Over the centuries the Church of England has developed a complex set of laws to deal with internal matters, and deals with them in its own courts. Those at a diocesan level are known as Consistory Courts; 'chancellors' act as judges. When consecrated ground is used for anything other than worship (and similar things), formal permission — a 'faculty' — should be obtained, according to ecclesiastical law. This was not widely known among Anglicans.

Before LGCM took up its office in the tower of St Botolph's, Malcolm Johnson should have applied for a faculty. When he found out, he contacted the Diocese of London's lawyers, who helped to prepare the paperwork: getting a licence seemed to be just a formality — in modern times it was practically unheard-of for a faculty to be refused. Johnson was therefore taken aback when the strongly homophobic Chancellor of London asked the new Archdeacon to intervene.

The Archdeacon of London, George Cassidy, who came from the Ulster Loyalist community, was not keen on compromise. Johnson wrote to him in December 1987, pleading with him for a meeting to settle the matter quietly to avoid lurid publicity in the mass media, and prevent damage to the church's work with homeless people. Cassidy did not respond. Legal proceedings went ahead.

Cassidy came up with a number of objections to the granting of a faculty. Among these he claimed that LGCM, by displaying a flyer for the *Gay Guide to London* in the office, encouraged promiscuity; that, by publishing a leaflet arguing for positive images in schools, it was promoting paedophilia; and that, by advertising the GLC booklets entitled *Changing the World* and *Tackling Heterosexism*, it was in opposition to the criminal law of England! More seriously, he quoted Synod's resolution on sexuality, and argued that an organisation whose beliefs and aims contradicted this should not be allowed to use church premises.

Johnson was told by his lawyers that he, the churchwardens, the Parochial Church Council and LGCM (all of whom had applied for the faculty) were likely to lose the case. They were facing a mounting legal bill, whereas Cassidy had behind him the huge resources of the diocese — much of it contributed by gays and lesbians. Moreover, the Chancellor's opinion was clear.

In spring 1988 Johnson asked for the case to be adjourned so that LGCM could move its office without appearing to have been thrown out. This was refused. In the end he, the churchwardens and the PCC applied to withdraw from the case, and LGCM reluctantly agreed to leave. At first it seemed that LGCM might be forced to pay the Archdeacon's legal costs as well as its own, which might leave it bankrupt. However, its barrister showed that it was not liable.

During the dispute, numerous people wrote letters protesting against the Diocese of London's behaviour. One of the Church of England's most eminent theologians criticised the Diocese for actions which suggested 'a positive eagerness to humiliate and exclude those whom the parish and LGCM seek to help', and 'a readiness to follow secular fashion in harassing and rejecting homosexuals.' Another wrote of 'a new resurgence of idolatrous religion' in which 'the church is valued, if it is valued at all, to the extent that it helps to shore up the values and culture of Thatcherism.'

Even among Anglicans who disagreed with LGCM's aims, some were shocked by what had happened. Seventy clergy in the Diocese publicly criticised the way it had handled the case. In turn, Cassidy enlisted the help of the *Mail on Sunday* to justify his behaviour. The newspaper published an article alleging that material distributed from St Botolph's has included 'the kind of stuff you would expect to find in a San Francisco bath-house, not a Church of England', and, more broadly, that 'militant clerical homosexuality has now spread to a point where many of the ancient City churches are open pick-up joints.' Tony Higton sent a copy of the article to every member of General Synod.

On the one hand, the Church of England had managed to insult and harass its lesbian and gay members (it is not known how many left in disgust), and had helped to justify to the public the upsurge in homophobic discrimination and violence which was taking place at the time. On the other hand, many heterosexual Christians had become less ignorant about the issues around sexuality, and lesbians and gays in the church had received an unprecedented show of solidarity.

LGCM survived and settled down in an office in Bethnal Green.

'To grow and develop in relationships'

Meanwhile rumours were circulating about a secret Church of England report on lesbians and gays. In February 1990 this was leaked, stirring up further controversy.

The report had been prepared by a working party set up in 1986 by the House of Bishops and chaired by Reverend June Osborne. As in the 1979 report, despite developments in Biblical scholarship, it asserted that throughout the Bible there was strong disapproval for homosexual practice but sinful human beings still have to make moral sense of their lives:

> 'Thus it might be argued that loving, committed and trusting relationships between homosexual people, whilst in some respects they are considered sinful and falling short of the pattern for our life as revealed in the Scripture, make the best moral sense of a situation which is, of itself, flawed.
>
> It is better for people to be able to grow and develop in relationships than to suffer the burdens of isolation and constant temptation and the threat of seeking relief through clandestine and casual relationships.'

The Osborne report went further, arguing that the

Church of England should not consider lesbian issues 'without considering its own social culture of male/female power relationships.' It was also tentatively suggested that services of blessing for lesbian and gay couples could be helpful.

Anti-discriminatory teaching in schools was endorsed:

> 'We need to take seriously the strength of argument that education opportunities should be used to undermine the power of homophobia in our society.'

The issue of discrimination in employment, too, was raised, and the practice of keeping secret files on lesbians and gays:

> 'Thus bodies like the Church exercise power over the individual on the basis of the knowledge they possess of that person. It is hard to justify such a relationship from a moral perspective.'

The bishops refused to comment on the leaked report.

A Matter of Time

By mid-1990 the Church of England's position on lesbian and gay sexuality was thoroughly confused. A new Archbishop of Canterbury was selected who took a public stance against clergy in gay and lesbian relationships, but who was persuaded to adopt a more flexible position, at least for the time being.

Inevitably, the Church of England will sooner or later announce officially that it is acceptable to express love and commitment to another woman or another man in a sexual relationship. Meanwhile, the church will continue to encourage in some of its members ignorance and prejudice against their 'brothers and sisters in Christ', while sowing fear and self-distrust in others.

Chapter 18
It Couldn't Happen Here

A European Perspective

Robert and Gerard

The Stop The Clause campaign received support throughout Europe, most visibly and actively in Amsterdam. Significant because of its gay culture and tradition of liberalism, Amsterdam also has a sense of recent history which is lacking in Britain. Witness its monuments to the dead of the Second World War: old synagogues are preserved, public buildings stand as memorials, and — unique in the world — Amsterdam has its own Homomonument, which commemorates and mourns the homosexual victims of fascism.

The Homomonument is both a sacred memorial and a place for celebration: during one weekend in early 1990 it was the setting for a Jewish memorial to the dead (the kaddish service) and a celebration of the Dutch Queen's birthday. This sense of a future and a past for homosexuality contrasts unfavourably with the British sense of history — it would be unfortunate if the only way for a society to learn from its own history was for it to be occupied by fascists! That point is explored elsewhere in this book.

Amsterdam is not typical, of course: most European countries treat their lesbian and gay citizens more harshly, and Britain is one of the worst. The opportunities of 1992, however, could lead to a progressive harmonisation of anti-discriminatory legislation, and the changes in Eastern Europe provide further cause for us to extend our solidarity to lesbians and gays all over Europe, as they did for us.

The following two pieces illustrate the way in which European involvement in the Stop The Clause campaign was necessitated both by horror of what appeared to be happening in Britain, and by a concern about what was also happening in Europe.

Interview with Robert G.

Robert G. is a Dutch gay activist who has lived in Amsterdam, England, Canada and Sweden. His employers consider homosexuality a 'security threat', and so he is interviewed here under a pseudonym.

How did you get involved with the European Stop The Clause Campaign?
R: I was living in a legalised communal squat in Amsterdam with a lesbian, a transsexual and two bisexual women. When the news of the British Clause 28 broke, a number of groups formed a campaign against it, but the main one was LAMBDA — later called DAQUA (Dykes and Queens United in Action). Our transsexual flatmate was one of the main organisers of the campaign, and we were all active supporters — not least by paying the rent for LAMBDA to set up an office in our squat.

What did the Campaign do?
R: LAMBDA was very active, very effective. Dutch activists started visiting England very early in 1988. They attended some of the London Stop The Clause meetings in order to gain information and strengthen communication — unfortunately, they often came away frustrated and unsuccessful because of internal difficulties within the London campaign. We didn't let that stop us, though — almost overnight, it seemed,

It Couldn't Happen Here

Amsterdam was covered with Stop The Clause graffiti, especially along the canal banks.

I took a boat trip round the canals in August 1988 and was amazed and touched by all the graffiti. It was unmissable, even the tourists couldn't ignore it.
R: Especially the tourists couldn't miss it — we made sure of that. I think Amsterdam dykes and queers deserve a lot of credit for spreading awareness of the Clause throughout Europe and the world. All our actions gained very widespread publicity. Our 16th April demo, for example, was attended by 7,000 people and attracted an incredibly positive response from passers-by. Ordinary Dutch citizens were lining the streets, smiling and clapping. I thought at the time, this simply couldn't happen in England. It was very pleasing, very liberating.

Even better was our 5th July 'Kiss The Queens' demo. Queen Elizabeth of England was visiting Amsterdam for the William and Mary celebrations — three-hundred years of English-Dutch friendship — so us Dutch queens planned our own reception for her. A few days before her arrival, I went with two friends to the Royal Palace, dressed up as the Three Musketeers. In broad daylight, and playing a trumpet fanfare, we ceremoniously lowered the British flag and hoisted in its place the International Flag of Lesbian and Gay Liberation. Nobody stopped us, our only witnesses were dozens of American tourists, all solemnly taking photos of this ethnic curiosity. Incidentally, I cycled past the Royal Palace at 2 a.m. the next morning and saw that all the flags had been taken down except ours — a gesture of regal solidarity, perhaps?!

Anyway, we desecrated the British flag — sewed on a pink triangle and painted on slogans — and took it along to the demo, which was very well attended. We got lots of international media coverage, far more than the Queen would have got without us, and again we were very well supported by the Dutch people. In fact, something amazing happened when Elizabeth arrived: the offices of the liberal newspaper *NRC Handelsblad* are next to the Royal Palace. With the cooperation of their management, staff unfurled a banner from the windows saying something like 'Liz, leave your queens alone'. This was actually rather brave considering the police marksmen lining the roofs!

I think in Britain we were all rather amazed at how much solidarity was extended to us from Europe. We were grateful, of course, but also rather ashamed, doubting that we would ever have put ourselves out so much for you ...

R: It's true that the British seem very lacking European solidarity, but you know our activity wasn't just about altruism, far from it. There was real fear that this English homophobia would spread, especially with European harmonisation. We needed to make a statement to Dutch society, a warning that we wouldn't take similar attacks lying down.

There was another factor, identified in a recent Dutch gay magazine as 'The Woolly Society' — woolly in the sense of cushioned, I think. This described Dutch society as one in which liberal consensus has smothered over expressions of homophobia, while leaving the underlying heterosexism intact. A good example of this has been the recent discussion over anti-discriminatory legislation. Our only area of difficulty was that the Christian Democrats initially argued against extending this policy to cover religious schools — but they have now given way. From the outside it can seem like the Netherlands is a gay paradise, and compared to Britain it probably is. But that doesn't mean we have no homophobia here — just that it is rather more amorphous, more difficult to pinpoint. I hate to say it, but Clause 28 was greeted with a high degree of elation and excitement mixed with horror, a feeling of yes it was terrible news but at least we have an obvious enemy figure, as last an easy target to mobilise against. The Dutch campaign was at least as much on our own behalf as on yours.

What was the feeling when the Clause became law, then — frustration, anticlimax, anger perhaps with the British campaign?
R: Everyone felt that the campaign had been worthwhile, but there had been a lot of tensions and problems to deal with and so that affected how we all felt at the end.

Within the Dutch campaign, or between British and Dutch activists?
R: Both. We had all the usual internal strife, including leadership problems, and the difficulties of working with volunteers. Then again there were a lot more women than men involved (*comme toujours*), and some of the men reacted very negatively to that.

And major differences emerged very early on between the English and European movements. England is of course an island, and has evolved its own brand of gay activism which — this is a generalisation but I think quite a valuable one — is far advanced of European politics in anti-racist and disability matters, but less radical, less sophisticated, on issues of sexuality. Two incidents caused particular problems, both connected with the Stop The Clause European Tour. This tour was a roving busload of activists who went all over Europe in the late summer of 1988, mobilising support and raising funds for the campaign. But even before the tour started there was a big row over its publicity poster, which was produced in Amsterdam. It was a very arty photo-montage of five naked people: two women, two men, and one transsexual holding a globe. The English delegation objected violently to this poster, saying it couldn't possibly be distributed, especially in the UK. There were three reasons for their protest. Firstly, that all the figures represented were white, young, thin and able-bodied. As I said before, this kind of political analysis has simply not advanced in Europe as it has in Britain. Secondly, they were scared that images of nudity would confirm society's view of homosexuality as being essentially to do with sexual activity: the Dutch thought this ridiculous, and it confirmed their view of the British gay scene as far too conservative artistically, politically and sexually. Finally, the UK contingent were adamant that transsexuality was not acceptable, and this really created a lot of bad feeling, as the transsexual in question was one of the main organisers of the campaign. Some of the Dutch took this very personally, feeling that the British were not willing to show reciprocal support for a hardworking ally, that their stance showed no respect or gratitude. The Dutch scene is far more libertarian, you know, it tends to embrace bisexuals, transsexuals and other 'sexual outlaws' in a way which you don't find in Britain.

The tour itself ran into bad trouble when it reached Stockholm. They arrived at the Pride Club tired and dusty after the long drive from Copenhagen, to find no refreshments or hospitality laid on. So there was bad feeling from the start: the tourists resentful of the Swedes, who looked down on them as a bunch of grubby anarchists. During the evening disco a British lesbian stole a half-empty bottle of whisky from behind the bar, and was caught. She finally settled the row by offering to pay for a new bottle, but then the police turned up and a scuffle ensued. Three British women were thrown through the bookshop window, arrested, taken into custody and treated rather badly. The tour went on without them, but all the heart had gone out of it. Although the European lesbian and gay community were angry at the police brutality, there was a widespread feeling that the women had behaved very stupidly, jeopardising themselves, their hosts, and the tour. Indeed, when I visited the Pride Club recently, I got talking to a gay man who had been present that night and remembered it with anger and disgust. 'They got what they deserved,' he told me, and that, I'm afraid, is what will be remembered of the European Tour.

To sum up, what was the legacy of Clause 28 for Dutch society?
R: Our initial fear that the Clause would spread proved to

be unfounded. Now there is a general consensus in the Netherlands that Britain is an economic backwater, and that Thatcher really can't be taken seriously — due in no small part to her resistance to British assimilation into the European Community. In fact, I would go so far as to say that there is almost a feeling of relief here that Clause 28 is associated with someone so widely discredited.

I hope that the international outcry over Clause 28 will make the British reactionaries think twice before making any new attacks on you. Certainly we were delighted at the public support we gained in Amsterdam, which really established as accepted fact that Clause 28 could not happen here. The general population has no stomach for such blatant bigotry, and the lesbian and gay communities would fight all the way to protect the limited freedoms we enjoy here.

Friends Over the Water

Gerard V.

(Gerard V. is the pseudonym of a Dutch gay activist.)

Despite years of gay struggle, not all West European governments have a positive regard for homosexuality. There are anti-discrimination laws in France and Germany, and discriminatory laws in Austria and Finland. Some countries, like Italy, have no explicit mention of homosexuality in their legislature, while others, like Germany and Ireland, do not acknowledge lesbian sexuality.

Governmental response to AIDS has also been varied, with some countries depicting the illness as a 'gay disease'. In a number of countries (like the Netherlands and Denmark) this tendency is modified by the emphasis on 'risk groups', including heterosexuals and drug addicts in prevention policy. In Sweden, government prevention policy has been directed to heterosexuals, so that the gay movement has had to look for its own information. The quality of advice on prevention also varies enormously: from the recommendation of safer sex and condom use (the Netherlands, Denmark), to the promotion of a monogamous lifestyle and the erosion of hard-won freedoms (Belgium, Italy).

Societal mentality is also an important factor in the quality of life experienced by lesbians and gay men, determining their ability to find work, accommodation and education. In many countries the majority of the population is intolerant of homosexuality. Even the recognised 'tolerant' societies of Denmark, Sweden, France and the Netherlands have not eradicated discrimination and violence against homosexual women and men.

In 1988 there were regional and national organisations promoting the interests of homosexual women and men in every country in Western Europe. After a period of blossoming in the 1970s, during which time homosexuals came into the public eye and fought militantly for their rights, the majority of gay organisations became institutionalised. Their main aim was acceptance and the assimilation of homosexuality into heterosexual society: their main tool was negotiation with the government.

Dependent on governmental funding and reluctant to lose establishment goodwill, these groups often came to rely on governments with extremely negative attitudes to homosexuality. Their acceptance of financial dependency and political negotiation led to constant adaptation and concession-making, delaying yet further the achievement of equality by an active homosexual movement. Even among lesbian and gay groups which resisted such institutionalisation, spirited resistance has been drained by lack of perspective, in-fighting, and exhaustion of energy, money and inspiration.

From the moment that Clause 28 appeared for discussion in the British Parliament, there was massive protest against this new law. Activists, artists and politicians

It Couldn't Happen Here

joined forces in opposition: a conference in Sheffield planned a Stop The Clause European Benefit Tour, to promote the organisation, co-operation and solidarity of lesbian and gay movements in Europe, and direct action protests were widespread. But despite the strength and size of the protest, the campaign against Clause 28 has certainly failed.

There are a number of reasons for this failure. In the first place, the British homosexual movement was badly organised and severely divided when Clause 28 appeared: there was no national organisation for lesbians and gays in England at the time.

Another reason was that Stop The Clause was a single-issue campaign, while Thatcherite policy pushed through a series of oppressive laws on a number of fronts, attacking homosexual women and men, but also black people, the unemployed, working women, disabled people and so on. Conservative legal reforms form an accurate mapped-out policy, designed to make the rich richer, remove from society those who are not economically useful, and idealise law, order and the family. The struggle against Clause 28 could only be effective seen within this context, and in alliance with other groups struggling against Thatcherism.

The situation in Britain appears miserable at this moment. Section 28 is a fact; but violence against homosexual women and men is getting out of hand. The fact that London gay bar owners and police officials are now cooperating on how to protect clients expresses the extent of this.

Section 28 must hold a warning for lesbians and gays elsewhere in Europe, particularly with an eye to 1992. We must prepare ourselves for the possibility that the situation for homosexual women and men will also worsen in our own countries. Section 28 is a warning of such a worsening, and we should lay the foundation of our defence now. We must fight for greater tolerance, and for legislation that protects against anti-gay discrimination, to ensure that something like Section 28 will never be brought into the rest of Europe. We must be careful that the harmonisation of individual legislatures is not achieved at the expense of those groups with little economic power. An example of this has already appeared in Holland, where the Minister of Justice refused to approve policy allowing lesbians and gays to adopt children, arguing that Holland should not deviate so far from general European policy.

While doing this we can learn from the struggle in Britain, and from the mistakes which have been made there. You simply cannot begin to talk about cooperation with other oppressed groups if the European gay movements are themselves badly organised.

We should remember that homosexuals form part of society, and they can exert their influence on the prevailing norms and values and therefore also on legislation. As long as they themselves take cover through fear of current laws and 'decent' norms, and lead, as it were, a double life, they allow society the option of discrimination and adherence to accepted morality. Those countries where public attitudes are most tolerant are those where homosexuals are most visible, and gay groups most active. All over Europe homosexuals are on the retreat from public activity: it is important that homosexual women and men do not let go of their responsibility for their own lives, as is now the case in England. They must strengthen themselves, show themselves, so that the prevailing morality is broken, so that good anti-discriminatory legislation can come to exist, so that there is no basis for the kind of developments that have occurred in Britain.

Homosexuals will have to put their struggle for tolerance and against heterosexist norms and morals in an international perspective. We need a gay movement with international contacts, so that we can inform, stimulate and support each other. This network must not be slowed down by bureaucracy, or allowed to become a 'gay elite' willing to make deals and compromises.

We have only two years in which to change the

'survival of the fittest' ideology into a social attitude which is tolerant of ethnic, political and other minority groups, and individuals who are threatened by the ruling moral standards.

Chapter 19
Porn Again

Colin Richardson

Pornography is the vice whose name we dare not speak. Every gay man I know owns something pornographic — a book, some postcards, a video — but none would ever say so. We would rather talk about art or literature. A friend of mine, should he find himself in a gay sex shop, will readily leaf through the glossy magazines, but he always puts them back on the shelf and leaves empty-handed. To buy one would be an admission of guilt. We know we should find porn utterly repellent but we cannot help finding it endlessly fascinating. We are so ashamed of ourselves that we keep quiet about the whole sorry business. It is an ominous silence; it must be broken.

Porn has never been so loved or so hated as it is now. In the United States, 1500 porn titles were released on video in 1988 compared to an annual total of around 100 in the 1970s.[1] The American gay magazine *The Advocate* reckons that US sales of gay porn videos have more than doubled in recent years.[2] It is not so easy to produce figures for Britain as so much porn is consumed illegally, but the trend is sure to mirror that of the States. In my experience, gay porn, most of it produced abroad, is increasingly widely available. In 1989, porn produced by and for lesbians in Britain appeared above ground with Sheba's publication of an anthology of 'lesbian erotic stories and poetry', *Serious Pleasure*, and the launch of the lesbian sex magazine *Quim*.

Porn Again

At the same time, anti-pornography forces are on the move again, demanding new laws. Their chances of success are looking good, because these days sex is out while law-and-order is in. A New Brutalist Conservative government has brought the moral Right in from the cold of post-60s permissive liberalism and has given it its head. Section 28 was one of the more noxious consequences of moralism's new-found influence and respectability. The Left is divided and confused in the face of such moral certitude. The Labour leadership at first welcomed Section 28, then opposed it. A number of Labour backbenchers are active in anti-pornography campaigns and are attempting to persuade the party to commit itself to new legislation. A prospective Labour government is unlikely to oppose such moves for fear of being dubbed 'the pornographer's friend'. ('We are not going to go to the wall for *Escort* and *Parade*', an 'associate' of Roy Hattersley told *The Observer*, 6th May 1990.)

Outside Parliament the pressure is being stepped up. In early 1989 the Campaign Against Pornography And Censorship (CPC) was formed. It scored a quick success in April that year, when Liberty (the National Council for Civil Liberties) voted at its AGM in favour of a CPC-sponsored motion which calls for new anti-porn legislation. Late in 1989, the Off The Shelf campaign was launched with support that ranges across the political divide. This direct action campaign aims to persuade newsagents, notably W.H. Smith, to stop stocking 'top shelf' porn magazines.

I take this personally. The top shelf is where *Gay Times* is traditionally to be found, nestling coyly next to *Penthouse*. Experience tells me that attacks on pornography quickly become attacks on the whole of lesbian and gay culture because the two are seen as one and the same. That is why we must oppose anti-porn forces in whatever guise they appear; which means being prepared to face up to pornography, to understand why we like it and why we find that so shameful.

Porn embarrasses us in part because of what we use it for. Porn's main function is to arouse. It's an aid to masturbation, hence all those jokes about the pages being stuck together. But we do not like to admit that we masturbate, because people might think that we cannot get ourselves a man or a woman of our own. To admit to using porn is to admit failure. We have a seedy image of people who use porn; men in raincoats, sleazy, pathetic inadequates who cannot get 'the real thing'. And we do not like to be associated with them. Yet, if we are honest, we know that wanking is an integral part of our sex lives. It is not a substitute for sex, it is a *kind* of sex, 'sex with someone you love', as Woody Allen once said. At last, thanks to safer sex, it is almost trendy to admit to self-abuse so long as porn had nothing to do with it.

Pornography was invented by the Victorians. They were so fascinated by sex that they elevated its study from the status of a hobby to that of a science. They invented most of the formal sex words we are now so familiar with, the better to study sex and the better to control it. The word 'pornography' was first coined in 1864 from the Greek root *porne*, meaning 'prostitute'. The *Oxford English Dictionary* gives the original definition:

> **Pornography** 1864. Description of the life, manners, etc., of prostitutes and their patrons; hence, the expression or suggestion of obscene or unchaste subjects in literature or art.[3]

From the start, the meaning of the word was loaded. Because of the connection with prostitutes, pornography means more than just the graphic depiction in words or pictures of sexual activity. The sex in porn is a particular kind of sex, that which the prostitute symbolises: sex outside marriage or the bounds of romantic love; sex as a transaction; sex with no other context than desire or reward. This was not the official Victorian view of sex nor, indeed, is it the modern line. As a result, the Victorians attempted to ban both prostitution and pornography.

Both were seen as sources of disease, bodily or spiritual, moral corruptions which were spreading throughout the land. Homosexuality, which was invented in 1869 also from a Greek root (*homo*, meaning 'same'), was seen in the same light and its male variety was banned in 1885. Pornography, prostitution and homosexuality continue to be seen as variations on a theme to this day, something we implicitly acknowledged when we adopted the word 'gay' as our own. For, as Neil Bartlett points out, that nice little word was corrupted long before we got our sticky fingers on it. He quotes the *New English Dictionary* of 1897-1900, a forerunner of the *OED*:

> **Gay** addicted to social pleasures and dissipations. Often euphemistically: of loose or immoral life. hence in slang use of a woman leading an immoral life, living by prostitution.[4]

Because it makes public that which should stay hidden, pornography is widely considered to be a form of sexual propaganda. And because it seeks to arouse, porn eroticises immorality which makes it especially dangerous to those who worry about these things. The fleshly temptations of porn pose a threat to public morality and so the law steps in. British law in this area is roughly based on the liberal precept that immorality may only be tolerated so long as it remains a wholly private matter. Ever since the 'permissive' sixties, the moral Right has been concerned that the distinctions between public and private morality have become blurred. The Conservative government has been sympathetic to these concerns and has launched a fierce rhetorical offensive against social liberalism, initiating or supporting measures designed to police the moral boundaries. Section 28 was thus in perfect tune with the times. By equating our culture with pornography it threw a *cordon sanitaire* around us and all our works so as to safeguard the public, of whom we are not considered part, from our corrupting influence.

It is remarkable how similarly the law treats both homosexuality and pornography. Just as it is not illegal to own porn, nor is it illegal to be lesbian or gay (unless you are a man under 21); but the rights of both porn and lesbian and gay people to exist are strictly limited. A number of laws, many of them based on principles of 'obscenity', 'indecency' and 'offence' are designed to prevent the distribution or display of homosexuality in the same way as porn is constrained. To make one's homosexuality public is to risk accusations of 'flaunting', of 'behaviour likely to cause a breach of the peace', of intent to corrupt, 'persistent importuning' or of 'gross indecency'.

Since the late 1970s there has been a marked tightening of the laws which regulate public order, public morality and porn in particular. Child porn was outlawed in 1978. Between 1981 and 1982 three Acts were passed which, taken together, give local authorities powers to license and control the siting of sex shops and cinemas. Indecent material may only be displayed in licensed sex shops which have no window display and cannot be seen into from the street, do not admit people under 18 years of age and which carry a warning sign to this effect over the door.

If ordinary newsagents want to display such material, they may only do so in a specially marked-off section of the shop, according to the Indecent Displays (Control) Act 1981. This suggests that the likes of *Playboy*, *Mayfair* and so on are not considered indecent by the law (or, at least, their covers are not, for only that part of the material which is 'exposed to view' is covered by this particular law). The existence of the 'top shelf', however, implies a certain uneasiness about this. Licensing thus gives some 'protection' to the general public but it offers no immunity to the retailer. Zipper, a gay sex shop in North London, has a licence but has been raided on numerous occasions by the Obscene Publications Squad.

The Video Recordings Act 1984 was intended to

Porn Again

outlaw the 'video nasties' which were causing such a panic at the time, by making it illegal to distribute films on video which have not received a certificate from the British Board of Film Classification. Most of the video nasties which gave rise to the Act have passed this test with flying colours, whilst most porn fails. The year after this Act was passed, Tory MP Winston Churchill tried to extend the scope of the Obscene Publications Act so that it would apply to television. The chief effect of his Bill would have been the banning of almost all images of homosexuality from the small screen. Though his Bill failed, the government has found another means to the same end. The 'taste and decency' clauses of the BBC and ITA charters are considered to be too weak by the moral tendency of the Conservative Party. Channel 4 has been a constant provocation with its film seasons, Gordon in 'Brookside', and 'Out On Tuesday', a whole series devoted to showing the world what respectable and cultured citizens we are. The BBC has let the side down too, what with 'EastEnders', 'Oranges Are Not The Only Fruit', and all. So, as part of its deregulation of television, the government has established a new TV watchdog, the Broadcasting Standards Council (BSC), to assume custodianship of the nation's morals.

The BSC will retrospectively censor the output of all mainland TV stations, but will have no jurisdiction over programmes beamed in by satellite from abroad. I call it retrospective censorship because the BSC will not preview programmes and has no powers to ban programmes. Instead, it will watch programmes as they are broadcast, along with the rest of us, and then pronounce on their suitability (or lack of it). It is clever because it effectively means that the broadcasters will have to censor themselves. With Sir William Rees-Mogg, who is on record as abjuring both pornography and homosexuality, at its head, the priorities of the BSC are already clear.

Not all the recent demands for new laws to deal with pornography have come from the moral Right. Feminist writings on sex and sexuality since the sixties have developed a powerful indictment of porn for its depiction of men's oppression of women. Because it portrays male dominance and, on occasion, male violence in a sexual context, porn, in this view, is far from being harmless smut. To some feminists, such as Andrea Dworkin,[5] pornography is a major cause of women's oppression; it *is* violence against women or, as the old slogan has it, 'porn is the theory, rape is the practice.' Other feminists, Rosalind Coward for instance,[6] oppose such a brutal cause-and-effect view of pornography. Rather, they argue that pornography has established the conventions by which we understand sexualised images of women as images of submission, images which invite violence. This pornographic genre is not confined to porn itself, but spreads through our culture from advertising through bodice-ripping fictions to soap operas. Porn, in other words, plays a part in conditioning our view of sexual roles and their relative importance. Despite their differences, both views tend to support a tightening of the law on pornography.

This raised a problem of definition: what exactly *is* porn for the purposes of any law? Some argue for a distinction between soft and hard porn; others for a distinction between erotica and pornography. Many dispense with such niceties, arguing that porn is porn however you look at it. Even those who attempt to split the difference are not too fussy about where the line is drawn. Take this from a *Spare Rib* interview with Catherine Itzin, founding member of the Campaign Against Pornography And Censorship (CPC), which prides itself on a definition of pornography which would leave 'erotica' untouched by any new law. Asked by Shaila Shah, 'Would the political approach you have outlined to what is largely heterosexual pornography apply to gay male or lesbian pornography?', Itzin replied:

> 'I actually don't know; I am not familiar with it. However, it's a very important issue and must be addressed properly. At the moment, we do not have the resources, knowledge or understanding with which to do so. But

from what little I do know of it, my understanding is that it basically dramatises the same power relationships, and so seems to appeal to the same inequalities. And it can't by definition be about sexual liberation simply because it duplicates and exploits those same power relationships.'[7]

In opposition to such worrying and cavalier approaches to the subject of pornography, a new group was launched towards the end of 1989. Feminists Against Censorship (FAC), in the words of group member Mary McIntosh, rejects the view:

'that somehow pornography is the root cause of oppression and that if you eliminated it, you would reduce the amount of violence against women. Pornographic images of women reflect the pattern of social relationships in which men are dominant and privileged, so that is what you really need to attack, not the images.'[8]

Linda Semple of FAC makes another important point:

'We think these campaigns (against porn) are forgetting one of the main points of the women's liberation movement, which is the right of women to make their own sexual definition ... We feel there is a very important place for sexually explicit material in women's lives. One of the main themes of lesbian feminism of the last years has been trying to create a forum in which women can talk about sex, feel happy about sex, and consume sexually explicit material without guilt.'[9]

Sexual images *can* be about liberation, which is why the moral Right wants to ban them. But it is almost impossible to produce such images without someone raising the cry, 'pornography'. Opposing censorship therefore leads us into the position of defending pornography. This is such a horrifying thought that most of us would rather not think about it. However, I believe that it is unavoidable if we are to have any hope of defending what is ours. So let us look at what pornography means to us.

Pornography tells the story of our lives. The language it uses seems very familiar, but it has other meanings. We have had to rethink sex, and our porn — however imperfectly — reflects this. Our sex is sex between people of the same gender, which automatically removes the actual or symbolic inequalities deriving from gender difference. The principle that sex is about masculine and feminine, fucker and fuckee, does not necessarily apply. And when it does we make it explicit that this is a matter of choice and consent. We ritualise it, make a game out of it and name it: butch and femme; top and bottom. We are used to seeing things differently. We grew up in a heterosexual culture which banishes positive images of homosexuality. So we read between the lines, take our own meanings from the books and films we are allowed access to and call it camp. Our first images of sex are heterosexual images, but we can still enjoy them. I remember when I first saw simulated sex on TV, putting myself in the place of the woman, the man on top of me. Lesbian and gay porn frees our imagination from such trickery. When I watch a gay video I can imagine myself as any or all of the participants, or just sit back and enjoy being a voyeur. When I look at a picture of a naked man, I can think like Richard Dyer: 'I'd like to feel that man and I'd like to be that man.'[10] Lesbian and gay sex porn demands to be looked at differently. It repays the compliment. Pornography is the only place we can create our own images of lesbian and gay sex which celebrate its joy and beauty. As John Preston, the American gay porn writer, puts it, for gay men:

> 'The first step toward personal and communal liberation is unlearning those lessons of socialisation which made our cocks and asses dirty. The acceptance of our bodies, the unhindered celebration of our sexuality and the act of loving other men spiritually, romantically, and *physically* is the necessary first step toward liberation. Anything that helps to free our repressed selves — including pornography — has a positive value.'[11]

Our porn challenges the received myths about our love-making, as Gillian Rodgerson pointed out when she argued that lesbians need to produce their own because 'then the myth that all lesbian sex is two women lounging around waiting for a man to join them, might finally be exploded.'[1 2]

In this way, our porn helps us to come out. My own experience was much like that described by Gregg Blachford:

> 'I remember the very exciting feeling I got when I first saw one of these magazines before I came out. There I saw men kissing and holding and loving each other; something that I never thought possible as the mainstream culture manifests itself in overwhelmingly heterosexual and macho terms. It was proof of a homosexual community and it was through porn that I learned of its existence.'[1 3]

Porn can teach us about the simple mechanics of lesbian and gay sex. It allows us to explore our fantasies and to accept our sex as natural. It enables us to produce images of sex that would otherwise be absent. In the end, porn matters to us because sex matters to us so much. As Preston says:

> 'One of the reasons we constantly return to sex is — I think — that we are always needing to know if this is enough to justify what we go through because of it. Often that's an emotional issue; are these emotions worth it? But because the repercussions are so enormous it becomes a political and social issue as well.'[1 4]

Now, in the age of AIDS, porn means more to us than ever before. Pornographic imagery has been crucial to the success of safer-sex campaigns. Simon Watney refers to the effects of videos produced by Gay Men's Health Crisis in New York, which eroticise the use of condoms as a form of 'pornographic healing'.[1 5] It is no accident that Watney cites an American example, because the self-same videos are illegal here. To import them is to take a huge risk. A friend of mine found this out when he brought a video back with him after a long weekend in Amsterdam. Naturally, he was stopped by British Customs; what gay men returning from Amsterdam (or San Francisco, or ...) is not? Although he had removed all trace of labelling from the cassette the Duty Men were not fooled. They keep a video cassette player nearby for just such an eventuality. They declared the video to be obscene, confiscated it and imposed an on-the-spot fine on my friend. When he protested they threatened to tell his employers. As a gay teacher, he had too much to lose, so he paid up. Even without the threat to his job, he had little choice. Had he contested the Customs Officers' decision, who would have supported him?

It is the same with printed material: questions have even been asked in Parliament. A Tory MP called on the government to 'take steps to cease the distribution by the Citizens' Advice Bureau in Wimbledon of the pamphlet *Sex*, published by the Terrence Higgins Trust, in view of its explicit promotion of exclusively homosexual activities.'[16] The Vice Squad have taken their cue and there have been reports of seizures of safer-sex literature on the grounds that it is obscene; e.g. 'Vice Squad rejects "crude" AIDS leaflet' (*The Guardian*, 15th April 1986).

They do things differently abroad. Gay bars show porn videos, many of which carry an explicit safer-sex message. In some countries, such as the Netherlands, the government has funded such videos. Explicit printed material, which makes what is available here look tame, is also widely available.

In Britain, the government has yet to place its safer-sex advertising aimed at 'men who have sex with men' in non-gay publications, thus by-passing those men who do not identify as gay and so are least likely to be well-informed because of their minimal contact with the gay scene. It remains the case in this country that safer-sex adverts which use pornographic imagery are largely produced by gay organisations and are confined to the gay press. Mainstream newspapers, many of which refuse to recognise that AIDS affects heterosexuals, will not touch them. This is a tragedy because the evidence suggests that 'pornographic healing' works. Certainly, the iceberg-and-tombstone approach, which relies on fear to get the message across, has proved to be a disastrous failure. The boom in the production and consumption of porn has a lot to do with AIDS. In the United States, the porn industry has started to come to terms with its new responsibilities. So many porn stars have died from AIDS that producers now insist on safer-sex techniques in the making of videos. A number of commercially produced porn videos now make the use of condoms explicit although, as *The Advocate* reported, some producers argue that there is still a place for fantasy, a release from the demands of real life.[17] In this view, people do not directly act out what they see on screen, but treat porn as a means of wish fulfilment. Both approaches have their place.

Writers of porn in the States have also been quick to acknowledge their role in helping us to face the epidemic. In 1985 Alyson Publications published *Hot Living*, a book of 'Erotic Stories about Safer Sex' edited by John Preston. This was the first book to explore in graphic terms the erotic possibilities of safer sex. Alyson followed this up with two books by Max Exander, *Safestud* and *Lovesex*. Although badly written and fairly unimaginative, they pass the 'wet test' in their descriptions of safer sex. This is why porn is uniquely placed to promote safer-sex messages, by giving the reader/viewer instant feedback. Preston again:

> 'Writing about sex is one of the best ways to inform the gay world about itself, including issues with which it should be concerned and potential problems it might face.'[18]

Lesbian and gay porn of any sort, let alone that which deals with safer sex, is not easy to obtain here. Very little of it is home-produced; it is nearly all imported, which is illegal. British law already places strong restrictions on pornography. Pornography is not defined as such by law, instead it applies standards of 'obscenity' and 'indecency'. Obscenity is the narrower test, referring to material which would tend to 'deprave and corrupt' those who actually seek it out and use it. The material must also be judged as a whole and in context. Indecency is a much broader and more widely used category of offence. It defines material which 'any reasonable person' (a judge, for example) would find 'shocking, disgusting and revolting', as Lord Denning the then Master of the Rolls defined it in 1976. The law allows enormous scope for interpretation and those who interpret are not friends of ours. Generally speaking, it is not illegal to possess pornography (except child porn) for personal use. But it is illegal to import it, send it through the post or display it to the general public. In Scotland, actual distribution or display must be shown to have occurred, whereas in England and Wales it is enough merely to establish 'intent'.

Censorship of pornography is already here. We have seen the future and we know how it will work. Because so little lesbian or gay pornography is produced in this country, HM Customs & Excise play a large part in the policing of our lives. The same powers which took my friend's video away from him at the airport and threatened his livelihood into the bargain, have routinely been used against our whole culture. The raid on Gay's The Word bookshop in 1984 was merely the largest and best publicised exercise in State censorship this decade. In the same year, other bookshops, mail order firms (one of which went bust as a result) and the International Feminist Book Fair were affected too, as lesbian and gay literature was seized en masse. Although the charges against Gay's The Word were eventually dropped, Customs' raids and seizures continue in smaller ways; Gay's The Word was able to win through because of its prestige as a well respected and established bookshop. The liberal literary establishment came to its aid. The individual gay man, arrested because of his video collection, is on his own. In the same way, it is possible to screen explicit safer-sex videos from abroad at the Institute for Contemporary Arts (ICA) as part of a one-off cultural event, but not on a routine basis to punters in gay bars. I know one gay bar in London which used occasionally to screen porn videos, including safer-sex videos, but that has stopped after discreet pressure from the local nick.

Even Art is losing its protective powers. Gay artist Philip Core died whilst fighting in court the Customs seizure of materials he had sent to his London home during a trip to America. The materials included a book on sale in this country, *Tom of Finland: A Retrospective*, personally inscribed to Core by the author. Core's defence relied on the claim that the materials were for artistic purposes, a defence recognised in British law. However, in a judgement with frightening implications, the magistrate rejected pleas to consider the materials in context or to take into account their intended purpose as artistic source material. Instead, he applied a narrow dictionary definition of the term obscene as that which is 'lewd, filthy and loathsome', and ordered the materials to be destroyed.[19]

Unless we are prepared to defend it ourselves we will stay forever at the mercy of the moralists, their inquisitions and their laws. It is easy to keep quiet — who wants to be thought of as someone with dirty habits or as a woman-hater? It is easy to get angry at some of the images produced in the name of sexual gratification and to imagine that the answer to our rage is to ban these images. To do so is to forget our history too easily.

Moralist and anti-porn campaigns are nothing new. In late Victorian Britain, the law-makers were gripped by a clean-up fervour, not unlike what is happening today, which sought to make the country safe for women, children and the family. The result was the total criminalisation of male homosexuality and the trial of Oscar Wilde. Obscenity laws were used in the 1920s to ban Radclyffe Hall's book, *The Well of Loneliness*. In the 1950s, anti-Communism and the ideology of the nuclear family combined to put women back in the kitchen and to launch a series of prosecutions of gay men which amounted to mass persecution.

Evidence suggests that the fifties are back with a

vengeance. Recent research by GALOP (the Gay London Policing Group), *Him* magazine, *Capital Gay* and *Gay Times* shows that in 1989, police in England and Wales arrested more men for consensual sex ('indecency between males') than in any other year this century save for 1954 and 1955.[20] This is no accident; it seems likely that it results from a deliberate policy decision taken somewhere on high.

Lives have been ruined because people have read the wrong books or looked at the wrong pictures. As I write, *Gay Times* reports:

> Eighteen homes raided in nationwide Customs clampdown. Customs & Excise officers launched a dramatic series of raids last month on the homes of gay men throughout Britain after finding their names and addresses in a Dutch contact magazine. A number of men have already been charged with a range of offences and at least two men received heavy fines when they appeared in court last month, charged with 'importing obscene material'. Other men will appear in court this month.[21]

One of the arrested men subsequently committed suicide.[22]

Now we need more than ever to remind ourselves of what Ellen Willis has written:

> The basic purpose of obscenity laws is and always has been to reinforce cultural taboos on sexuality and suppress feminism, homosexuality and other forms of sexual dissidence. No pornographer has ever been punished for being a woman-hater, but not too long ago information about female sexuality, contraception and abortion was assumed to be obscene. In a male supremacist society the only obscenity law that will not be used against women is no law at all.[23]

Pornography serves to divide and contain us. Because we define ourselves by our sexuality we are automatically considered 'immoral' and 'obscene' by the rest of society. But precisely because of that, sex and sexual representations are important to us, and so we cannot allow a simple-minded anti-pornography consensus to stifle us. Pornography means more than most people would have us believe, but the word has become so weighed down with negative associations that we tend to shy away from it. We try to talk about what we like as erotica, but no-one can agree, one person's erotica being another's porn. We try to pretend that sex isn't so important, that we are just like everyone else, just as we sought to distance ourselves from books like *The Milkman's On His Way* during the Section 28 debates. It didn't wash, and we lost. We cannot tell our stories without talking dirty or without shocking or offending someone.

So I think, like Ellen Willis, that 'it would be clearer and more logical simply to acknowledge that some sexual images are offensive and some are not.'[2][4] We should recognise that sexual imagery can challenge as much as uphold prevailing sexual orthodoxies and that the law has no place in deciding what is good and what is bad, because it will always get it wrong. By allowing the open production and distribution of explicit sexual imagery, we are taking the risk that some of the images produced will be unacceptable. But only by allowing such openness can we effectively establish any kind of good practice. We need to be able to show that being explicit about sex is not inherently bad or damaging, that the pornographic view of sex is not the only one. Censorship merely confirms the view that sex is dirty and must be hidden away, out of sight and — cross fingers — out of mind.

But it doesn't work like that: we live in a society where pornography takes most of the burden of talking about sex and where talking about sex is considered pornographic. So sex education becomes crucially important, but while the 1986 Education Act and Section 28 remain in place, sex education in Britain will consist of little more than a hymn to family life, largely devoid of any education about sex. Only with the repeal of these measures, the abolition of all laws based upon precepts of 'obscenity' and 'indecency', and the opening up of the narrow, prescriptive sexual teachings insisted upon by the moralists, can we get on and live our lives, talk about our desires and argue about them without feeling ashamed or guilty. The fight against censorship starts in our own heads.

Postscript

Since I started to work on this chapter somewhere back in early 1989 a lot has happened. My original purpose in writing this was to warn of the dangers of censorship and to provoke debate in the lesbian and gay communities. Debate is now starting to take place in both the lesbian and gay and the straight press; the advocates of censorship are not going unchallenged. Significantly, following lobbying by Feminists Against Censorship amongst others, Liberty narrowly voted at its 1990 AGM to reverse the position adopted a year earlier in favour of anti-pornography legislation. Lesbian and gay speakers played an important part in the debate.

There will undoubtedly be more battles like this in the coming years, whether or not the Conservatives hold on to power. Censorship will continue to threaten Britain's lesbian and gay communities from within as well as from without. But I hope that the debate will not rest there. We have spent so long fighting against a political tide which is pushing us ever backwards that it is a victory just to stand still. The nineties have yet to prove themselves a kinder and gentler decade, but that should not stop us from looking forward again. It is time to promote ourselves and if that makes us pornographers, too bad.

Porn Again

Acknowledgements

With grateful thanks to Philip Derbyshire for his valuable comments and criticisms and for the loan of so many of his books; Tara and Paul for their patience; Becky Gardener, Mark McNestry, Ian McIntyre and Lizzy Owen for listening, arguing and encouraging; and my mother, Molly Richardson, for her understanding and her typing.

Notes

1. *Sunday Correspondent*, 5th November 1989.
2. 'Changing Times for Gay Erotic Videomakers: Growing Markets and New Expectations in Age of AIDS' from Henry Fenwick, *The Advocate* No.491, 2nd February 1988.
3. *Oxford English Dictionary*
4. 'Who Was That Man? A Present for Mr Oscar Wilde', Serpent's Tail, 1988.
5. See 'Pornography: Men Possessing Women' by Andrea Dworkin, Women's Press, 1981.
6. See 'Sexual Violence and Sexuality' from Rosalind Coward (ed.) 'Sexuality: A Reader', *Feminist Review*, Virago, 1987.
7. 'Fighting Pornography' from *Spare Rib* No.201., May 1989.
8. Quoted in 'Should Pornography Come Off The Shelf?' from *The Guardian*, 15th February 1990.
9. *The Guardian* op.cit.
10. 'A Conversation About Pornography' by Richard Dyer, from *Coming on Strong — Gay Politics and Culture*, eds. Simon Shepherd and Mick Wallis, Unwin Hyman, 1989.
11. 'Goodbye Sally Gerhart', reprinted in *The View from Christopher Street*, Chatto, 1984.
12. 'Images for Action' by Gillian Rodgerson, from *Gay Times*, August 1989.
13. 'Looking At Pornography' by Gregg Blachford, from *Pink Triangles*, ed. Pam Mitchell, Alyson Publications, 1980.
14. 'On Writing Pornography', epilogue to *I Once Had A Master*, Alyson Publications, 1984.
15. *Policing Desire* by Simon Watney, Comedia, 1987.
16. *Hansard*, 17th February 1988, quoted by Simon Watney in

    Taking Liberties — AIDS and Cultural Politics, eds Simon Watney, Serpent's Tail, 1989.
17. 'Changing Times for Gay Erotic Videomakers' from *The Advocate*, op.cit.
18. 'On Writing Pornography', Preston, op.cit.
19. See the report in *Gay Times*, February 1990. Philip Core died on 12th November 1989, several days after he appeared in court and before the verdict was announced.
20. 'Sex Arrests Hit 34-Year High' from *Capital Gay*, 18th May 1990.
21. *Gay Times*, February 1990.
22. *Capital Gay*, 2nd February 1990.
23. 'Feminism, Moralism and Pornography' by Ellen Willis, from *Desire — the Politics of Sexuality*, eds. Ann Snitow, Christine Stansell and Sharon Thompson, Virago, 1983.
24. Willis, op.cit.

Chapter 20
New Year Revolutions

Debby Klein

This article first appeared in the *Pink Paper*, 1989.

January 1st
Today I became a radical lesbian Separatist. Last night at a party in Clapham I met Snowater Clitwomon for the first time. One look into those icy blue eyes and my political position did a somersault. I offered her my body and she dismissed me as a liberal, male-identified gay girl. Ha!

January 2nd
I feel like a new wombyn. I may be still penniless and unsuccessful, but it is not my fault. It's such a relief to know that everything in the world including war, pollution, my novel not being published (or written), modern architecture and salmonella in eggs can be blamed on men. For the first time in my life I am living in a guilt-free zone.

January 3rd
This morning I rang Snowater and persuaded her to come over tomorrow and enlighten me on the more subtle aspects of separatist ideology. Spent the evening in tremulous anticipation. Watched 'Mildred Pierce' and ate a box of Milk Tray. I must stop eating chocolate.

January 4th
Snowater proves difficult to seduce. Last night she

refused chilled champagne on the grounds that consumption of alcohol dulls her capacity for revolutionary anger. We drank hibiscus tea and Snowater said she looked forward to our spiritual bonding. So, of course, did I.

January 5th
Subtlety is obviously a male-centred way of thinking. Snowater is so thrillingly dogmatic. She says all men are the enemy. 'What about my friend Raymond?' I retorted. Snowater suggested I replace the word 'man' with 'prick' or 'woman-killer' and remember the times when Raymond had been abusive. I thought hard and dredged up an incident last year when he borrowed my best party frock and it came back covered in nasty little stains, which he swore was lighter fuel. 'Ah yes,' said Snowater, 'talking of frocks ...'

January 6th
This afternoon, Snowater has disposed of all the 'oppressive' items in my wardrobe. Then she threw out my make-up. I look into the mirror and wonder how I'll live the rest of my life without mascara.

January 7th
Snowater agreed to spend the night! I told her three of my favourite sexual fantasies to put her in the mood. It did, but it was the wrong mood. Apparently all my fantasies are sick, twisted, perverted and anti-lesbian, and that's even before we get to the good bits.

January 8th
Snowater is 're-educating' me about sex. Penetration (by anything) is out. Lying on top of each other is out. Bondage and toys are definitely out. Any sort of touching which implies a power relationship is out. After I had renounced my odious past, Snowater agreed to come to bed. We held hands passionately ...

January 9th
Saw Raymond today and told him he was a Prick and a

New Year Revolutions

Womanhater. If Snowater hadn't assured me that men don't have feelings, I could have sworn he looked upset.

January 10th
My address book now resembles the aftermath of a Stalinist purge. Snowater says I will only find true support among the bosoms of my separatist sisters.

January 20th
I have been transformed. I have turned my back on Hollywood movies, Annie Lennox, Puccini, Chocolate, Doris Lessing and 'Brookside'. They are all products of a wymyn-hating culture. I have begun reading wimmons poetry and last week I went to a conference and Snowater showed me how to spot the enemy within. Tonight I am joining Snowater on the picket of an undesirable night-club. I've just finished polishing my boots; the morally perfect don't need mascara. Must rush as I'm meeting Snowater at the Ball And Chain in half an hour. How I love our Nights on the Town.

Continuing the Confessions of A Girl About Town 'Boys Will be Boys'

February 1st
I am through with separatism! Snowater is doing it with Marigold Womblove: a woman whose sense of humour has been surgically removed and who looks like the back end of a labyris. Snowater accused me of being looksist. I suggested looksist was 'wombynspeak' for honest. I have been excommunicated from the sisterhood.

February 2nd
Decided to stop listening to Patsy Cline and get politically active. Rang Raymond, who told me to come along to tomorrow's meeting of a new vibrant group called Lesbian And Gay Men Intent On Creating Solidarity Between Different Factions Of The Gay Community, or L.G.M.I.O.C.S.B.D.F.G.C. Doesn't exactly roll off the

tongue, but Raymond assures me it will be challenging.

February 4th
Was late for the meeting as my mother phoned, convinced I was dead. Was still taking down her recipe for Chicken Soup at ten to eight. Arrived at the upstairs room of the Pie And Chicken to find fifteen gay men sitting amongst empty beer crates talking about sex. The Queen Mother at an orgy couldn't have had more dramatic effect. Fifteen pairs of lips clamped shut over the words 'cock size'. I flashed Raymond one of my best 'I'll get you for this later' looks and slunk into a corner. However, invisibility is not the lot of a 'token', I was aurally accosted by impassioned speeches on how hard they'd tried not to be a male-dominated group. Where had they gone wrong? I told the assembled throng that if I'd wanted to spend my time absolving guilt, I'd have run for Pope. Nobody laughed.

February 6th
Raymond rang beseeching me not to give up on L.G.M.I.O.C.S.B.D.F.G.C. He promised there would be some more lesbians at the next meeting. From the tone of his voice it sounded as though he had personally gone out on safari and netted them. Told me the latest gossip. *Capital Gay* is being taken over by *Gardener's Weekly* and the LLGC [Lesbian and Gay Centre] is being financed by a member of the Royal Family — usual stuff.

February 10th
A long meeting. Raymond had recruited one other dyke and a transsexual. We're organising a benefit for the group. Problems with the cabaret. 'Starturns' (a lesbian band) have been asked to perform, but want ten pounds each expenses! Philip offered them their return bus fare to Hackney, saying this was their chance to put something back into the Gay Community who have supported all their gigs. They were very rude and now they're not appearing. Performers are so temperamental. Stacey (the other dyke) says she's got a friend who will read her

poetry and doesn't even need her bus fare. The boys agreed to organise another act. In a fit of butch affection I volunteered to be bouncer.

February 20th
The benefit was last night. I am now in hiding. Personally I blame the whole fiasco on Raymond's home brew: I sold twenty barrels. Stacey's poet friend was not a success. During her fifty-minute rendition in free verse of the intricacies of her monthly cycle, thirteen men walked out, one passed out, and the rest indulged in some rather unbrotherly sneering. Top billing went to 'Divine Desiree' who sported false tits and a lurex mini skirt strategically covering a leather jockstrap. He mimed to Kylie Minogue. Among howls of 'Get him off' from the women, two dykes made a surprise attack on his falsies, and assorted faggots leapt into the fray. I had no idea who to start bouncing so I caught the last bus home.

February 21st
I'm not answering the phone. Raymond left a message saying that Stacey and Philip have been arrested for breach of the peace, and did I want to get involved in their defence campaign. The boy's a fool.

Afterword

On 12th July, 1990 the Princess of Wales gave a speech to the right-wing, anti-feminist, anti-abortion, homophobic delegates attending the International Congress For The Family, in Brighton. As she sat down, the stage was invaded by a number of lesbians and one gay man, from Brighton Area Action Against Section 28. They handed the Princess a leaflet, and paraded a banner across stage declaring 'Lesbian mothers are not pretending'.

One month earlier, the Organisation for Lesbian and Gay Action announced its demise, having never achieved its aim to unite Britain's lesbians and gays in one national campaign. Many of its activists have helped set up OutRage, a new organisation dedicated to applying the science of direct action to lesbian and gay concerns. An early victory has been the eviction of 'pretty police' from Hyde Park. In the same month, the Calcutt Enquiry's code of professional and ethical standards for newspapers proposed that the press should avoid prejudicial or pejorative references to a person's sexual orientation, or mention that orientation unless it is of direct relevance to the story. And HRH Prince Edward announced that he *isn't* gay!

More disturbingly, GALOP (the gay policing project) uncovered a sinister recriminalisation of gay sexuality, publishing statistics which showed that in 1988 over 5000 gay men were convicted under Britain's discriminatory anti-gay laws. This was the highest total since the mid-1950s, and at least three times greater than the number convicted in the three years before the 1967 Sexual Offences Act (designed to decriminalise male

Afterword

homosexuality in England and Wales).

Most of these 'crimes' have no heterosexual equivalent: others illustrate how 'neutral' police powers (like the 1986 Public Order Act) can be used to harass gay citizens. The figures include men who have kissed in the street, men who have had sex with others aged between 16 and 21 (eleven of whom received prison sentences of between eighteen months and four years), and lesbians and gays who were discharged and/or court-martialled by the armed forces (receiving prison terms of up to twelve months) for the 'crime' of being homosexual.

These figures add up to a damning portrait of officially sanctioned homophobia and victimisation. At a time when figures for reported violent crime and sexual assaults are soaring, the police are concentrating resources on victimless, often witnessless, crimes which provide an easy target for a force frustrated with its low detection rate. 'Gay crime' and violent crimes are collapsed into the amorphous category of 'sexual offences', which begs the question: 'Offences against whom?'.

All these are illustrations of the post-Clause landscape, a world in which homosexuality is more visible, more accepted, and yet more feared than ever before. And yet the political development which, above all others, exemplified the discourse which underpinned Clause 28 has been largely neglected: it was the attempt to criminalise lesbian motherhood via the Human Fertilisation and Embryology Bill.

A Storm In A Spermbank

> 'If we get the family right ... our prisons will not be bursting; our rates of abortion will not be higher than anywhere else; marriages will not break down; and divorce will not be higher than anywhere else. The cause of the problem is that marriages go wrong. I recommend that the Government focus on the cause of the problem and do not spend their life trying to shore up holes in the

dyke as they occur.'[1]

Throughout the Stop The Clause campaign, lesbian and gay activists voiced dire warnings of what was to follow: 'They'll be recriminalising homosexuality next', was the popular choice. 'They' didn't, of course. Clause 28 confirmed the suspicions of both activists and reactionaries: that the best weapon against homosexuality is not straightforward criminalisation — even after ten years of Thatcherism, that would be too much for the British liberal stomach — but by undermining homosexual representation and cultural legitimation.

Tory backbenchers had done their homework. Once again they hitched their cause onto a Government bill addressing complex, vital issues, in order to maximise confusion and political inefficiency:

> 'The Bill is appallingly constructed and worded in the most impenetrable legalistic jargon. Much like Section 28, it seeks to intimidate and add to a general climate of reaction, as well as specifically proscribe.'[2]

Once again, 'they' exploited media-orchestrated moral panic over the homosexual menace to children by discouraging the 'promotion [of] pretended family relationships'.

Their target was clinic provision of donor insemination (DI) to lesbians, a simple, low-tech method of achieving pregnancy which is practised in about six of the sixty clinics offering DI services in this country, and by countless women in the privacy of their own homes.

The *Sunday Express* spearheaded the media smear campaign in the autumn of 1989, attacking the charities PAS (Pregnancy Advisory Service) and BPAS (British Pregnancy Advisory Service) for providing non-discriminatory DI services. Ann Winterton MP then laid an Early Day Motion condemning these services as a threat to 'the status of marriage, corrupting the family unit, and leaving the ensuing children at grave risk of subsequent emotional harm', and calling on the Secretary

Afterword

of State to prohibit the provision of DI to lesbians.

A formidable cast of old enemies — David Wilshire, Dame Jill Knight, Harry Greenaway *et al* — lined up to introduce a new amendment to the Government's Human Fertilisation and Embryology Bill, aiming to criminalise any clinic which dared to help lesbians become mothers.

Eugenics and Embryos

The Human Fertilisation and Embryology Bill, which became law in late 1990, is designed to bring all embryology and assisted reproductive techniques under ethical and political control. Working from the ideological premise that stable, heterosexual couples provide the best environment for child-rearing, the Bill establishes a Statutory Licensing Authority to regulate, license and monitor the use of reproductive methods such as IVF (In Vitro Fertilisation) and DI. It will become a criminal offence — punishable by up to two years' imprisonment — for clinics to offer DI without a licence (unless the woman treated is married to her donor). Self-insemination is not prohibited.

Although regulation of private medicine is to be welcome, it should function in the interests of consumer protection, not State control. In this case, there are very real fears that compromising the autonomy of DI clinics will erode their already pitifully inadequate provision for unmarried women. Clinics will no longer be able to guarantee complete confidentiality: all records will be available for the inspection of the Licensing Authority, and a central register of sperm donors will be established. Children born as a result of assisted conception will in future be able to gain access to non-identifying genetic information about the donor. It also seems unlikely that the Licensing Authority will *not* follow routine NHS policy — and Warnock's recommendation — that DI should not be available to lesbians. In any case, the imposition of licence fees may drive out of business those very clinics which currently provide a non-discriminatory service: the non-profit-making charities.

Concern for the purity of aristocratic lineage motivated Lady Saltoun of Abernethy to introduce a number of amendments to the Bill in January 1990: among these was the prohibition of any assisted reproductive technique to unmarried women. They were narrowly defeated — by one vote — on 6th February.

The attack was taken up in the Commons by David Wilshire (nice touch!), but his success was limited despite widespread sympathy throughout the House. The Government headed the homophobes off at the pass, with a compromise amendment requiring doctors to take the future child's welfare into account when deciding whether to administer IVF or DI treatment. Wilshire managed to amend this to include 'the child's need for a father', but the Health Minister insisted that this would not necessarily exclude lesbians and single women from treatment (in practice, of course, the new Licensing Authority is likely to take a jaundiced view of lesbian appropriation of reproduction autonomy).

Why the Embryo Bill?

As a muck-raking follow-up to Clause 28, this latest attack had obvious value for our opponents. It drew upon very deep-seated public distaste for 'artificial' separation of sexuality and procreation, and 'unnatural' methods of conception. It also exploits homophobic concern to 'protect' children from non-nuclear family life, and utilises the current moral panic over the growth of single-parent families which is fuelling Government attacks on State benefits.

DI is not a widespread practice, and few would feel personally affected enough to take action on this issue — particularly in the context of concurrent attacks on abortion rights, also attached to the Embryo Bill. Many lesbians are hostile to DI clinics because they operate

Afterword

within the private sector: others oppose all reproductive technologies as an extension of the male scientific establishment's exploitation of women's bodies and appropriation of their reproduction powers.

Liberal opinion may favour toleration of some notional homosexual 'rights', may even support lesbian mothers engaged in custody battles: but deliberate conception of a child with the express intent of bringing it up in a lesbian environment will not win the support of many.

It is, of course, impossible to prevent women arranging to become pregnant: all that Lady Saltoun and friends could hope for was to restrict the options available to women. Those women who cannot, or prefer not, to self-inseminate; those women who want counselling and professional support; those women who want the donor screened and tested for HIV, syphilis and other diseases, would find another avenue of choice closed to them. Saltoun and Wilshire's amendments would have formed an additional guarantee that the reproductive freedom of unmarried women would be restricted, and that the charity clinics would be forces to withdraw DI services.

Conspiracy theories are rarely helpful, but there can be little doubt that the Embryo Bill represented an act of State appropriation of the medical establishment's control of women's bodies. The growth of legalised abortion and family planning provision in the 1960s and '70s was a clear reflection of worldwide concern over the 'population boom': in the context of the current decline in the birthrate (and racist fears of 'swamping' by the global non-white majority), we should not be surprised that these services are now facing massive cuts.

Single mothers, too, are under attack as the storm-troopers of the dreaded 'new underclass'. Ignoring the evidence that one-parent family life is not *per se* disadvantageous for children,[3] resisting the reality that traditional nuclear families are increasingly rare in our society, conservatives continue to assert that 'pretended family relationships' are directly causative of crime, poverty and moral degradation.

Inevitable, then, is this attack on donor insemination at a time when women are making changes to their traditional role within the family, and 'alternative' lifestyles are becoming increasingly visible, acceptable, and popular. Self-insemination cannot be stopped, but propaganda and legal reforms can enshrine as official doctrine the concept of lesbian and gay family life as unnatural, undesirable, and dangerous.

So why did the Government move to rein in those elements of its political constituency which were simply seeking to enshrine Tory 'pro-family' ideology in legislation?

They were mindful, no doubt, of the Liberty (the National Council For Civil Liberties) briefing which argued that adoption of such invasive, discriminatory powers would be in breach of the European Convention on Human Rights. State influence over human sexuality and reproduction is an inescapable fact of modern life, but it is usually only totalitarian regimes which seek to deny reproductive choice so flagrantly, so coercively, so abusively.

Concern was also centred on humanitarian arguments, as exemplified by Baroness Ewart-Biggs, who argued:

> '... many children have already been born by donor insemination. If this amendment were carried it would attach a retrospective stigma of criminality to the circumstances of their birth.'

Even Lord Hailsham weighed in on a point of pragmatism:

> 'There is a total anomaly about trying to prohibit AID [Artificial Insemination by Donor] by the methods of this Bill, with criminal sanctions, while refusing to go the whole hog ... in prohibiting, as the Puritans did in the seventeenth century, both adultery and fornication.'

Lesbians and Gays Fight Back

But what was our influence on this debate? What was the

Notes on Contributors

Kirsten Hearn 'I'm a 34-year-old, fat, proud, angry, blind dyke who is active in the lesbian, gay and disability communities. My recreational activities include eating, lying in hot perfumed baths, swimming, making sculptures, playing clarinet and saxophone, singing and writing songs, listening to Regency historical romances, "The Archers" and Abba.'

Savitri Hensman works at the Black Lesbian and Gay Centre, and is active in the Lesbian and Gay Christian Movement.

Tara Kaufmann was born in 1964 and grew up in South London, where she still lives. For two years she worked for LAGER (Lesbian And Gay Employment Rights), and is now public relations manager for a national charity.

Debby Klein is a writer, performer and a counsellor. She is best known as the tall red-headed half of double act 'Parker and Klein', and script-writer for their latest play 'Blood On The Lino', seen at Drill Hall Arts Centre in 1990.

Paul Lincoln was born in London in 1955, where he continues to live. His earliest involvement in gay politics was in 1982, when he was a member of London Gay Workshops. He was also a member of the London Stop The Clause campaign, and of Jews Against The Clause.

Jonathan Louw was a member of the Stop The Clause Education Group. He is also a longtime volunteer at London Lesbian and Gay Switchboard. Previously a Deputy Headmaster, he now works in local government developing HIV/AIDS and Drugs services.

Peter Nevins has lived in London since 1987. 'I work for Islington MIND and am currently training as a psychotherapist. I am a founder member of "Let's Rap", the Blackgay men's discussion group.'

Kath Pringle is an independent film editor living and working in York.

Sarah Roelofs is a lesbian feminist socialist, active in the Labour Party since 1980. Involved in Women For Socialism, the Labour Campaign for Lesbian and Gay Rights, and the Socialist Lesbian Group, she was a member of the London Labour Party Executive for over three years, until resigning in protest in 1989.

High Risk Lives

Colin Richardson Born in 1959, Colin eventually fell into film and video-making following a series of odd jobs and a long and intermittent association with the DSS. He worked for Converse Pictures Ltd, a lesbian and gay film production house, in time becoming a director of the company, and ultimately presiding over its sad demise in the wake of local government cutbacks. Colin is now a freelance writer, researcher and programme-maker.

Sue Sanders is a white, currently able-bodied lesbian who teaches part-time in a girls' school in London, where she is 'out'. She is also a psychotherapist, management consultant and trainer. She has been active in both the women's and the lesbian and gay movements for over fifteen years.

Christopher Scott was born in County Durham in the early 1960s, and educated in the Midlands. Christopher moved to London in 1982, and after qualifying as a registered nurse went on to study counselling. He has been working with people affected by HIV and AIDS since 1985 in various capacities. Christopher is actively involved in lesbian and gay politics, and is currently an undergraduate at the University of London.

Heather Smith is a working-class, Irish Socialist feminist who grew up in Blackburn, Lancashire, and now lives in London. A Sussex graduate, Heather works as a Women's Officer in local government. 'I write, take photographs, and dream of making films.'

Caroline Spry Fifteen years of working in film and television have included independent production, working as a cameraman, co-founding Cinema of Women Film distributors, and, for the last five years, commissioning programmes on Channel 4.

Carole Woddis is a freelance journalist and writer. Her work includes eight years at *City Limits* as editor for both health and theatre. She has been co-author of two books, *The Herpes Manual* and *The Bloomsbury Theatre Guide*. A third book, based on conversations with leading actresses, is due to be published by Virago in the spring of 1991.

our community's in-fighting has at times become desperate. Our response to external threat has so often been to retreat into special interest groups, batten down the hatches, lash out in fury at the easy targets. So easy to deny the amorphous nature of sexual identity, the difficulty of constructing a coherent political programme on the basis of shared sexual impulse, the self-destruction inherent in political purism. How often have we mobilised identity in an apolitical way, preferring to promote ourselves as victims of oppression in glorious isolation?

All credit, then, to the Stop The Clause campaign for achieving some form of effective coalition activism. Particularly interesting was the widespread collaboration between women and men — often women who had spent their political lives in autonomous lesbian campaigns, men who had thrived on bar culture. This was not without cost — many feminists were alarmed at the drain on feminist resources, citing analogies with the situation in AIDS work, where women rush to the rescue of their gay brothers, performing a disproportionate share of the grassroots work for little recognition or reciprocal care.

This sacrifice of separatism may have been the inevitable political price of an effective damage limitation campaign. Yet in most parts of the country the power, the exhilaration, the solidarity we found at that time have largely dissipated. The Campaign Against Clause 28 seemed a wonderful opportunity for us to build a cohesive and influential lesbian and gay movement — nearly three years on, lesbian and gay activists are as divided, as frustrated as we ever were. But perhaps it would have been unrealistic to expect the level of lesbian and gay activity spawned by the Clause to achieve any state of permanency. United by a common threat, we created a rather fragile coalition whose demise merely reflects the internal health of a fragmentary and disunited lesbian and gay movement. We are a common interest group only in our status as sexual outlaws, after all, and our ultimate aim — paradoxically — must be to make that fragile bond superfluous and irrelevant.

Afterword

response of the lesbian and gay community to this fundamental attack — protests in the streets, direct actions, arts benefits? No. A small London-based Campaign for Access to Donor Insemination struggled to win community support, but was dogged by apathy, internal strife and, at times, political naivety. Their support — and effect — was minimal.

Why did this issue not capture the lesbian and gay imagination in the way that Clause 28 did? Because it was seen as a 'women's issue'? Because we could not reconcile our support for State regulation of private medicine with our fears about State encroachment on reproductive choice? Or maybe we have internalised society's conviction that we are harmful to children, that only heterosexuals should be permitted to produce tomorrow's citizens?

Has the Stop The Clause campaign really taught us so little about how to interpret, challenge and defeat legislative attacks on our communities? It is ironic that, in the same month that the Rumanian people were celebrating their newly won liberation by legalising abortion, British lesbian and gay activists were barely noticing a sinister restriction on one of our most basic human rights.

Thriving, Surviving, Learning for the Future

Clause 28 is a yardstick for our strengths, and our failings. Its very introduction marks the extent to which lesbians and gay men have succeeded in redefining homosexuality in our terms — not as a sickness, not as a crime, but as an active and valid lifestyle choice, with community, culture and creed. No longer the pitiable image of lonely men in toilets, we had achieved a high level of public visibility, inevitably attracting both tolerance and hostility.

The Thatcher government became very adept at playing different social groups off against each other, and

NOTES ON CONTRIBUTORS

James Baaden is an American journalist and AIDS worker.

David Benedict has worked as a director, writer and actor since 1980 for companies including New End Hampstead, Solent People's Theatre, Red Shift, the National Theatre, Channel Four, and Gay Sweatshop, for whom he is Joint Artistic Director. In addition to freelance researching, he is currently writing a musical and choreographing a series of dance works.

Bob Cant became a socialist in Tanzania in the late 1960s and came out as gay in London in 1971. He was a founder member of Teachers in FE/HE Lesbian and Gay Group, a member of the Gay Left Collective, and actively involved in the struggles around Positive Images in Haringey in the mid-1980s; he co-edited, with Susan Hemmings, *Radical Records* (1988). Bob is a community worker in Wester Hailes and a volunteer on Edinburgh Gay Switchboard.

Nicola Field lives in London and is a writer, researcher and video-maker. She worked on the award-winning 'Framed Youth' and researched for 'Desire — Sexuality in Germany 1910-45' and 'Comrades In Arms', a drama/documentary about British lesbians and gays in World War II. Recently she worked on Channel 4's 'Women HIV and AIDS', and is currently developing a documentary about bisexuality and HIV. She is a member of the Aids Coalition To Unleash Power, London.

Ian Fraser was born in Scotland in 1951. He worked and travelled in the Far East 'to gain my sanity and self-confidence after British education.' Now working as a Designer for a Government Regeneration Authority.

Diane Hamer is an Australian lesbian living in London. She teaches Women's Studies and Media Studies in adult education, and also works as a researcher. Her TV work includes 'Out On Tuesday', 'The Media Show' and 'Verdict'.

Afterword

Notes

1. Lord Ashbourne speaking on DI in the House of Lords, 6th February 1990.
2. Briefing by the Labour Campaign for Lesbian and Gay Rights.
3. See, for example, Golombok, Spencer & Rutter, 'Children in Lesbian and Single Parent Households: Psychosexual and Psychiatric Appraisal', from *Journal of Child Psychology and Psychiatry* Vol.24, No.4, 1983.

dyke as they occur.'[1]

Throughout the Stop The Clause campaign, lesbian and gay activists voiced dire warnings of what was to follow: 'They'll be recriminalising homosexuality next', was the popular choice. 'They' didn't, of course. Clause 28 confirmed the suspicions of both activists and reactionaries: that the best weapon against homosexuality is not straightforward criminalisation — even after ten years of Thatcherism, that would be too much for the British liberal stomach — but by undermining homosexual representation and cultural legitimation.

Tory backbenchers had done their homework. Once again they hitched their cause onto a Government bill addressing complex, vital issues, in order to maximise confusion and political inefficiency:

> 'The Bill is appallingly constructed and worded in the most impenetrable legalistic jargon. Much like Section 28, it seeks to intimidate and add to a general climate of reaction, as well as specifically proscribe.'[2]

Once again, 'they' exploited media-orchestrated moral panic over the homosexual menace to children by discouraging the 'promotion [of] pretended family relationships'.

Their target was clinic provision of donor insemination (DI) to lesbians, a simple, low-tech method of achieving pregnancy which is practised in about six of the sixty clinics offering DI services in this country, and by countless women in the privacy of their own homes.

The *Sunday Express* spearheaded the media smear campaign in the autumn of 1989, attacking the charities PAS (Pregnancy Advisory Service) and BPAS (British Pregnancy Advisory Service) for providing non-discriminatory DI services. Ann Winterton MP then laid an Early Day Motion condemning these services as a threat to 'the status of marriage, corrupting the family unit, and leaving the ensuing children at grave risk of subsequent emotional harm', and calling on the Secretary

Afterword

homosexuality in England and Wales).

Most of these 'crimes' have no heterosexual equivalent: others illustrate how 'neutral' police powers (like the 1986 Public Order Act) can be used to harass gay citizens. The figures include men who have kissed in the street, men who have had sex with others aged between 16 and 21 (eleven of whom received prison sentences of between eighteen months and four years), and lesbians and gays who were discharged and/or court-martialled by the armed forces (receiving prison terms of up to twelve months) for the 'crime' of being homosexual.

These figures add up to a damning portrait of officially sanctioned homophobia and victimisation. At a time when figures for reported violent crime and sexual assaults are soaring, the police are concentrating resources on victimless, often witnessless, crimes which provide an easy target for a force frustrated with its low detection rate. 'Gay crime' and violent crimes are collapsed into the amorphous category of 'sexual offences', which begs the question: 'Offences against whom?'.

All these are illustrations of the post-Clause landscape, a world in which homosexuality is more visible, more accepted, and yet more feared than ever before. And yet the political development which, above all others, exemplified the discourse which underpinned Clause 28 has been largely neglected: it was the attempt to criminalise lesbian motherhood via the Human Fertilisation and Embryology Bill.

A Storm In A Spermbank

> 'If we get the family right ... our prisons will not be bursting; our rates of abortion will not be higher than anywhere else; marriages will not break down; and divorce will not be higher than anywhere else. The cause of the problem is that marriages go wrong. I recommend that the Government focus on the cause of the problem and do not spend their life trying to shore up holes in the